Asgard to Athens

The AmblesideOnline Book of Mythology

Edited and Annotated
by Anne E. White

Asgard to Athens: The AmblesideOnline Book of Mythology
Copyright © 2025 by Anne E. White www.annewrites.ca
Cover photograph and design by Bryan White.

All rights reserved. No part of this publication may be reproduced, stored in a retrieval system or transmitted in any form by any means, electronic, mechanical, photocopy, recording or otherwise, without the prior permission of the publisher, except as provided by Canadian copyright law.

ISBN 978-1-990258-30-5

Contents

YEAR FOUR: *THE HEROES OF ASGARD: TALES FROM SCANDINAVIAN MYTHOLOGY*, BY ANNIE AND ELIZA KEARY — I

From the Kearys' Introduction to *The Heroes of Asgard* — ii

Notes for the AmblesideOnline Edition — iii

Term Examinations on *The Heroes of Asgard* — iv

Chapter One: The Aesir — 1

(Lesson 1) A Giant, a Cow, and a Hero (First Half) — 1

(Lesson 2) A Giant, a Cow, and a Hero (Second Half) — 4

(Lesson 3) Air Throne, the Dwarfs, and the Light Elves (First Half) — 7

(Lesson 4) Air Throne, the Dwarfs, and the Light Elves (Second Half) — 9

(Lesson 5) Niflheim (First Half) — 11

(Lesson 6) Niflheim (Second Half) — 14

(Lesson 7) The Children of Loki — 16

(Lesson 8) Bifrost, Urda, and the Norns (First Half) — 19

(Lesson 9) Bifrost, Urda, and the Norns (Second Half) — 21

(Lesson 10) Odhaerir (First Part) — 23

(Lesson 11) Odhaerir (Second Part) — 26

(Lesson 12) Odhaerir (Third Part) — 29

Poetic Interlude: Some Things Odin Wrote When Inspired by Odhaerir — 34

Chapter Two: How Thor Went to Jotunheim — 35

(Lesson 13) From Asgard to Utgard (Part One) — 35

(Lesson 14) The Serpent and the Kettle — 43

Chapter Three: Frey	48
(Lesson 15) On Tiptoe in Air Throne	48
(Lesson 16) The Gift	50
(Lesson 17) Fairest Gerd	52
(Lesson 18) The Wood Barri	55
Chapter Four: The Wanderings of Freyja	57
(Lesson 19) The Necklace Brisingamen	57
(Lesson 20) Loki—The Iron Wood—A Boundless Waste	61
(Lesson 21) The King of the Sea and his Daughters	64
Chapter Five: Iduna's Apples	66
(Lesson 22) Reflections in the Water	66
(Lesson 23) The Winged-Giant (First Half)	69
(Lesson 24) The Winged-Giant (Second Half)	72
(Lesson 25) Hela	75
(Lesson 26) Through Flood and Fire	78
Chapter Six: Baldur	81
(Lesson 27) The Dream	81
(Lesson 28) The Peacestead	85
(Lesson 29) Baldur Dead	88
(Lesson 30) Helheim	90
(Lesson 31) Weeping	92
Chapter Seven: The Binding of Fenrir	95
(Lesson 32) The Might of Asgard	95

(Lesson 33) The Secret of Svartheim	99
(Lesson 34) Honour	102
(Lesson 35) Chapter Eight: The Punishment of Loki	104
(Lesson 36) Chapter Nine: Ragnarok, or, The Twilight of the Gods	108
Poetic Epilogue: Tegnér's Drapa, by Henry Wadsworth Longfellow	115
YEAR FIVE: *THE AGE OF FABLE*, BY THOMAS BULFINCH	**117**
Preface/Introduction	118
Term Examinations on *The Age of Fable*	120
Chapter One	121
(Lesson 1) Introductory Chapter (First Part)	121
(Lesson 2) Introductory Chapter (Second Part)	124
(Lesson 3) Introductory Chapter (Third Part)	128
Chapter Two	133
(Lesson 4) Earth, Man, and a Gift	133
(Lesson 5) Pandora, and the Golden Age	135
(Lesson 6) Prometheus and Deucalion	139
Chapter Three	143
(Lesson 7) Apollo and Daphne	143
(Lesson 8) Pyramus and Thisbe	147
(Lesson 9) Cephalus and Procris	151
Chapter Four	153
(Lesson 10) Juno and Her Rivals	153
(Lesson 11) Diana and Actaeon	159

(Lesson 12) Latona and the Rustics ... 161

Chapter Five ... 164

(Lesson 13) Phaeton (First Part) ... 164

(Lesson 14) Phaeton (Second Part) ... 168

(Lesson 15) Phaeton (Third Part) ... 170

Chapter Six ... 174

(Lesson 16) Midas ... 174

(Lesson 17) Baucis and Philemon ... 177

Chapter Seven ... 181

(Lesson 18) Proserpine (First Part) ... 181

(Lesson 19) Proserpine (Second Part) ... 184

(Lesson 20) Glaucus and Scylla ... 188

Chapter Eight ... 191

(Lesson 21) Pygmalion ... 191

(Lesson 22) Venus and Adonis ... 194

Chapter Nine ... 197

(Lesson 23) Ceyx and Halcyone (First Half) ... 197

(Lesson 24) Ceyx and Halcyone (Second Half) ... 201

Chapter Ten ... 205

(Lesson 25) Vertumnus and Pomona ... 205

Chapter Eleven ... 210

(Lesson 26) Cupid and Psyche (First Half) ... 210

(Lesson 27) Cupid and Psyche (Second Half) ... 214

Chapter Twelve	220
(Lesson 28) Cadmus	220
(Lesson 29) The Myrmidons	224
Chapter Thirteen	229
(Lesson 30) Three Stories of Love in Vain	229
(Lesson 31) Two Short Stories About Love	235
Chapter Fourteen	237
(Lesson 32) Minerva and Arachne	237
(Lesson 33) The Sad Story of Niobe	241
(Lesson 34) Special Lesson: Statues of the Gods	245

YEAR SIX: *THE AGE OF FABLE*, BY THOMAS BULFINCH — 249

Introduction to the Year Six Readings	250
Chapter Twenty-Two	251
(Lesson 1) The Rural Deities and Erisichthon	251
(Lesson 2) Gods of Water and Winds	256
Chapter Twenty-Three	260
(Lesson 3) Achelous and Hercules	260
(Lesson 4) Admetus and Alcestis	263
(Lesson 5) Antigone	266
Chapter Twenty-Four	270
(Lesson 6) Orpheus and Eurydice	270
(Lesson 7) Aristaeus the Bee-Keeper	275
(Lesson 8) Who Can Tell the Strangest Story?	278

Chapter Twenty-Five	280
(Lesson 9) Arion and the Pirates	280
(Lesson 10) Ibycus: A Greek Whodunit	285
Chapter Twenty-Six	289
(Lesson 11) Two Stories About Diana	289
(Lesson 12) Aurora, Tithonus, and Memnon	292
Postscript: In Which Bulfinch Tells of Ovid, a Poet of Mythology	296

FOR FURTHER READING 298

Year Four: *The Heroes of Asgard: Tales from Scandinavian Mythology*, by Annie and Eliza Keary

Introductory Things

From the Kearys' Introduction to *The Heroes of Asgard*

The little tales which follow, drawn from the most striking and picturesque of the Northern myths, are put together in the simplest possible form, and were written only with a design to make the subject interesting to children.

A good deal of this courageous spirit of conflict and self-surrender comes into the Scandinavian myths and heroic tales. We read of one of the gods' messengers, who, when implored to desist from an undertaking because danger threatened, replied, "For one day was my age decreed and my whole life determined." In a lay of Odin, it says, "We ourselves die, but the fair fame never dies of him who has earned it"; and this reminds us of the Scandinavian custom of engraving the records of their warlike deeds upon their shields. "When a young warrior was at first enlisted," it is said, "they gave him a white and smooth buckler, which was called the 'shield of expectation,' which he carried until he had earned its record."

It is related of one of the celebrated Jomsburg sea-rovers called Bui, that finding himself defeated in an engagement, and seeing that all further resistance was fruitless, he took his treasure—two chests full of gold—and, calling out "Overboard all Bui's men," plunged into the sea and perished. But better far is the following: "A warrior having been thrown upon his back in wrestling with his enemy, and the latter finding himself without arms, the vanquished person promised to wait without changing his posture while the other fetched a sword to kill him, and he faithfully kept his word."

The *Younger Edda*…begins by telling a sort of story. [It] says "there was once a King called Gylfi, renowned for his wisdom and skill in magic"; he being seized with a desire to know all about the gods, and wishing also to get his information first-hand, sets off on a journey to Asgard itself, the gods' own abode. When he gets there he finds a mysterious Three seated upon three thrones—the High, the Equally High, and the Third. The story-teller is supposed to have taken this picture from a temple at Upsal, where the thrones of Odin, Thor, and Frey were placed in the same manner, one above another. Gylfi…proceeded to question the Three upon the origin of the world, the nature and adventures of the gods, etc., etc. [His] questions, and the answers which he receives, will, with reference to the *Elder Edda* tales, help us to get just the short summary we want of the Scandinavian mythology…

But we, who are not so presumptuous as to enquire into the future of the ages, and are neither learned nor over-inquisitive like King Gylfi, will go on listening to the great-grandmothers' stories, giant stories and god stories—a little bit that one remembers, and a little bit that another remembers, and so on; and all the time we will try to make the story tellers clear to one another and to ourselves as they go on, translating their old fashioned words into our own common everyday words and modes of speech, so that we may have at least a chance of understanding them.

Notes for the AmblesideOnline Edition

On Transcription and Spellings

The stories, or **sagas**, you are about to hear were first written down in two main books called the Elder, or Poetic *Edda*, and the Younger, or Prose *Edda*. (There are other, shorter sources as well.) Before that, they were handed down orally, throughout the Norse countries, by storytellers called **skalds**. Therefore, the proper pronunciation of any of the names and places is that used in Iceland. (At least according to people in Iceland.)

However…that's hard. Even a seemingly simple name like **Thor** sounds quite different when given an Icelandic rolling "R" at the end.

And since the stories have also been told in English (and have become even more popular in recent years because of comic books, games, and movies), English speakers have developed accepted, though technically incorrect, pronunciations for many of the names. Even when we try to look up the "right" pronunciations, though, sources vary. Two videos on pronunciations for **Aesir** suggest either "AH-sihr" or "AY-sihr." The suggestions given in this guide will therefore try to use the versions that are simplest for English-speaking students to pronounce.

The Old Norse orthography (alphabet and spelling) is quite different from English, and, therefore, the English spellings of names, places, and other words have varied greatly over the years. When the Keary sisters published *The Heroes of Asgard* in 1857, it was usual (especially in Britain) to use ligatures (the A-E and O-E letters squished together), along with other accent symbols. Over the years, particularly in North America, it has become increasingly common to change Æ to AE or Ae, and ö to a simple o. While the ligatures and umlauts lend Norse flavour and mystery to the stories, it does simplify the reading to use Anglicized spellings. Therefore, if you are using an original version of *Heroes*, you will see **Æsir**, **Mímir**, and **Jötunheim**. In our version, you will read those names as **Aesir**, **Mimir,** and **Jotunheim**.

The original text has not been much changed, with one exception: the end-of-chapter notes have been abridged where noted. The Kearys' long paragraphs have been broken up somewhat for ease of reading; and as they seem (unusually, for Victorian writers) to have been wary of overusing commas, I have added a bit of extra punctuation where it seemed helpful.

Some Words You Will Need to Know

In one of the first chapters of *Heroes of Asgard*, we are given the word **Asa**, and in a footnote, told that it is the singular of **Aesir**. While true enough, it seems we could use a bit more explanation. The word spelled **Asa** in this book comes from words meaning "deity," or "god." As noted above, the plural of that (and one of the most-used names in this book) is **Aesir**. Female **Aesir**, or goddesses, are the **Asyniur**, sometimes spelled **Asynjur**. (A single goddess is an **Asynja**, but that word doesn't come up in the book.)

Introductory Things

However, just to complicate things, there were more than one group or family of deities in Norse mythology. The **Aesir** are one tribe; the **Vanir** are another; and a third are the giants and "wicked witches" who live in **Jotunheim**. (**Heim** can be translated "home" or "land." The elves, for example, go to live in **Alfheim**.)

The word **Asa** or **Van** is often used before the name of a god, for instance, Asa Thor, or Van Frey. A **Vana**, like Freyja, is a female **Van**.

Nicknames

Longer names are sometimes shortened to single syllables. Examples: Gerda/Gerd; Hela/Hel; Hodur/Hod. This is not so much a matter of giving someone a casual nickname, as it is a difference in transcription from the original language.

A few miscellaneous points

Runes, as anyone who has read *The Hobbit* knows, are a kind of alphabet, and were used to write the *Eddas*. However, almost any time the word is used in this book, it refers to verbal spells and incantations.

Yggdrasil (IGG-dra-zill, IGG-dra-sill) is the Norse "Tree of Life." It is a giant ash tree, which holds all the kingdoms of gods and humans, including the other-worldly places such as heaven and hell.

Valhalla is the great hall in the Palace of Gladsheim where dead warriors are received. Not all the dead were believed to go to Valhalla, as explained in the stories; some went to the underworld land called **Niflheim**, which also contained a miserable, cold realm called **Hel** or **Helheim**.

Term Examinations on *The Heroes of Asgard*

The original examination questions provided for this book (and also for *The Age of Fable*) were a bit different from typical "Tell what you know of the death of Baldur" questions. In the original PNEU exams, they are found under the topic of "Composition," and the students were asked to write a story in either prose or verse, about one given character (depending on what was covered during the term): for instance, Iduna, Baldur, Svartheim, Odin, Heimdall, Thor, and Freyja/Baldur. As this seems a simple and useful pattern to follow, we will not suggest more detailed questions.

However, for older students or those who want a little more, the following may be an interesting alternative:

Below are two stanzas from Henry Wadsworth Longfellow's poem "The Challenge of Thor."

> I am the God Thor,
> I am the War God,
> I am the Thunderer!
> Here in my Northland,
> My fastness and fortress,
> Reign I forever!
>
> Here amid icebergs
> Rule I the nations;
> This is my hammer,
> Miölner the mighty;
> Giants and sorcerers
> Cannot withstand it!

Either a) continue the poem, in the style of Longfellow, or b) write the opening stanzas of a similar poem but about another character.

Chapter One: The Aesir

(Lesson 1) A Giant, a Cow, and a Hero (First Half)

Introduction

This is the Norse story of how all things—especially the Aesir—had their beginnings.

Vocabulary

tirewomen: maidservants

damask: a woven fabric

precipice: cliff

Vanir: a tribe of supernatural beings, slightly different from the **Aesir**

Aesir (AH-sihr): The tribe of gods (supernatural beings) to which **Odin** belonged.

Names

a giant: the ancestor of other giants, called Ymir. The *Eddas* tell how Odin and the others used various parts of Ymir to form the earth itself: his bones for the mountains, his brains for the clouds, and so on.

Odin: the chief among the Norse gods; referred to as **All-father**; the husband of **Frigga**

Thor: a god associated with strength and storms (his siblings are also listed here)

Niord: the chief of the **Vanir**

Places

Ginnungagap: the bottomless chasm from which all things were said to have come.

Reading

Prologue

"What was the beginning of things?"…an ancient poem says:

"Once was the age
When all was not—

No sand, nor sea,

No salt waves,

No earth was found,

Nor over-skies,

But yawning precipice

And nowhere grass." (*The Younger Edda*)

Part One

In the beginning of ages there lived a cow, whose breath was sweet, and whose milk was bitter. This cow was called Audhumla, and she lived all by herself on a frosty, misty plain, where there was nothing to be seen but heaps of snow and ice piled strangely over one another. Far away to the north it was night, far away to the south it was day; but all around where Audhumla lay a cold, grey twilight reigned.

By-and-by **a giant** came out of the dark north, and lay down upon the ice near Audhumla. "You must let me drink of your milk," said the giant to the cow; and though her milk was bitter, he liked it well, and for him it was certainly good enough.

After a little while the cow looked all round her for something to eat, and she saw a very few grains of salt sprinkled over the ice; so she licked the salt, and breathed with her sweet breath, and then long golden locks rose out of the ice, and the southern day shone upon them, which made them look bright and glittering.

The giant frowned when he saw the glitter of the golden hair; but Audhumla licked the pure salt again, and a head of a man rose out of the ice. The head was more handsome than could be described, and a wonderful light beamed out of its clear blue eyes. The giant frowned still more when he saw the head; but Audhumla licked the salt a third time, and then an entire man arose—a hero majestic in strength and marvellous in beauty.

Part Two

Now, it happened that when the giant looked full in the face of that beautiful man, he hated him with his whole heart, and, what was still worse, he took a terrible oath, by all the snows of **Ginnungagap**, that he would never cease fighting until either he or Bur, the hero, should lie dead upon the ground. And he kept his vow; he did not cease fighting until Bur had fallen beneath his cruel blows. I cannot tell how it could be that one so wicked should be able to conquer one so majestic and so beautiful; but so it was, and afterwards, when the sons of the hero began to grow up, the giant and his sons fought against them, too, and were very near conquering them many times.

But there was, of the sons of the heroes, one of very great strength and wisdom, called **Odin**, who, after many combats, did at last slay the great old giant, and pierced his body through with his keen spear, so that the blood swelled forth in a mighty torrent, broad and deep, and all the hideous giant brood were drowned in it excepting one, who ran away panting and afraid.

Part Three

After this Odin called round him his sons, brothers, and cousins, and spoke to them thus: "Heroes, we have won a great victory; our enemies are dead, or have run away from us. We cannot stay any longer here, where there is nothing evil for us to fight against."

The heroes looked round them at the words of Odin. North, south, east, and west there was no one to fight against them anywhere, and they called out with one voice, "It is well spoken, Odin; we follow you."

"Southward," answered Odin, "heat lies, and northward night. From the dim east the sun begins his journey westward home."

"Westward home!" shouted they all; and westward they went.

Odin rode in the midst of them, and they all paid to him reverence and homage as to a king and father. On his right hand rode **Thor**, Odin's strong, warlike, eldest son. On his left hand rode Baldur, the most beautiful and exalted of his children; for the very light of the sun itself shone forth from his pure and noble brow. After him came Tyr the Brave; the Silent Vidar; Hodur, who, alas! was born blind; Hermod, the Flying Word; Bragi, Hoenir, and many more mighty lords and heroes; and then came a shell chariot, in which sat **Frigga**, the wife of Odin, with all her daughters, friends, and **tirewomen**.

[For] eleven months they journeyed westward, enlivening the way with cheerful songs and conversation, and at the twelfth new moon they pitched their tents upon a range of hills which stood near the borders of an inland sea.

Part Four

[For] the greater part of one night, they were disturbed by mysterious whisperings, which appeared to proceed from the sea-coast, and creep up the mountain side. But as Tyr, who got up half a dozen times, and ran furiously about among the gorse and bushes, always returned saying that he could see no one, Frigga and her maidens at length resigned themselves to sleep, though they certainly trembled and started a good deal at intervals. Odin lay awake all night, however; for he felt certain that something unusual was going to happen. And such proved to be the case; for in the morning, before the tents were struck, a most terrific hurricane levelled the poles, and tore in pieces the **damask** coverings, swept from over the water furiously up the mountain gorges, round the base of the hills, and up again all along their steep sides right in the faces of the heroes.

Thor swung himself backwards and forwards, and threw stones in every possible direction. Tyr sat down on the top of a **precipice**, and defied the winds to displace him; whilst Baldur vainly endeavoured to comfort his poor mother, Frigga. But Odin stepped forth calm and unruffled, spread his arms towards the sky, and called out to the spirits of the wind, "Cease, strange **Vanir** (for that was the name by which they were called), cease your rough play, and tell us in what manner we have offended you that you serve us thus."

The winds laughed in a whispered chorus at the words of the brave king, and, after a few low [chuckles], sank into silence. But each sound in dying grew into a shape: one by one the strange, loose-limbed, uncertain forms stepped forth from caves, from gorges, dropped from the tree tops, or rose out of the grass—each wind-gust a separate Van.

Then **Niord**, their leader, stood forward from the rest of them, and said, "We know, O mighty Odin, how you and your company are truly the **Aesir**—that is to say, the lords of the whole earth—since you slew the huge, wicked giant. We, too, are lords, not of the earth, but of the sea and air, and we thought to have had glorious sport in fighting one against another; but if such be not your pleasure, let us, instead of that, shake hands." And, as he spoke, Niord held out his long, cold hand, which was like a windbag to the touch.

Odin grasped it heartily, as did all the Aesir; for they liked the appearance of the good-natured, gusty chief, whom they begged to become one of their company, and live henceforth with them. To this Niord consented, whistled good-bye to his kinsfolk, and strode cheerfully along amongst his new friends.

Narration and Discussion

How is this "beginnings" story different from others you have heard? Are there any ways in which it is similar?

Creative narration: Imagine that you are one of Odin's great-grandchildren, and you have asked him to tell the story of where your people came from. You can act this out, draw it, or tell it in some other way.

For further thought: Odin says, "We cannot stay any longer here, where there is nothing evil for us to fight against." What does this say about the Aesir?

(Lesson 2) A Giant, a Cow, and a Hero (Second Half)

Introduction

The Aesir are now a family, and they build a beautiful city called Asgard.

A note: where do humans come into the story?

The Kearys, trying to follow the story of the Aesir, do not include the myth relating to the creation of human beings. Briefly, the gods formed a man and a woman from logs of wood, and Odin breathed life into them. They and their descendants lived in the land called **Midgard**, behind a wall made from the giant Ymir's eyelashes (or eyebrows).

Vocabulary

> **mortar:** a mixture of lime, cement, sand, and water, used to hold bricks or stones together
>
> **Air Throne:** also called the Lidskyalf
>
> **Valhalla:** the hall where dead warriors were welcomed (see introductory notes)
>
> **coats of mail:** suits of armor
>
> **smithy:** a place for metal-working
>
> **forge their arms:** make their weapons
>
> **orator:** speech-maker

Names

> **that giant who fled from us:** named Bergelmir

Places

> **Niflheim:** a cold, misty underworld realm
>
> **Jotunheim:** the place where frost giants and other unfriendly beings live

Reading

Part One

After this they journeyed on and on steadily westward until they reached the summit of a lofty mountain, called the Meeting Hill. There they all sat round in a circle, and took a general survey of the surrounding neighbourhood.

As they sat talking together Baldur looked up suddenly, and said, "Is it not strange, Father Odin, that we do not find any traces of **that giant who fled from us**, and who escaped drowning in his father's blood?"

"Perhaps he has fallen into **Niflheim**, and so perished," remarked Thor.

But Niord pointed northward, where the troubled ocean rolled, and said, "Yonder, beyond that sea, lies the snowy region of **Jotunheim**. It is there the giant lives, and builds cities and castles, and brings up his children—a more hideous brood even than the old one."

"How do you know that, Niord?" asked Odin.

"I have seen him many times," answered Niord, "both before I came to live with you, and also since then, at night, when I have not been able to sleep, and have made little journeys to Jotunheim, to pass the time away."

"This is indeed terrible news," said Frigga; "for the giants will come again out of Jotunheim and devastate the earth."

"Not so," answered Odin, "not so, my dear Frigga; for here, upon this very hill, we will build for ourselves a city, from which we will keep guard over the poor earth, with its weak men and women, and from whence we will go forth to make war upon Jotunheim."

"That is remarkably well said, Father Odin," observed Thor, laughing amidst his red beard. Tyr shouted, and Vidar smiled, but said nothing; and then all the Aesir set to work with their whole strength and industry to build for themselves a glorious city on the summit of the mountain.

Part Two

For days, and weeks, and months, and years they worked, and never wearied; so strong a purpose was in them, so determined and powerful were they to fulfil it. Even Frigga and her ladies did not disdain to fetch stones in their marble wheelbarrows, or to draw water from the well in golden buckets, and then, with delicate hands, to mix the **mortar** upon silver plates. And so that city rose by beautiful degrees, stone above stone, tower above tower, height above height, until it crowned the hill.

Then all the Aesir stood at a little distance, and looked at it, and sighed from their great happiness. Towering at a giddy height in the centre of the city rose Odin's seat, called **Air Throne**, from whence he could see over the whole earth. On one side of Air Throne stood the Palace of Friends, where Frigga was to live; on the other rose the glittering Gladsheim, a palace roofed entirely with golden shields, and whose great hall, **Valhalla**, had a ceiling covered with spears, benches spread with **coats of mail**, and five hundred and forty entrance-gates, through each of which eight hundred men might ride abreast. There was also a large iron **smithy**, situated on the eastern side of the city, where the Aesir might **forge their arms** and shape their armour. That night they all supped in Valhalla, and drank to the health of their strong, new home, "The City of Asgard," as Bragi, their chief **orator**, said it ought to be called.

Narration and Discussion

What sort of place is Asgard? Would you like to live there?

Do you think the giants in Jotunheim might become a problem for the Aesir?

Creative narration: As an ongoing or occasional narration project, create the first page of the very first edition of the *Asgard Daily News* (or whatever title you like). What are the biggest headlines today? Are there any advertisements? Weather predictions?

(Lesson 3) Air Throne, the Dwarfs, and the Light Elves (First Half)

Introduction

Odin feels he has some responsibility towards the human world as well, especially when it comes to dealing with mischievous dwarfs and elves.

Vocabulary

puny: small, weak

dwarfs: smaller creatures closely related to the elves.

husbandman: farmer

furrows: grooves or trenches made in the earth, for sowing seeds

sent his compliments: "Sending one's compliments" was a polite greeting.

ladybirds: ladybugs

propensities: tendencies

Names

one, the wisest of men: As is described here, **Kvasir** was a special, wise creature made from the joining of the **Aesir** and the **Van**. Kvasir's murder, and the jars (three jars in this version, "two vats and a kettle" in others), will come up again later.

Flying Word: Hermod is the messenger of the gods (like Mercury in the Greek myths)

Reading

Part One

In the morning Odin mounted Air Throne, and looked over the whole earth, whilst the Aesir stood all round waiting to hear what he thought about it

"The earth is very beautiful," said Odin, from the top of his throne, "very beautiful in every part, even to the shores of the dark North Sea; but, alas! the men of the earth are **puny** and fearful. At this moment I see a three-headed giant striding out of Jotunheim. He throws a shepherd-boy into the sea, and puts the whole of the flock into his pocket. Now he takes them out again one by one, and cracks their bones as if they were hazel-nuts, whilst, all the time, men look on, and do nothing."

"Father," cried Thor in a rage, "last night I forged for myself a belt, a glove, and a hammer, with which three things I will go forth alone to Jotunheim." Thor went, and Odin looked again.

Part Two

"The men of the earth are idle and stupid," said Odin. "There are **dwarfs** and elves, who live amongst them, and play tricks which they cannot understand, and do not know how to prevent. At this moment I see a **husbandman** sowing grains of wheat in the **furrows**, whilst a dwarf runs after him, and changes them into stones. Again, I see two hideous little beings, who are holding under water the head of **one, the wisest of men**, until he dies; they mix his blood with honey; they have put it into three stone jars, and hidden it away."

Then Odin was very angry with the dwarfs, for he saw that they were bent on mischief; so he called to him Hermod, his **Flying Word**, and despatched him with a message to the dwarfs and light elves, to say that Odin **sent his compliments**, and would be glad to speak with them, in his palace of Gladsheim, upon a matter of some importance. When they received Hermod's summons the dwarfs and light elves were very much surprised, not quite knowing whether to feel honoured or afraid. However, they put on their pertest manners, and went clustering after Hermod like a swarm of **ladybirds**.

Part Three

When they were arrived in the great city they found Odin descended from his throne, and sitting with the rest of the Aesir in the Judgment Hall of Gladsheim. Hermod flew in, saluted his master, and pointed to the dwarfs and elves hanging like a cloud in the doorway to show that he had fulfilled his mission. Then Odin beckoned the little people to come forward. Cowering and whispering they peeped over one another's shoulders; now running on a little way into the hall, now back again, half curious, half afraid; and it was not until Odin had beckoned three times that they finally reached his footstool.

Then Odin spoke to them in calm, low, serious tones about the wickedness of their mischievous **propensities**. Some, the very worst of them, only laughed in a forward, hardened manner; but a great many looked up surprised and a little pleased at the novelty of serious words; whilst the light elves all wept, for they were tender-hearted little things. At length Odin spoke to the two dwarfs by name whom he had seen drowning the wise man. "Whose blood was it," he asked, "that you mixed with honey and put into jars?"

"Oh," said the dwarfs, jumping up into the air, and clapping their hands, "that was **Kvasir's** blood. Don't you know who Kvasir was? He sprang up out of the peace made between the Vanir and yourselves, and has been wandering about these seven years or more; so wise he was that men thought he must be a god. Well, just now we found him lying in a meadow drowned in his own wisdom; so we mixed his blood with honey, and put it into three great jars to keep. Was not that well done, Odin?"

"Well done!" answered Odin. "Well done! You cruel, cowardly, lying dwarfs! I myself saw you kill him. For shame! for shame!" And then Odin proceeded to pass sentence upon them all. Those who had been the most wicked, he said, were to live, henceforth, a long way underground, and were to spend their time in throwing fuel upon the great earth's central fire; whilst those who had only been mischievous were to work in the gold and diamond mines, fashioning precious stones and metals. They might all come up at night, Odin said; but must vanish at the dawn.

Then he waved his hand, and the dwarfs turned round, shrilly chattering, scampered down the palace-steps, out of the city, over the green fields, to their unknown, deep-buried earth-homes.

Narration and Discussion

What do the Aesir think about human beings? How do they plan to help them?

How does this account fit with other stories about where dwarfs live or what they do?

Creative narration: What is happening in the *Asgard Daily News*? Sports? Headlines? Help-wanted ads for dwarf businesses?

(Lesson 4) Air Throne, the Dwarfs, and the Light Elves (Second Half)

Introduction

The dwarfs have been severely punished for the murder of Kvasir; but the elves receive a different treatment.

Vocabulary

genius: spirit

Names

Frey (or Freyr, pronounced fray): a Van, associated with peace, prosperity, good weather, and a good harvest

Freyja (fray-yah or froy-yah): a Vana, associated with love, beauty, gold, and war

Places

Alfheim: Elfland

Reading

Part One

But the light elves still lingered, with upturned, tearful, smiling faces, like sunshiny morning dew. "And you," said Odin, looking them through and through with his serious eyes, "and you–" "Oh! indeed, Odin," interrupted they, speaking all together in quick, uncertain tones; "Oh! indeed, Odin, we are not so very wicked. We have never done anybody any harm."

"Have you ever done anybody any good?" asked Odin.

"Oh! no, indeed," answered the light elves, we have never done anything at all."

"You may go, then," said Odin, "to live amongst the flowers, and play with the wild bees and summer insects. You must, however, find something to do, or you will get to be mischievous like the dwarfs."

Part Two

"If only we had any one to teach us," said the light elves, "for we are such foolish little people." Odin looked round inquiringly upon the Aesir; but amongst them there was no teacher found for the silly little elves. Then he turned to Niord, who nodded his head good-naturedly, and said, "Yes, yes, I will see about it." And then he strode out of the Judgment Hall, right away through the city gates, and sat down upon the mountain's edge.

After awhile he began to whistle in a most alarming manner, louder and louder, in strong wild gusts, now advancing, now retreating; then he dropped his voice a little, lower and lower, until it became a bird-like whistle—low, soft, enticing music, like a spirit's call; and far away from the south a little fluttering answer came, sweet as the invitation itself, nearer and nearer until the two sounds dropped into one another. Then through the clear sky two forms came floating, wonderfully fair— a brother and sister—their beautiful arms twined round one another, their golden hair bathed in sunlight, and supported by the wind.

"My son and daughter," said Niord, proudly, to the surrounding Aesir, "Frey and

Freyja, Summer and Beauty, hand in hand."

Part Three

When Frey and Freyja dropped upon the hill, Niord took his son by the hand, led him gracefully to the foot of the throne, and said, "Look here, dear brother Lord, what a fair young instructor I have brought for your pretty little elves." Odin was very much pleased with the appearance of Frey; but, before constituting him king and schoolmaster of the light elves, he desired to know what his accomplishments were, and what he considered himself competent to teach.

"I am the **genius** of clouds and sunshine," answered Frey; and as he spoke, the essences of a hundred perfumes were exhaled from his breath. "I am the genius of clouds and sunshine, and if the light elves will have me for their king, I can teach them how to burst the folded buds, to set the blossoms, to pour sweetness into the swelling fruit, to lead the bees through the honey-passages of the flowers, to make the single ear a stalk of wheat, to hatch birds' eggs, and teach the little ones to sing. All this, and much more," said Frey, "I know, and will teach them."

Then answered Odin, "It is well"; and Frey took his scholars away with him to **Alfheim**, which is in every beautiful place under the sun.

Narration and Discussion

Do you think Odin's decision was wise?

For further thought: Odin says, "You must, however, find something to do, or you will get to be mischievous like the dwarfs." Is that true of children as well?

Creative narration: What is happening in the *Asgard Daily News*? Headlines? Handicrafts and music Lesson s with the Vans?

(Lesson 5) Niflheim (First Half)

Introduction

In this story, we meet Loki, a troublemaker who nevertheless lives with the Aesir, and who does occasionally come in handy for his sharp thinking and his ability to change into anything needed.

Vocabulary

How he came amongst the Aesir…: Some storytellers give Loki more back-story, but we will go with the Kearys' version.

progeny: children

vigilant: sharp-eyed, watchful

Names

Loki (LO-kee): one of the gods, but, as stated here, "utterly unlike to them"; he often causes trouble. Oxford professor Gabriel Turville-Petre (a student of J. R. R. Tolkien) once said that "more ink has been spilled on Loki than on any other figure in Norse myth." More recently, Neil Gaiman wrote in *Norse Mythology* that "Loki makes the world more interesting but less safe."

Angrboda: second wife of Loki (he was also married to Siguna or Sigyn); mother to three strange creatures

Fenrir: also called Fenris, or Fenris Wolf

Reading

Part One

Now, in the city of Asgard dwelt one called **Loki**, who, though amongst the Aesir, was not of the Aesir, but utterly unlike to them; for to do the wrong, and leave the right undone, was, night and day, this wicked Loki's one unwearied aim. **How he came amongst the Aesir no one knew, nor even whence he came.** Once, when Odin questioned him on the subject, Loki stoutly declared that there had been a time when he was innocent and noble-purposed like the Aesir themselves; but that, after many wanderings up and down the earth, it had been his misfortune, Loki said, to discover the half-burnt heart of a woman; "since when," continued he, "I became what you now see me, Odin." As this was too fearful a story for anyone to wish to hear twice over Odin never questioned him again.

Whilst the Aesir were building their city, Loki, instead of helping them, had been continually running over to Jotunheim to make friends amongst the giants and wicked witches of the place. Now, amongst the witches there was one [named **Angrboda**], so fearful to behold in her sin and her cruelty, that one would have thought it impossible even for such a one as Loki to find any pleasure in her companionship: nevertheless, so it was that he married her, and they lived together a long time, making each other worse and worse out of the abundance of their own wicked hearts, and bringing up their three children to be the plague, dread, and misery of mankind.

These three children were just what they might have been expected to be from their parentage and education. The eldest was Jormungand, a monstrous serpent; the second **Fenrir**, most ferocious of wolves; the third was Hela, half corpse, half queen. When Loki and his witch-wife looked at their fearful **progeny** they thought within themselves, "What would the Aesir say if they could see?" "But they cannot see," said Loki; "and, lest they should suspect, Witch-wife, I will go back to Asgard for a little while, and salute old Father Odin bravely, as if I had no secret here." So saying, Loki wished his wife good-morning, bade her hide the children securely indoors, and set forth on the road to Asgard.

Part Two

But all the time he was travelling, Loki's children went on growing, and long before he had reached the lofty city, Jormungand had become so large that his mother was obliged to open the door to let his tail out. At first it hung only a little way across the road; but he grew. Oh, how fearfully Jormungand grew! Whether it was from sudden exposure to the air, I do not know; but, in a single day he grew from one end of Jotunheim to the other, and early next morning began to shoot out in the direction of Asgard.

Luckily, however, just at that moment Odin caught sight of him, when, from the top of Air Throne, the eyes of this **vigilant** ruler were taking their morning walk. "'Now," said Odin, "it is quite clear, Frigga, that I must remain in idleness no longer at Asgard, for monsters are bred up in Jotunheim, and the earth has need of me."

So saying, descending instantly from Air Throne, Odin went forth of Asgard's golden gates to tread the earth of common men, fighting to pierce through Jotunheim, and slay its monstrous sins.

Narration and Discussion

Tell what you know of Loki and his family.

Can you think of other stories where a small thing grows large and dangerous?

Something to think about: Loki and his wife were "making each other worse and worse out of the abundance of their own wicked hearts." Do you think it is true that our sins tend to rub off on each other? Can the opposite be true as well?

Creative narration: What is in the *Asgard Daily News*? Headlines? Fashion advice, recipes, business, sports? (From now on, this suggestion will appear only at the ends of chapters, but it can be used any time.)

The AO Book of Mythology

(Lesson 6) Niflheim (Second Half)

Introduction

Odin, being a hands-on, feet-on sort of god, travels around to see if he can learn more about the good and evil realms, and if he can become a wiser and more noble Asa. His quest costs him heavily, but he also acquires an "inward light."

Vocabulary

draught (draft): drink, swallow

specters: ghostly shapes

Hvergelmir: a deep spring which is the source of rivers; the home of **Nidhogg**

Names

Mimir (MEE-mir): a character famous for his wisdom

Nidhogg (or Nidhoggr): a worm or dragon who gnaws at the roots of the tree Yggdrasil. A close-enough pronunciation is "Need-hock."

Places

Niflheim: the underworld. "Niflheim was colder than cold…" (Neil Gaiman, *Norse Mythology*)

Reading

Part One

In his journeyings Odin mixed freely with the people of the countries through which he passed; shared with them toil and pleasure, war and grief; taught them out of his own large experience, inspired them with his noble thoughts, and exalted them by his example. Even to the oldest he could teach much; and in the evening, when the labours of the day were ended, and the sun cast slanting rays upon the village green, it was pleasant to see the sturdy village youths grouped round that noble chief, hanging open mouthed upon his words, as he told them of his great fight with the giant of long ago, and then pointing towards Jotunheim, explained to them how that fight was not yet over, for that giants and monsters grew round them on every side, and they, too, might do battle bravely, and be heroes and Aesir of the earth.

One evening, after thus drinking in his burning words, they all trooped together to the village smithy, and Odin forged for them all night arms and armour, instructing them, at the same time, in their use. In the morning he said, "Farewell, children; I have further to go than you can come; but do not forget me when I am gone, nor how to fight as I have taught you. Never cease to be true and brave; never turn your arms against one another; and never turn them away from the giant and the oppressor."

Then the villagers returned to their homes and their field-labour, and Odin pressed on, through trackless uninhabited woods, up silent mountains, over the lonely ocean, until he reached that strange, mysterious meeting-place of sea and sky.

Part Two

There, brooding over the waters like a grey sea fog, sat **Mimir**, guardian of the well where wit and wisdom lie hidden.

"Mimir," said Odin, going up to him boldly, "let me drink of the waters of wisdom."

"Truly, Odin," answered Mimir, "it is a great treasure that you seek, and one which many have sought before, but who, when they knew the price of it, turned back."

Then replied Odin, "I would give my right hand for wisdom willingly."

"Nay," rejoined the remorseless Mimir, "it is not your right hand, but your right eye you must give."

Odin was very sorry when he heard the words of Mimir, and yet he did not deem the price too great; for plucking out his right eye, and casting it from him, he received in return a **draught** of the fathomless deep. As Odin gave back the [drinking] horn into Mimir's hand, he felt as if there were a fountain of wisdom springing up within him—an inward light; for which you may be sure he never grudged having given his perishable eye.

Now, also, he knew what it was necessary for him to do in order to become a really noble Asa, and that was to push on to the extreme edge of the earth itself, and peep over into **Niflheim**. Odin knew it was precisely that [which] he must do; and [it was] precisely that [which] he did. Onward and northward he went over ice-bound seas, through twilight, fog, and snow, right onward in the face of winds that were like swords until he came into the unknown land, where sobs, and sighs, and sad, unfinished shapes were drifting up and down. "Then," said Odin, thoughtfully, "I have come to the end of all creation, and a little further on Niflheim must lie."

Part Three

Accordingly he pushed on further and further until he reached the earth's extremest edge, where, lying down and leaning over from its last cold peak, he looked into the gulf below. It was Niflheim. At first Odin imagined that it was only empty darkness; but, after hanging there three nights and days, his eye fell on one of Yggdrasil's mighty stems. Yggdrasil was the old earth-tree, whose roots sprang far and wide, from Jotunheim, from above, and this, the oldest of the three, out of Niflheim. Odin looked long upon its time-worn, knotted fibres, and watched how they were for ever gnawed by **Nidhogg** the envious serpent, and his brood of poisonous diseases.

Then he wondered what he should see next; and one by one **spectres** arose from Nastrond, the Shore of Corpses—arose and wandered pale, naked, nameless, and without a home.

Then Odin looked down deeper into the abyss of abysses, and saw all its shapeless, nameless ills; whilst far below him, deeper than Nastrond, Yggdrasil, and Nidhogg, roared **Hvergelmir**, the boiling cauldron of evil.

Nine nights and days this brave wise Asa hung over Niflheim pondering. More brave and more wise he turned away from it, than when he came. It is true that he sighed often on his road thence to Jotunheim; but is it not always thus that wisdom and strength come to us weeping.

Narration and Discussion

What do you think of Odin's advice to the village people? What might it have meant to the first hearers of these stories?

Something more to think about: "It is true that he sighed often on his road thence to Jotunheim; but is it not always thus that wisdom and strength come to us weeping." What do you think this means?

Creative narration: Some students may enjoy acting out parts of this story. Caution, of course, is advised.

(Lesson 7) The Children of Loki

Introduction

Odin begins to deal with the dangerous creatures threatening Asgard. He also meets Heimdall, the keeper of the rainbow bridge.

Vocabulary

   imperial: royal, commanding

   tractable: yielding, controllable

   tremulous: shaking, quivering

Names

Heimdall: His job was to watch for invaders or other danger from his home at the end of the rainbow bridge called **Bifrost**.

Nornir: also called the **Norns**. Three women who weave the threads of fate (similar to the Fates in other European mythologies); they also take care of the tree **Yggdrasil**.

Places

Bifrost (also called Bilröst): a bridge that reached between **Midgard** (Earth) and **Asgard** (the home of the Aesir).

Urda fountain: also called **Urdarbrunnr**, a spring or well, located beneath **Yggdrasil**

Reading

Part One

When, at length, Odin found himself in the land of giants—frost giants, mountain giants, three-headed and wolf-headed giants, monsters and iron witches of every kind—he walked straight on, without stopping to fight with any one of them, until he came to the middle of Jormungand's body. Then he seized the monster, growing fearfully as he was all the time, and threw him headlong into the deep ocean. There Jormungand still grew, until, encircling the whole earth, he found that his tail was growing down his throat, after which he lay quite still, binding himself together; and neither Odin nor any one else has been able to move him thence.

When Odin had thus disposed of Jormungand, henceforth called the "Midgard Serpent," he went on to the house of Loki's wife. The door was thrown open, and the wicked Witch-mother sat in the entrance, whilst on one side crouched Fenrir, her ferocious wolf-son, and on the other stood Hela, most terrible of monsters and women.

A crowd of giants strode after Odin, curious to obtain a glance of Loki's strange children before they should be sent away. At Fenrir and the Witch-mother they stared with great eyes, joyfully and savagely glittering; but when he looked at Hela each giant became as pale as new snow, and cold with terror as a mountain of ice. Pale, cold, frozen, they never moved again; but a rugged chain of rocks stood behind Odin, and he looked on fearless and unchilled.

"Strange daughter of Loki," he said, speaking to Hela, "you have the head of a queen, proud forehead, and large, **imperial** eyes; but your heart is pulseless, and your cruel arms kill what they embrace. Without doubt you have somewhere a kingdom; not where the sun shines, and men breathe the free air, but down below in infinite depths, where bodiless spirits wander, and the cast-off corpses are cold."

Then Odin pointed downwards towards Niflheim, and Hela sank right through the earth, downward, downward, to that abyss of abysses, where she ruled over spectres, and made for herself a home called Helheim, nine lengthy kingdoms wide and deep.

Part Two

After this, Odin desired Fenrir to follow him, promising that if he became **tractable** and obedient, and exchanged his ferocity for courage, he should not be banished as his brother and sister had been. So Fenrir followed, and Odin led the way out of Jotunheim, across the ocean, over the earth, until he came to the heavenly hills, which held up the southern sky tenderly in their glittering arms. There, half on the mountain-top and half in air, sat **Heimdall**, guardian of the **tremulous** bridge **Bifrost**, that arches from earth to heaven.

Heimdall was a tall, white Van, with golden teeth, and [he had] a wonderful horn, called the Giallar Horn, which he generally kept hidden under the tree Yggdrasil; but when he blew it the sound went out into all worlds.

Now, Odin had never been introduced to Heimdall—had never even seen him before; but he did not pass him by without speaking on that account. On the contrary, being altogether much struck by his appearance, he could not refrain from asking him a few questions. First, he requested to know whom he had the pleasure of addressing; secondly, who his parents were, and what his education had been; and thirdly, how he explained his present circumstances and occupation.

"My name is Heimdall," answered the guardian of Bifrost, "and the son of nine sisters am I. Born in the beginning of time, at the boundaries of the earth, I was fed on the strength of the earth and the cold sea. My training, moreover, was so perfect, that I now need no more sleep than a bird. I can see for a hundred miles around me as well by night as by day; I can hear the grass growing and the wool on the backs of sheep. I can blow mightily my horn Giallar; and I forever guard the tremulous bridge-head against monsters, giants, iron witches, and dwarfs."

Then asked Odin, gravely, "Is it also forbidden to the Aesir to pass this way, Heimdall? Must you guard Bifrost, also, against them?"

"Assuredly not," answered Heimdall "All Aesir and heroes are free to tread its trembling, many-coloured pavement, and they will do well to tread it, for above the arch's summit I know that the **Urda fountain** springs; rises, and falls, in a perpetual glitter, and by its sacred waters the **Nornir** dwell—those three mysterious, mighty maidens, through whose cold fingers ran the golden threads of Time."

"Enough, Heimdall," answered Odin. "Tomorrow we will come."

Narration and Discussion

Did Odin treat Loki's children fairly? What do you think will happen with Fenrir?

What do you think of Heimdall?

Creative narration: You are Odin, returning home. Tell what you have been doing, and what the plans are for tomorrow.

(Lesson 8) Bifrost, Urda, and the Norns (First Half)

Introduction

In this reading, Odin does return home and tell where he has been. He also introduces Fenrir, "yon hideous and unmannerly animal." The next day, the Aesir set out for Heimdall's bridge.

Vocabulary

undertake the office: take the job

discourse: conversation, speech

fare: travel

Names

Asyniur: female deities (goddesses)

Tyr: said in this book to be a son of Odin, but sometimes called the son or grandson of a jotun named Hymir. He corresponds somewhat with Mars, the Roman god of war; and while Romance languages call one day of the week "mardi" or "martes," in English we say "Tuesday," in honour of Tyr.

Reading

Part One

Odin departed from Heimdall, and went on his way, Fenrir obediently following, though not now much noticed by his captor, who pondered over the new wonders of which he had heard. "Bifrost, Urda, and the Norns—what can they mean?"

Thus pondering and wondering he went, ascended Asgard's Hill, walked through the golden gates of the City into the palace of Gladsheim, and into the hall Valhalla, where, just then, the Aesir and **Asyniur** were assembled at their evening meal. Odin sat down to the table without speaking, and, still absent and meditative, proceeded to carve the great boar, Saehrimnir, which every evening eaten, was every morning whole again. No-one thought of disturbing him by asking any questions, for they saw that something was on his mind, and the Aesir were well-bred. It is probable, therefore, that the supper would have been concluded in perfect silence if Fenrir had not poked his nose in at the doorway, just opposite to the seat of the lovely Freyja. She, genius of beauty as she was, and who had never in her whole life seen even the shadow of a wolf, covered her face with her hands, and screamed a little, which caused all the Aesir to start and turn round, in order to see what was the matter. But Odin directed a reproving glance at the ill-mannered Fenrir, and then gave orders that the wolf should be fed. "After which," concluded he, "I will relate my adventures to the assembled Aesir."

"That is all very well, Asa Odin," answered Frey; "but who, let me ask, is to **undertake the office** of feeding yon hideous and unmannerly animal?" "That will I, joyfully," cried **Tyr**, who liked nothing better than an adventure; and then, seizing a plate of meat from the table, he ran out of the hall, followed by Fenrir, who howled, and sniffed, and jumped up at him in a most impatient, un-Aesir-like manner.

After the wolf was gone Freyja looked up again, and when Tyr was seated once more, Odin began. He told them of everything that he had seen, and done, and suffered; and, at last, of Heimdall, that strange white Van, who sat upon the heavenly hills, and spoke of Bifrost, and Urda, and the Norns. The Aesir were very silent whilst Odin spoke to them, and were deeply and strangely moved by this conclusion to his **discourse**.

"The Norns," repeated Frigga, "the Fountain of Urd, the golden threads of time! Let us go, my children," she said, rising from the table, "let us go and look at these things."

But Odin advised that they should wait until the next day, as the journey to Bifrost and back again could easily be accomplished in a single morning.

Part Two

Accordingly, the next day the Aesir and Asyniur all rose with the sun, and prepared to set forth. Niord came from Noatun, the mild sea-coast, which he had made his home, and with continual gentle puffings out of his wide, breezy mouth, he made their journey to Bifrost so easy and pleasant that they all felt a little sorry when they caught the first glitter of Heimdall's golden teeth. But Heimdall was glad to see them; glad, at least, for their sakes. He thought it would be so good for them to go and see the Norns. As far as he himself was concerned he never felt dull alone. On the top of those bright hills how many meditations he had! Looking far and wide over the earth how much he saw and heard!

"Come already!" said Heimdall to the Aesir, stretching out his long, white hands to welcome them; "come already! Ah! this is Niord's doing. How do you do, cousin," said he; for Niord and Heimdall were related.

"How sweet and fresh it is up here!" remarked Frigga, looking all round, and feeling that it would be polite to say something. "You are very happy, Sir," continued she, "in having always such fine scenery about you, and in being the guardian of such a bridge."

And in truth Frigga might well say "such a bridge"; for the like of it was never seen on the ground. Trembling and glittering it swung across the sky, up from the top of the mountain to the clouds, and down again into the distant sea.

"Bifrost! Bifrost!" exclaimed the Aesir, wonderingly; and Heimdall was pleased at their surprise.

"At the arch's highest point," said he, pointing upward, "rises that fountain of which I spoke. Do you wish to see it today?"

"That do we, indeed," cried all the Aesir in a breath. "Quick, Heimdall, and unlock the bridge's golden gate."

Then Heimdall took all his keys out, and fitted them into the diamond lock till he found the right one, and the gate flew open with a sound at the same time sad and cheerful, like the dripping of leaves after a thunder-shower.

Narration and Discussion

Why are the Aesir so interested in seeing the bridge and what lies beyond?

Have you ever listened to the dripping of leaves after a thunder-shower? Can you think of any other sounds that are both sad and cheerful?

> "Leaves dropped with a whisper to the earth, and acorns plopped like heavy drops of rain...The woods were full of a ghostly, hollow knocking as though dozens of brittle knuckles beat upon closed doors. He lay down flat on his back and looked up into the purpling roof of leaves. How high it was, and beyond it how tremendous was the sky." (Elizabeth Enright, *The Four-Story Mistake*)

Creative narration: Draw one of these: a) Tyr feeding Fenrir, b) Heimdall and the bridge Bifrost.

(Lesson 9) Bifrost, Urda, and the Norns (Second Half)

Introduction

The Aesir finally reach the Norns, who are "mighty and wilful," but not very talkative.

Vocabulary

> **summit:** highest point
>
> **woof:** in weaving, the crosswise threads; also called the **weft**

Names

> **Urd, Verdandi, Skuld:** Urd represents the past; Verdandi, the present; and Skuld, the

future.

Reading

Part One

The Aesir pressed in; but, as they passed him, Heimdall laid his hand upon Thor's shoulder, and said "I am very sorry, Thor; but it cannot be helped. You must go to the fountain alone by another way; for you are so strong and heavy, that if you were to put your foot on Bifrost, either it would tremble in pieces beneath your weight, or take fire from the friction of your iron heels. Yonder, however, are two river-clouds, called Kormt and Ermt, through which you can wade to the Sacred Urd, and you will assuredly reach it in time, though the waters of the clouds are strong and deep."

At the words of Heimdall, Thor fell back from the bridge's head, vexed and sorrowful. "Am I to be sent away, then, and have to do disagreeable things," said he, "just because I am so strong? After all, what are Urda and the Norns to me, and Kormt and Ermt? I will go back to Asgard again."

"Nay, Thor," said Odin, "I pray you, do not anything so foolish. Think again, I beseech you, what it is that we are going to see and hear. Kormt and Ermt lie before you, as Bifrost before us. It is yonder, above both, that we go. Neither can it much matter, Thor, whether we reach the Fountain of Urd over Bifrost or through the cloud." Then Thor blushed with shame at his own weakness, which had made him regret his strength; and, without any more grumbling or hanging back, he plunged into the dreadful river-clouds, whose dark vapours closed around him and covered him. He was hidden from sight, and the Aesir went on their way over the glittering bridge.

Part Two

Daintily and airily they trod over it; they swung themselves up the swinging arch; they reached its **summit** on a pale, bright cloud. Thor was there already waiting for them, drenched and weary, but cheerful and bold. Then, all together, they knocked at the door of the pale, bright cloud; it blew open, and they passed in. Oh! then what did they see! Looking up to an infinite height through the purple air, they saw towering above them Yggdrasil's fairest branches, leafy and of a tender green, which also stretched far and wide; but, though they looked long, the Aesir could distinguish no topmost bough, and it almost seemed to them that, from somewhere up above, this mighty earth-tree must draw another root, so firmly and so tall it grew. On one side stood the Palace of the Noras, which was so bright that it almost blinded them to look at it, and on the other the Urda fountain plashed its cool waters—rising, falling, glittering, as nothing ever glitters on this side [of] the clouds.

Part Three

Two ancient swans swam under the fount, and around it sat the Three. Ah! how shall I describe them—**Urd, Verdandi, Skuld**. They were mighty, they were wilful, and one was veiled.

Sitting upon the Doomstead, they watched the water as it rose and fell, and passed golden threads from one to another. Verdandi plucked them with busy fingers from Skuld's reluctant hand, and wove them in and out quickly, almost carelessly; for some she tore and blemished, and some she cruelly spoiled. Then Urd took the **woof** away from her, smoothed its rough places, and covered up some of the torn, gaping holes; but she hid away many of the bright parts, too, and then rolled it all round her great roller, Oblivion, which grew thicker and heavier every moment. And so they went on, Verdandi drawing from Skuld, and Urd from Verdandi; but whence Skuld drew her separate bright threads no one could see. She never seemed to reach the end of them, and neither of the sisters ever stopped or grew weary of her work.

The Aesir stood apart watching, and it was a great sight. They looked in the face of Urd, and fed on wisdom; they studied the countenance of Verdandi, and drank bitter strength; they glanced through the veil of Skuld, and tasted hope.

At length, with full hearts, they stole away silently, one by one, out by the pale, open door, re-crossed the bridge, and stood once more by the side of Heimdall on the heavenly hills; then they went home again. Nobody spoke as they went; but ever afterwards it was an understood thing that the Aesir should **fare** to the Doomstead of the Nornir once in every day.

Narration and Discussion

Why was Thor so annoyed about not being able to cross the bridge? Can you think of any stories where someone wished to be different (or *not* different), but then discovered that their shape/size/talents were valuable?

Why do the Aesir decide to travel to the fountain every day?

Creative narration: Tell about (or draw) the Fountain of Urd, and the Norns.

(Lesson 10) Odhaerir (First Part)

Introduction

Do you remember the story about the killing of Kvasir? The sweet drink made from his blood has become something precious but also dangerous—especially to the rebellious dwarfs.

Vocabulary

mead: an alcoholic beverage. This mead, however, had very special properties.

three...draughts: drinks (because of the three jars into which it had been poured)

Odhaerir (OH-de-reer): also called the Poetic Mead or Mead of Poetry.

Names

Vafthrudnir (or Vafthruthnir): a giant (or **jotun**) whose name means "mighty weaver" or "mighty riddler."

Father of Hosts: that is, Odin

Gilling (or Gillingr): a giant, the father of **Suttung**.

Jotuns (or jotnar): A jotun is a being unlike the gods, but also different from the dwarves, elves and other non-human figures in Norse mythology. The word is often translated "giant," but not all the **jotuns** were super-sized.

Reading

Part One

Now upon a day it happened that Odin sat silent by the Well of Urd, and in the evening he mounted Air Throne with a troubled mind. All-father could see into Dwarf Home from his high place, as well as over man's world; his keen eye pierced, also, the mountains and darkness of Jotunheim.

On this evening, a tear, the fate-sisters' gift, swam across his vision, and—behold, is that an answering tear which he sees down there in Dwarf Home, large, luminous, golden, in the dark heart of the earth? "Can dwarfs weep?" exclaimed All-father, surprised as he looked a second and a third time, and went on looking. Fialar and Galar, the cunning dwarfs who had killed Kvasir, were kneeling beside the tear. "Is it theirs?" said All-father again, "and do they repent?"

No; it was not a tear; Odin knew it at last. More precious still, it was Kvasir's blood —golden **mead** now, because of the honey-drops from Earth's thousand bees and flowers which these thoughtless mischief-schemers (but wonder workers) had poured into it. "It is **three**," said Odin, "three precious **draughts**!— **Odhaerir** is its name— and now the dwarfs will drink it, and the life and the light, and the sweetness of the world will be spilt, and the heart of the world will die!"

But the dwarfs did not drink it; they could only sip it a little, just a drop or two at a time. The Father of Hosts watched how they were amusing themselves. Fialar and Galar, and a whole army of the little [*omission*] crooked-limbed creatures, were tilting the big jars over to one side, whilst first one, and then another, sucked the skim of their golden sweetness, smacking their lips after it, grinning horribly, leaping up into the air with strange gestures; falling backwards with shut eyes, some of as if asleep; tearing at the earth and the stones of their cavern homes; others, like wild beasts; rolling forth beautiful, senseless, terrible words. It was Fialar and Galar who did that; and behold, in a little while, one after another, the dwarfs gathered round them as they spoke, and listened, open-mouthed, with clenched fists, stamping, and roaring applause until at last they seized the weapons that lay near [*omission*], and marched in warlike fashion, led on by Fialar and Galar, straight up through their cavernous ways, to Manheim, and across it into the Frozen Land.

Part Two

Giant **Vafthrudnir**, that "Ancient Talker," he who sits ever in his Hall weaving new and intricate questions for the gods, saw them; and looking up towards the brooding heavens, he exchanged glances with the **Father of Hosts**. But the dwarfs did not come near Vafthrudnir's Halls; they never looked aside at him, nor up to the Air Throne of the Asa; only rushed heedlessly on till they stumbled over the Giant **Gilling**, who was taking a nap upon the green bank of Ifing.

Ifing looks a lazy stream; one can hardly see at first sight that it flows at all: but it flows, and flows quietly, unceasingly, and is so deep that neither god nor giant has ever yet been able to fathom it. It is, in fact, that stream which divides for ever the **Jotuns** from the Gods, and of it Odin himself once said:—

"Open shall it run

Throughout all time,

On that stream no ice shall be."

So the dwarfs found Gilling asleep; they knew how deep Ifing was, they knew that if they could once roll the giant Gilling in there he would never get out again, and then they should have done something worth speaking about. "I have killed a giant," each dwarf might say, and, who knows, even the Aesir might begin to feel a little afraid of them. "It all comes from drinking Kvasir's blood," they said, and then with their thousand little swords and spears, and sticks and stones, they worked away until they had plunged the sleeping giant into the stream.

All-father's piercing eye saw it all, and how the silly dwarfs jumped and danced about afterwards, and praised themselves, and defied the whole world, gods, giants and men. "It is not for us," they said, "any more to run away before Skinfaxi the shining horse that draws day over humankind, whose mane sheds light instead of dew. We will dance before him and crown ourselves with gold, as the gods and as men do every morning."

But, in the midst of all their gleeful folly, the ground they stood upon began to shake under them, and an enormous darkness grew between them and the sky. Then the dwarfs stopped their rejoicing as if a spell had fallen upon them, dropping their weapons, huddling close to one another, cowering, whispering. Giant **Suttung**, son of that Gilling whom they had just slain, was coming upon them in great fury to avenge his father's death.

Narration and Discussion

Why did the dwarfs kill the giant Gilling?

What did they mean when they said they would no longer run away from the shining horse of the morning?

Something to think about: When Fialar and Galar drank the mead, they began "rolling forth beautiful, senseless, terrible words…[and] the dwarfs gathered round them as they spoke, and listened, open-mouthed, with clenched fists, stamping, and roaring applause…" How can language (even poetry!) be misused?

(Lesson 11) Odhaerir (Second Part)

Introduction

The mead called Odhaerir changes hands once again. But Odin is worried: what if the golden gift is held captive in "frozen halls?" How can it be rescued?

Vocabulary

sea mews: seagulls

intoxicated: drunk

dells: valleys

rime, **hoar:** frost (also called hoarfrost)

ominous: threatening; carrying bad news

Reading

Part One

They were dreadfully frightened. Giant Gilling asleep had been easy to manage, but a giant awake, a giant angry—they were not the same dwarfs that they had seemed half an hour ago— and so it happened that they quite easily let Suttung carry them all off to a low rock in the sea which was dry just then, but would be washed over by the morning tide. "There you are," said Suttung as he threw them all down upon the rock, "and there you shall stay until the hungry grey wave comes." "But then we shall be drowned," they all screeched at once, and the **sea mews** started from their nests ashore and swooped round the lonely rock, and screeched as well.

Suttung strode back to the shore and sat on the high rocks over the sea mews' nests, and poked his fingers into the nests and played with the grey-winged birds, and paddled his feet in the breakers, and laughed and echoed the dwarfs and the sea mews. "Drowned, drowned, yes, then you will be drowned."

Then the dwarfs whispered together and consulted, they all talked at once, and every one of them said a different thing, for they were in fact a little **intoxicated** still by the sips they had taken of Odhaerir. At last Fialar and Galar said the same thing over so often that the others began to listen to them. "The sky is getting quite grey," they said, "and the stars are going out, and Skinfaxi is coming, and the waves are gathering and gathering and gathering; hoarse are the voices of the Sea-king's daughters; but why do we all sit chattering here instead of getting away as we might easily do, if we did but bribe the giant Suttung with a gift." "Yes, yes, yes," shouted the silly little people, "shall we give him our cap jewels, or our swords, or our pick-axes, or our lanterns, or shall we promise to make him a necklace out of the fire of the sun and the flowers of the earth, or shall we build him a ship of ships?"

"Nonsense," said Fialar and Galar; "How should a giant care for such things as these? Our swords could not help him; he does not want pick-axes nor lanterns who lives amongst the mountain snows, nor ships who can stride across the sea, nor necklaces—Bah! A giant loves life, he drinks blood, he is greedy besides and longs to taste the gold mead of the gods."

Then all the dwarfs shouted together, "Let us give him our gold mead, our wondrous drink, Odhaerir, our Kvasir's blood in the three stone jars."

Part Two

Odin heard from Air Throne's blue deep. He brooded over the scene. "The sweetness, and the life, and the light of the world, then," he said, "are to satiate a giant's greediness of food and blood"—and it was for mankind that he became Terror in the trembling Height. All-father feared nothing for the gods at that time: could he not pierce into Jotunheim, and Svartheim, and Manheim alike?

Suttung heard also from the Rock. "And what may this Odhaerir be worth, that you boast of so much?" he shouted to the dwarfs. "Wisdom, and labour, and fire, and life, and love," said the dwarfs. "Tut, tut, tut," answered Suttung. "Does it taste well?" "Honey and wine; like the blood of a God and the milk of the Earth." Then Suttung got up slowly from the rock, pressing it down with his hands into two little **dells** as he rose, and strode to the island, from which he took up all the dwarfs at a grasp—they clinging to his fists and wrists like needles to a magnet; and, with one swoop, threw them ashore just as the hungry waves began to lap and wash about the "dwarfs'-peril."

So the dwarfs jumped, and leaped, and laughed, and sang, and chattered again, and ran on before Suttung, to fetch him the golden mead, Odhaerir. Three big stone jars, all full; the "Spirit-mover," the "Peace-offer," the "Peace-kiss." Suttung lifted the lids, and looked into the jars. "It doesn't look much," he said. "And, after all, I don't know that I shall care to taste it; but I'll take the jars home to my daughter Gunnlod, and they will make a pretty treasure for her to keep."

Part Three

Odin brooded over the scene. It was a grey winter's morning in Jotunheim—ice over all the rivers, snow upon the mountains, **rime**-writing across the woods, weird **hoar**-letters straggling over the bare branches of the trees, writing such as giants and gods can read, but men see it only as pearl-drops of the cold.

Suttung could read it well enough as he trudged along to his Mountain Home— better than he had ever read it before; for was he not bearing upon his shoulders the wondrous Kvasir's life-giving blood, Odhaerir?

Odin read it. "This is **ominous**, Odin; this is dark. Shall the gold mead be made captive in frozen halls?" For behold, the life-tear becomes dark in the dark land, as Suttung's huge door opened to let him in, him and his treasure, and then closed upon them both. Suttung gave the mead to his daughter Gunnlod to keep, to guard it well, and—the heart of Manheim trembled, it was empty and cold.

Part Four

Then Odin looked north and south and east and west, over the whole world. "Come to me," he said, and two swift-winged ravens flew towards him. It seemed as if they came out of nothing; for in a moment they were not there and they were there. Their names were Hugin and Munin, and they came from the ends of the earth, where Odin sent them every morning. Every evening he was wont to say of them—

"I fear me for Hugin,

Lest he come not back,

But much more for Munin."

Yet they never failed to come back, both of them, at the dim hour in which they recounted to the Father of Hosts the history of the day that was past, and the hope of the day that was to come.

On this evening, Munin's song was so terrible that only the strength of a god could possibly have endured to its end. Hugin struck another note, profounder and sweet. Then said Odin, when cadence after cadence had filled his ears, and he had descended from Air Throne, "Night is the time for new counsels; let each one reflect until the morrow who is able to give advice helpful to the Aesir."

But when the jewelled horse ran up along the sky, from whence his mane shed light over the whole world, when giants and giantesses, and ghosts and dwarfs crouched beneath Yggdrasil's outer Root, when Heimdall ran up Bifrost and blew mightily his horn in Heaven's height, there was only one found who gave counsel to Odin, and that was Odin himself.

"Odhaerir," he said, "which is a god-gift, must come [back] up to men's earthly dwellings. Go forth, Hugin, go forth, Munin," said the Asa, and he also went forth alone, none knowing where he went, nor how.

Narration and Discussion

What do you think of the dwarfs' bargain with the giant Suttung? Was there anything else they could have done?

Creative narration: Odin says that only he can give himself counsel in this matter. Imagine a conversation between Odin and Odin, talking about the problem and figuring out what to do next.

Further thought (for older students and adults): What was Manheim like without the Odhaerir, and why did Odin think the people needed it back? Wasn't the "mead of poetry" a bit dangerous? (Look what happened to the dwarfs…)

(Lesson 12) Odhaerir (Third Part)

Introduction

Odin plans to enter the cave and rescue the Odhaerir—but just getting in there is going to take some time. And what will he do about the giant's daughter who guards it?

Vocabulary

> **whetting:** sharpening
>
> **scythes:** tools for cutting grain
>
> **thralls:** slaves, bond-servants
>
> **defrauded:** cheated
>
> **discordant:** harsh, disagreeable

Names

> **Baugi:** the brother of **Suttung**

Reading

Part One

So Odin journeyed for a long, long while towards Suttung's Hall, across the windy, wintry ways of Jotunheim, seeing well before him the yellow mead as he went, through rocks, and woods, and rivers, and through night itself, until at last it happened that Odin came into a meadow upon a summer morning in Giant Land. Nine slaves were mowing in the meadow, **whetting** some old rusty **scythes** which they had, working heavily, for they were senseless fellows, and the summer day grew faster upon them than their labour grew to completion. "You seem heavy-hearted," said Odin to the **thralls**; and they began to explain to him how rusty and old their scythes were, and that they had no whetstone to sharpen them with. Upon this Odin offered to whet their scythes for them with his whetstone; and no sooner had he done so than the scythes became so sharp that they could have cut stones as easily as grass.

Instead of mowing, however, the thralls began to clamour round Odin, beseeching him to give his whetstone to them. "Give it to me! give it to me! give it to me!" cried one and another; and all the time Odin stood quietly amongst them, throwing his whetstone up in the air, and catching it as it fell. Then the thralls tried if they could catch it, leaning stupidly across one another, with their scythes in their hands. Was All-father surprised at what happened next? He could hardly have been that; but he was sorry when, looking down as the whetstone fell, he saw all the thralls lying dead at his feet, killed by each other's sharpened weapons. "This is an Evil Land," said Odin, as he looked down on the dead thralls, "and I am a bringer of evil into it."

So he journeyed on till he came to the house of Suttung's brother, **Baugi**. Odin asked Baugi to give him a night's lodging, and Baugi, who knew no more than the thralls had done who this traveller was, consented, and began to talk to Odin of the trouble he was in. "This is hay harvest," he said, "as you must have seen, walking here through the meadows; and I have a mighty field to gather in, but how to do it puzzles me, because my nine slaves whom I sent out sound and well this morning, all fell dead about the middle of the day. How they managed it, I can't imagine, and it puts me out sadly, for summer days don't last long in Jotunheim."

"Well," said Odin, "I'm not a bad hand at mowing, and I don't mind undertaking to do the work of nine thralls for you, Baugi, for a certain reward you may give me, if you will."

"What is that?" inquired Baugi, eagerly.

"A draught of that golden mead, Odhaerir, which Suttung obtained from the dwarfs, and which his daughter Gunnlod keeps for him."

"Oh! that," said Baugi, "isn't so good as my homebrewed [beer] for a thirsty mower; but you shall have it. It is a bargain between us."

So Odin worked for Baugi the whole summer through, with the labour of nine instead of with the labour of one; and when the last field was reaped, and wintry mists were gathering, the god and the giant began to talk over their bargain again. "We will come together to Suttung's house," said Baugi, "and my brother shall give you the draught which you desire so much."

Part Two

But when the two came to Suttung's house, and asked him for the mead, Suttung was exceedingly angry, and would not hear a word about it from either of them.

"You don't drink it yourself, brother," pleaded Baugi, "although you might do so every day if you liked, without asking anybody's leave, or doing one stroke of work for it, whilst this man has toiled night and day for nine months that he might taste it only once."

"Odhaerir is for us giants, nevertheless," answered Suttung, "and well does my daughter Gunnlod guard it from dwarfs and from men, from spectres, from Asyniur, and from Aesir. Have I not sworn that so it shall be guarded by all the snows of Jotunheim, and by the stormy waves, and by the yawning chasm of the abyss?"

Then Baugi knew that nothing more was to be said, and he advised Odin to go back with him at once and drink beer. But Odin was not to be turned from his purpose so easily. "You promised me a draught of the gold mead, Baugi," he said, "and I can see it through the rock in its three treasure jars; sit down by me and look through the rock till you can see it too."

So Odin and Baugi sat down together, and pierced the rock with their glances all that day until they had made a small hole in it; and at night, when Suttung was asleep, and when Gunnlod was asleep, and whilst the gold mead shone steadily in the heart of the cave, Odin looked up towards Asgard, and said,—

"Little get I here by silence:

Of a well-assumed form I will make good use;

For few things fail the wise."

And then this strong wise Asa picked up from the ground the little, mean, wriggling form of a worm, and put it on and crept noiselessly into the hole which he and Baugi had made.

"The giant's ways are under me,

The giant's ways are over me,"

said Odin as he wriggled through the stone.

Part Three

But when he had got quite through to the inner side, to Gunnlod's room, Odin took his proper form again.

"I see her upon her golden seat," he said as he looked upon the sleeping Gunnlod where she lay, and Odin was surprised to see a giant-maid so beautiful. Surprised and sorry. "For I must leave her weeping," he mused. "How shall she not weep, **defrauded** of her treasure in an Evil Land?" And Odin loved and pitied the beautiful maiden so much, that he would have returned to Asgard without the mead had that been possible.

Alas for Gunnlod, it was less possible than ever since All-father had seen her. For Gunnlod awoke in the light of Odin's glance and trembled, she did not know why, she did not know at first that he was an Asa, but, when he asked her for her treasure she could not keep it from him, she could not have kept anything from him.

She rose from her golden couch, her blue eyes melted into the tenderness of a summer sky, she undid the bars and bolts and coverings of Odhaerir, which she had guarded so faithfully till then, and knelt before Odin and stretched her hands towards him and said, "Drink, for I think you are a god."

A draught, a draught, a long, deep draught, and the spirit of the Asa was shaken through its height and through its depth. And again a draught of love flowing forth to the outermost, to the abysses. And one draught again—peace—in rushing, still [omission].

"It is for the Aesir, it is for men," said Odin. "It is Odin's [prize], it is Odin's gift"; and immediately, in haste to share it, the Asa spread eagle's wings, and flew far up, away from the barren rock, and the black, cold halls of Suttung, towards his heavenly home. The dwarfs sold it for their lives; the giantess lost it of her love; gods win it for the world.

Alas for Gunnlod! she has lost her treasure and her Asa too. How cold the cavern is now in which she sits! her light is gone out; she is left alone; she is left weeping upon her golden throne.

Part Four

But Odin soared upwards—flew on toward Asgard, and the Aesir came crowding upon the city's jewelled walls to watch his approach. And soon they perceived that two eagles were flying towards the city, the second pursuing the first. The pursuing eagle was Suttung, who, as soon as he found that his mead was gone, and that Odin, eagle-wise, had escaped his vengeance, spread also his eagle's wings, very strong and very swift, in pursuit. Suttung appeared to gain upon Odin. Frigga feared for her beloved The Asyniur and the Aesir watched breathlessly. Frost giants and Storm giants came crowding up from the deeps to see. "Does Odin return amongst the gods?" they asked, "or will Suttung destroy him?"

It was not possible, however, that the struggle should end in any way but one. The Divine bird dropped from the height upon his Hall—the High One's Hall—and then there burst from him such a flood of song that the widest limits of Aesir Land were overflowed—some sounds even spilt themselves upon the common earth.

"It is Poetry herself, it is Odin's [prize], it is Odin's gift. It is for the Aesir, it is for the Aesir," said a thousand and a thousand songs. "And for men," answered All-father, with his million ringing, changing voices; "it is for men."

("Such as have sufficient wit to make a right use of it," said Loki. And this was the first **discordant** note that troubled Asgard after Odin's return.)

Narration and Discussion

We have come to the end of the first chapter of *Heroes of Asgard*. (The other chapters will be much shorter.) What do you know now about Norse mythology that you didn't before? Which parts (or characters) do you like best?

What do you make of Loki's final remark?

Creative narration #1: On slips of paper, write the names of characters or places that have been described so far in the story. If you are learning in a group, put the slips in a bowl, have each student take one, and tell what they remember.

Creative narration #2: What is in the *Asgard Daily News* today? Headlines? Fashion advice, business, sports? Odin's Advice Column?

One note about the story: Other versions of this adventure add more earthy details. For instance, some say that Odin, before leaving on his journey, asks his people to build three enormous barrels, and keep them by the gates until his return. As he arrives in the shape of an eagle, he opens his beak over the vats and spits the mead into the barrels. "Ever since then," writes Neil Gaiman, "we know that those people who can make magic with their words, who can make poems and sagas and weave tales, have tasted the mead of poetry." (*Norse Mythology*)

Poetic Interlude: Some Things Odin Wrote When Inspired by Odhaerir

One of the *Edda* songs is called the "High One's Lay," and we may conclude it was inspired by Suttung's mead. The following are selected from the "Lay."

"Cattle die,
Kindred die,
We ourselves also die;
But I know one thing
That never dies—
Judgment on each one dead."

"A firmer friend
No man ever gets
Than great sagacity."

"Givers and requiters
Are longest friends."

"I was once young,
I was journeying alone,
And lost my way;
Rich I thought myself
When I met another.
Man is the joy of man."

Chapter Two: How Thor Went to Jotunheim

(Lesson 13) From Asgard to Utgard (Part One)

Introduction

In the first term's readings, we heard a great deal about Odin. In this story we move on to Thor and Loki, and an adventure that they had together.

Note: This reading is quite a bit longer than the previous ones, so you may prefer to read it in more than one sitting.

Vocabulary

cumbrous: heavy, awkward

marrow: the soft substance inside bones

runes: incantations (see notes at the beginning of this book)

Miolnir: Thor's hammer

mannikin: small person

drain at a draught: drink in one swallow

acquit yourself: succeed, show your stuff

mortified: deeply embarrassed

cleft: split

verdant: green, fruitful

Names

Thialfi (or Tjalfi, Thjalfi): a boy who became the servant of Thor

Roskva (or Roska): the sister of Thialfi

Skrymir: a "jotun" or giant, also known as **Utgarda-Loki**

Ving-Thor: Winged Thor

crone Elli: In the d'Aulaires' *Norse Gods and Giants*, she is called **Granny Elle**.

Places

Jotunheim: the giants' land (see previous notes)

Reading

Part One

Once on a time, Asa Thor and Loki set out on a journey from Asgard to **Jotunheim**. They travelled in Thor's chariot, drawn by two milk-white goats. It was a somewhat **cumbrous** iron chariot, and the wheels made a rumbling noise as it moved, which sometimes startled the ladies of Asgard, and made them tremble; but Thor liked it, thought the noise sweeter than any music, and was never so happy as when he was journeying in it from one place to another.

They travelled all day, and in the evening they came to a countryman's house. It was a poor, lonely place; but Thor descended from his chariot, and determined to pass the night there. The countryman, however, had no food in his house to give these travellers; and Thor, who liked to feast himself and make every one feast with him, was obliged to kill his own two goats and serve them up for supper. He invited the countryman and his wife and children to sup with him; but before they began to eat he made one request of them.

"Do not, on any account," he said, "break or throw away any of the bones of the goats you are going to eat for supper."

"I wonder why," said the peasant's son, **Thialfi**, to his sister **Roskva**. Roskva could not think of any reason, and by and by Thialfi happened to have a very nice little bone given him with some **marrow** in it. "Certainly there can be no harm in my breaking just this one," he said to himself; "it would be such a pity to lose the marrow," and as Asa Thor's head was turned another way, he slyly broke the bone in two, sucked the marrow, and then threw the pieces into the goats' skins, where Thor had desired that all the bones might be placed. I do not know whether Thialfi was uneasy during the night about what he had done; but in the morning he found out the reason of Asa Thor's command, and received a Lesson on "wondering why," which he never forgot all his life after.

As soon as Asa Thor rose in the morning he took his hammer, Miolnir, in his hand, and held it over the goat-skins as they lay on the floor, whispering **runes** the while. They were dead skins with dry bones on them when he began to speak; but as he said the last word, Thialfi, who was looking curiously on, saw two live goats spring up and walk towards the chariot, as fresh and well as when they brought the chariot up to the door (Thialfi hoped).

But no; one of the goats limped a little with his hind leg, and Asa Thor saw it. His brow grew dark as he looked, and for a minute Thialfi thought he would run far, far into the forest, and never come back again; but one look more at Asa Thor's face, angry as it was, made him change his mind He thought of a better thing to do than running away. He came forward, threw himself at the Asa's feet, and, confessing what he had done, begged pardon for his disobedience. Thor listened, and the displeased look passed away from his face.

"You have done wrong, Thialfi," he said, raising him up; "but as you have confessed your fault so bravely, instead of punishing you, I will take you with me on my journey, and teach you myself the Lesson of obedience to the Aesir which is, I see, wanted." Roskva chose to go with her brother, and from that day Thor had two faithful servants, who followed him wherever he went.

Part Two

The chariot and goats were now left behind; but, with Loki and his two new followers, Thor journeyed on to the end of Manheim, over the sea, and then on, on, on in the strange, barren, misty land of Jotunheim. Sometimes they crossed great mountains; sometimes they had to make their way among torn and rugged rocks, which often, through the mist, appeared to them to wear the forms of men, and once for a whole day they traversed a thick and tangled forest In the evening of that day, being very much tired, they saw with pleasure that they had come upon a spacious hall, of which the door, as broad as the house itself, stood wide open.

"Here we may very comfortably lodge for the night," said Thor; and they went in and looked about them. The house appeared to be perfectly empty; there was a wide hall, and five smaller rooms opening into it. They were, however, too tired to examine it carefully, and as no inhabitants made their appearance, they ate their supper in the hall, and lay down to sleep. But they had not rested long before they were disturbed by strange noises, groanings, mutterings, and snortings, louder than any animal that they had ever seen in their lives could make. By and by the house began to shake from side to side, and it seemed as if the very earth trembled. Thor sprang up in haste, and ran to the open door; but, though he looked earnestly into the starlit forest, there was no enemy to be seen anywhere.

Loki and Thialfi, after groping about for a time, found a sheltered chamber to the right, where they thought they could finish their night's rest in safety; but Thor, with **Miolnir** in his hand, watched at the door of the house all night As soon as the day dawned he went out into the forest, and there, stretched on the ground close by the house, he saw a strange, uncouth, gigantic shape of a man, out of whose nostrils came a breath which swayed the trees to their very tops. There was no need to wonder any longer what the disturbing noises had been.

Thor fearlessly walked up to this strange monster to have a better look at him; but at the sound of his footsteps the giant-shape rose slowly, stood up an immense height, and looked down upon Thor with two great misty eyes, like blue mountain-lakes.

"Who are you?" said Thor, standing on tiptoe, and stretching his neck to look up; "and why do you make such a noise as to prevent your neighbours from sleeping?"

"My name is **Skrymir**," said the giant sternly; "I need not ask yours. You are the little Asa Thor of Asgard; but pray, now, what have you done with my glove? "

As he spoke he stooped down, and picked up the hall where Thor and his companions had passed the night, and which, in truth, was nothing more than his glove, the room where Loki and Thialfi had slept being the thumb.

Thor rubbed his eyes, and felt as if he must be dreaming. Rousing himself, however, he raised Miolnir in his hand, and, trying to keep his eyes fixed on the giant's face, which seemed to be always changing, he said, "It is time that you should know, Skrymir, that I am come to Jotunheim to fight and conquer such evil giants as you are, and, little as you think me, I am ready to try my strength against yours."

"Try it, then," said the giant. And Thor, without another word, threw Miolnir at his head.

"Ah! Ah!" said the giant; "did a leaf touch me?" Again Thor seized Miolnir, which always returned to his hand, however far he cast it from him, and threw it with all his force.

The giant put up his hand to his forehead. "I think," he said, "that an acorn must have fallen on my head." A third time Thor struck a blow, the heaviest that ever fell from the hand of an Asa; but this time the giant laughed out loud.

"There is surely a bird on that tree," he said, "who has let a feather fall on my face." Then, without taking any further notice of Thor, he swung an immense wallet over his shoulder, and, turning his back upon him, struck into a path that led from the forest. When he had gone a little way he looked round, his immense face appearing less like a human countenance than some strange, uncouthly-shaped stone toppling on a mountain precipice.

"**Ving-Thor**," he said, "let me give you a piece of good advice before I go. When you get to Utgard don't make much of yourself. You think me a tall man, but you have taller still to see; and you yourself are a very little **mannikin**. Turn back home whence you came, and be satisfied to have learned something of yourself by your journey to Jotunheim."

"Mannikin or not, *that* will I never do," shouted Asa Thor after the giant. "We will meet again, and something more will we learn, or teach each other."

The giant, however, did not turn back to answer, and Thor and his companions, after looking for some time after him, resumed their journey. Before the sun was quite high in the heavens they came out of the forest, and at noon they found themselves on a vast barren plain, where stood a great city, whose walls of dark, rough stone were so high, that Thor had to bend his head quite far back to see the top of them. When they approached the entrance of this city they found that the gates were closed and barred; but the space between the bars was so large that Thor passed through easily, and his companions followed him.

Part Three

The streets of the city were gloomy and still. They walked on for some time without meeting any one; but at length they came to a very high building, of which the gates stood open. "Let us go in and see what is going on here," said Thor; and they went.

After crossing the threshold they found themselves in an immense banqueting hall. A table stretched from one end to the other of it; stone thrones stood round the table, and on every throne sat a giant, each one, as Thor glanced round, appearing more grim, and cold, and stony than the rest. One among them sat on a raised seat, and appeared to be the chief; so to him Thor approached and paid his greetings.

The giant chief just glanced at him, and, without rising, said, in a somewhat careless manner, "It is, I think, a foolish custom to tease tired travellers with questions about their journey. I know without asking that you, little fellow, are Asa Thor. Perhaps, however, you may be in reality taller than you appear; and as it is a rule here that no one shall sit down to table till he has performed some wonderful feat, let us hear what you and your followers are famed for, and in what way you choose to prove yourselves worthy to sit down in the company of giants."

At this speech, Loki, who had entered the hall cautiously behind Thor, pushed himself forward. "The feat for which I am most famed," he said, "is eating, and it is one which I am just now inclined to perform with right good will. Put food before me, and let me see if any of your followers can despatch it as quickly as I can."

"The feat you speak of is one by no means to be despised," said the King, "and there is one here who would be glad to try his powers against yours. Let Logi," he said to one of his followers, "be summoned to the hall."

At this, a tall, thin, yellow-faced man approached, and a large trough of meat having been placed in the middle of the hall, Loki sat to work at one end, and Logi at the other, and they began to eat. I hope *I* shall never see any one eat as they ate; but the giants all turned their slow-moving eyes to watch them, and in a few minutes they met in the middle of the trough. It seemed, at first, as if they had both eaten exactly the same quantity; but, when the thing came to be examined into, it was found that Loki had, indeed, eaten up all the meat, but that Logi had also eaten the bones *and* the trough. Then the giants nodded their huge heads, and determined that Loki was conquered.

The King now turned to Thialfi, and asked what he could do. "I was thought swift of foot among the youth of my own country," answered Thialfi; "and I will, if you please, try to run a race with any one here."

"You have chosen a noble sport, indeed," said the King; "but you must be a good runner if you could beat him with whom I shall match you."

Then he called a slender lad, Hugi by name, and the whole company left the hall, and, going out by an opposite gate to that by which Thor had entered, they came out to an open space, which made a noble race-ground. There the goal was fixed, and Thialfi and Hugi started off together. Thialfi ran fast—fast as the reindeer which hears the wolves howling behind; but Hugi ran so much faster that, passing the goal, he turned round, and met Thialfi half-way in the course.

"Try again, Thialfi," cried the King; and Thialfi, once more taking his place, flew along the course with feet scarcely touching the ground—swiftly as an eagle when, from his mountain-crag, he swoops on his prey in the valley; but with all his running he was still a good bow-shot from the goal when Hugi reached it.

"You are certainly a good runner," said the King; "but if you mean to win you must do a little better still than this; but perhaps you wish to surprise us all the more this third time."

The third time, however, Thialfi was wearied, and though he did his best, Hugi, having reached the goal, turned and met him not far from the starting-point. The giants again looked at each other, and declared that there was no need of further trial, for that Thialfi was conquered.

Part Four

It was now Asa Thor's turn, and all the company looked eagerly at him, while the Utgard King asked by what wonderful feat he chose to distinguish himself. "I will try a drinking-match with any of you," Thor said, shortly; for, to tell the truth, he cared not to perform anything very worthy in the company in which he found himself.

King Utgard appeared pleased with this choice, and when the giants had resumed their seats in the hall, he ordered one of his servants to bring in his drinking-cup, called the "cup of penance," which it was his custom to make his guests **drain at a draught**, if they had broken any of the ancient rules of the society. "There!" he said, handing it to Thor, "we call it well drunk if a person empties it at a single draught. Some, indeed, take two to it; but the very puniest can manage it in three."

Thor looked into the cup; it appeared to him long, but not so very large after all, and being thirsty he put it to his lips, and thought to make short work of it, and empty it at one good, hearty pull. He drank, and put the cup down again; but, instead of being empty, it was now just so full that it could be moved without danger of spilling.

"Ha! Ha! You are keeping all your strength for the second pull, I see," said Utgard, looking in. Without answering, Thor lifted the cup again, and drank with all his might till his breath failed; but, when he put down the cup, the liquor had only sunk down a little from the brim.

"If you mean to take three draughts to it," said Utgard, "you are really leaving yourself a very unfair share for the last time. Look to yourself, Ving-Thor; for, if you do not **acquit yourself** better in other feats, we shall not think so much of you here as they say the Aesir do in Asgard."

At this speech Thor felt angry, and, seizing the cup again, he drank a third time, deeper and longer than he had yet done; but, when he looked into the cup, he saw that a very small part only of its contents had disappeared. Wearied and disappointed he put the cup down, and said he would try no more to empty it.

Part Five

"It is pretty plain," said the King, looking round on the company, "that Asa Thor is by no means the kind of man we always supposed him to be."

"Nay," said Thor, "I am willing to try another feat, and you yourselves shall choose what it shall be."

"Well," said the King, "there is a game at which our children are used to play. A short time ago I dare not have named it to Asa Thor; but now I am curious to see how he will acquit himself in it. It is merely to lift my cat from the ground—a childish amusement truly."

As he spoke a large, grey cat sprang into the hall, and Thor, stooping forward, put his hand under it to lift it up. He tried gently at first; but by degrees he put forth all his strength, tugging and straining as he had never done before; but the utmost he could do was to raise one of the cat's paws a little way from the ground.

"It is just as I thought," said King Utgard, looking round with a smile; "but we all are willing to allow that the cat *is* large, and Thor but a little fellow."

"Little as you think me," cried Thor, "who is there who will dare to wrestle with me in my anger?"

"In truth," said the King, "I don't think there is any one here who would choose to wrestle with you; but, if wrestle you must, I will call in that old **crone Elli**. She has, in her time, laid low many a better man than Asa Thor has shown himself to be."

The crone came. She was old, withered, and toothless, and Thor shrank from the thought of wrestling with her; but he had no choice. She threw her arms round him, and drew him towards the ground, and the harder he tried to free himself, the tighter grew her grasp. They struggled long. Thor strove bravely, but a strange feeling of weakness and weariness came over him, and at length he tottered and fell down on one knee before her. At this sight all the giants laughed aloud, and Utgard coming up, desired the old woman to leave the hall, and proclaimed that the trials were over. No one of his followers would now contend with Asa Thor, he said, and night was approaching. He then invited Thor and his companions to sit down at the table, and spend the night with him as his guests. Thor, though feeling somewhat perplexed and **mortified**, accepted his invitation courteously, and showed, by his agreeable behaviour during the evening, that he knew how to bear being conquered with a good grace.

Part Six

In the morning, when Thor and his companions were leaving the city, the King himself accompanied them without the gates; and Thor, looking steadily at him when he turned to bid him farewell, perceived, for the first time, that he was the very same Giant Skrymir with whom he had met in the forest.

"Come, now, Asa Thor," said the giant with a strange sort of smile on his face, "tell me truly, before you go, how you think your journey has turned out, and whether or not I was right in saying that you would meet with better men than yourself in Jotunheim."

"I confess freely," answered Asa Thor, looking up without any false shame on his face, "that I have acquitted myself but humbly, and it grieves me; for I know that in Jotunheim henceforward it will be said that I am a man of little worth."

"By my troth! no," cried the giant, heartily. "Never should you have come into my city if I had known what a mighty man of valour you really are; and now that you are safely out of it, I will, for once, tell the truth to you, Thor. All this time I have been deceiving you by my enchantments. When you met me in the forest, and hurled Miolnir at my head, I should have been crushed by the weight of your blows had I not skilfully placed a mountain between myself and you, on which the strokes of your hammer fell, and where you **cleft** three deep ravines, which shall henceforth become **verdant** valleys.

"In the same manner I deceived you about the contests in which you engaged last night. When Loki and Logi sat down before the trough, Loki [did], indeed, eat like hunger itself; but Logi is Fire, who, with eager, consuming tongue, licked up both bones and trough. Thialfi is the swiftest of mortal runners; but the slender lad, Hugi, was my Thought; and what speed can ever equal his? So it was in your own trials. When you took such deep draughts from the horn, you little knew what a wonderful feat you were performing. The other end of that horn reached the ocean, and when you come to the shore you will see how far its waters have fallen away, and how much the deep sea itself has been diminished by your draught. Hereafter, men watching the going out of the tide will call it the ebb, or draught, of Thor.

"Scarcely less wonderful was the prowess you displayed in the second trial. What appeared to you to be a cat, was, in reality, the Midgard serpent, which encircles the world. When we saw you succeed in moving it we trembled lest the very foundations of earth and sea should be shaken by your strength. Nor need you be ashamed of having been overthrown by the old woman Elli, for she is Old Age; and there never has, and never will be, one whom she has not the power to lay low.

"We must now part, and you had better not come here again, or attempt anything further against my city; for I shall always defend it by fresh enchantments, and you will never be able to do anything against me. "

At these words Thor raised Miolnir, and was about to challenge the giant to a fresh trial of strength; but, before he could speak, [King] Utgard vanished from his sight; and, turning round to look for the city, he found that it, too, had disappeared, and that he was standing alone on a smooth, green, empty plain.

"What a fool I have been," said Asa Thor, aloud, "to allow myself to be deceived by a mountain giant!"

"Ah," answered a voice from above, "I told you, you would learn to know yourself better by your journey to Jotunheim. It is the great use of travelling." Thor turned quickly round again, thinking to see Skrymir behind him; but, after looking on every side, he could perceive nothing, but that a high, cloud-capped mountain, which he had noticed on the horizon, appeared to have advanced to the edge of the plain.

Narration and Discussion

Skrymir/Utgard said to Thor, "I told you, you would learn to know yourself better by your journey to Jotunheim." Was that the case?

Why did Skrymir say that Thor must not ever try to come back to the giants' city? It seemed as if Thor had earned a little respect, but the ending did not seem very friendly.

Something to think about: Have you ever had to play a game against someone much better or stronger than you? Even if you didn't win, was it worthwhile trying?

Creative narration: This story lends itself very well to drama, if you can work out a way to show Thor, Loki and Thialfi visiting the giants. Drawing/painting your favourite scene would also be a good choice.

(Lesson 14) The Serpent and the Kettle

Introduction

This is another (again slightly longer) adventure for Thor, this time accompanied by Tyr. It begins as an errand to borrow a beer-kettle; takes in a whale-fishing trip; and ends with a smashing-dishes fight. Just a typical day for those two.

Vocabulary

- **reclined at the board:** As at Greek and Roman dinner parties, the guests are lounging on couches behind the table, rather than sitting upright on chairs.

- **the sound of a sullen swell:** a noise like an angry wave rolling in

- **surly:** grouchy, unfriendly

- **resounded:** echoed the sound of the footsteps

- **burst asunder:** split apart

- **great relish:** enjoyment

- **host:** army

Names

- **Aegir the Old:** the **jotun** or deity who represents the sea. He is married to **Ran**, and the father of numerous daughters and a son. Also associated with the brewing of ale (as in this story).

- **Tyr:** See notes in **Lesson 8**.

- **Hymir:** In some versions of this story, Hymir is Tyr's grandfather.

Reading

Part One

Thor turned away from Giant-land, and on the road homeward he passed through the Sea-King's dominions. There he found that **Aegir the Old** was giving a banquet to all the Aesir in his wide coral-caves. At a little distance Thor stood still to listen and to look. It was a fair sight: cave within cave stretched out before him decked with choicest shells, whilst far inward lay the banqueting-hall, lighted with shining gold; white and red coral-pillars stood at uneven distances; the bright-browed Aesir **reclined at the board** on soft water couches; Aegir's daughters—the fair-haired waves—murmured sweet music as they waited on their guests; and little baby-ripples ran about laughing in all the corners.

Thor walked through the caves and entered the hall. As he did so Odin looked up from his place at Aegir's right hand, and said,—

"Good evening, son Thor; how has it fared with you in Jotunheim?"

Thor's face grew a little cloudy at this question, and he only answered,—

"Not as it ought to have done, father." Then he placed himself amongst Aegir's guests.

"In my dominions," said King Aegir, looking all round, "an extraordinary thing has happened."

"And what may that be, brother?" asked Niord.

"From the shores of Jotunheim," answered Aegir, "the sea has run back a quarter of a mile, drawing itself away as if a giant were drinking it in."

"Is that all you have got to say, father?" said a tall Wave, as she swept her hair over the Sea-King's shoulder, and peeped up from behind him; "is that all you know of the wonders which are going on in your deep home? Listen." Then Aegir bent forward on his seat; the all ceased speaking, and drew in their breath; the waves raised their arched necks, and were still, listening. From a great way off came **the sound of a sullen swell**.

"Who is that speaking?" asked Odin,

"That is Jormungand speaking," said Thor.

"And what does he say, Thor?"

"He says that I could not conquer him."

"Pass round the foaming mead," cried Aegir, who saw that it was time to turn the conversation. But alas! Aegir's mead-kettle was so small, that before it had gone half down the table it stood empty before **Tyr**.

"There is a giant called **Hymir**," remarked Tyr, "who lives far over the stormy waves to eastward at the end of heaven." The Aesir all looked up.

"He has a kettle," Tyr went on to say, "which is a mile deep, and which would certainly hold mead enough for all this company."

"If Hymir would lend it to us," said Aegir, "we could finish our supper; but who would go to the end of heaven to borrow a kettle?" Then Thor rose from the table, and began to tighten round him his belt of power; he put on his iron gloves, and took

Miolnir in his hand.

"What! off again to Giant-land, Ving-Thor?" cried Aegir.

"Didn't you say you wanted Mile-deep?" said Thor. "I am going to borrow it [from] Hymir for you. Will you come with me, Tyr?" Tyr sprang up joyfully, and the two brothers started on their journey.

Part Two

When they arrived at Hymir's dwelling, which was a roughly-hewn cavern on the shore of a frozen sea, the first person they met was a wonderful giantess with nine hundred heads, in which glittered fiery eyes, and which grew out from all parts of her body, so that it was impossible to tell whether she was walking upon her head or her heels. As Thor and Tyr were looking at her trying to discover this, a woman came out of the giant's home quite as lovely as the giantess was hideous. She greeted them on the threshold. Her golden hair fell thick upon her shoulders; her mild eyes shone upon them; and with words of welcome she held out her hands and led them into the cavern. There she offered them meat and drink, and bade them rest until her husband, Hymir, should come home.

As the darkness came on, however, and the time of his expected return drew near, she became silent and anxious; and at last she said, "I am very much afraid that my husband will be angry if he sees strangers here when he comes in. Take my advice, now, Asa Thor and Asa Tyr, and hide behind one of these pillars in the rock. My lord, I assure you, is **surly** sometimes, and not nearly so hospitable as I could wish."

"We are not accustomed to hide ourselves," remarked Thor.

"But you shall come forth when I call you," answered the woman.

Part Three

So the Aesir did as she desired. By and by they heard heavy footsteps far off, over the frozen sea, coming nearer and nearer every moment. The distant icebergs **resounded**, and at last Hymir burst open the door of his cavern, and stalked angrily in. He had been unsuccessful that day in the chase, his hands were frost-bitten, and a "hard-frozen wood stood upon his cheek."

As soon as the fair-browed woman saw what mood he was in she went gently towards him, placed her hand in his, and told him of the arrival of the guests; then, with a sweet smile and voice, she entreated him to receive the strangers kindly, and entertain them hospitably.

Hymir made no answer; but, at one glance of his eye towards the place where the Aesir were hidden, the pillar **burst asunder**, and the cross-beam which it supported fell with a crash to the ground. Eight ponderous kettles had been hanging on the beam, and all but one were shivered to atoms.

Thor and Tyr then stepped forth into the middle of the hall, and Hymir received them civilly, after which he turned his attention to supper; and, having cooked three whole oxen, he invited the Aesir to eat with him. Thor fell to work with **great relish**, and when he had eaten the whole of one ox, prepared to cut a slice out of another.

"You eat a great deal," said Hymir, sulkily, but Thor was still very hungry, and went on with his supper until he had eaten two entire oxen. Then said Hymir, "Another night, Ving-Thor, you must provide your own supper; for I can't undertake to keep so expensive a guest."

Part Four

Accordingly, early the next morning, Hymir prepared to go out fishing, and offered Thor a place in his boat. On their way to the shore they passed a herd of oxen feeding.

"Have you provided a bait for me?" said Thor to the giant

"You must get one for yourself," answered Hymir, surlily.

So Thor was obliged to cut off the head of one of the oxen for a bait.

"You'll never be able to carry *that* head," said Hymir; for, in truth, the ox to which it had belonged was an enormous animal, called "Heaven Breaking." But Thor made nothing of the head, slung it over his shoulder, and carried it down to the boat. As they got under way, Thor and Hymir each took an oar; but Thor pulled so fast, and with such mighty strokes, that the giant was obliged to stop for breath, and beg that they might go no further.

"We have already reached the spot," he said, "where I always catch the finest whales."

"But I want to go further out to sea," said Thor.

"That will be dangerous, Ving-Thor," said Hymir; "for if we row any further we shall come to the waters under which Jormungand lies." Thor laughed, and rowed on. At last he stopped, baited his hook with the ox's head, and cast the line out into the sea, whilst Hymir leant over the other side of the boat, and caught two whales.

Now, when the great Jormungand smelt Thor's bait he opened wide his monstrous jaws, and eagerly sucked in both head, and hook, and line; but no sooner did he feel the pain than he struggled so fiercely, and plunged so wildly, that Thor's hands were in an instant dashed against the sides of the boat. Still Thor did not lose his hold, but went on pulling with such wondrous force that his feet burst through the boat, and rested on the slippery rocks beneath. At last the venomous monster's mountain-high head was hauled above the waves, and then, indeed, it was a dreadful sight to see Thor, in all the power of his god-like strength, casting his fiery looks on the serpent, and the serpent glaring upon him, and spitting forth poisoned venom. Even Hymir's sun-burnt cheek changed colour as he beheld beneath his feet the sinking boat, and at his side the deadliest monster of the deep. At last, in the wildness of his fear, he rushed before Thor, and cut his line [in half]. Immediately the serpent's head began to sink; but Thor hurled Miolnir with fearful force after it into the waters.

Then did the rocks burst; it thundered through the caverns; old mother earth all shrank; even the fishes sought the bottom of the ocean; but the serpent sank back, with a long, dull sound, beneath the waves, a deep wound in his head, and smothered vengeance in his heart. Ill at ease and silent, Hymir then turned to go home, and Thor followed him, carrying boat and oars, and everything else, on his shoulders.

Part Five

Now, every fresh sight of Thor increased the giant's envy and rage; for he could not bear to think that he had shown so little courage before his brave guest, and, besides, losing his boat and getting so desperately wet in his feet by wading home through the sea, did not by any means improve his temper. When they got home, therefore, and were supping together, he began jeering and taunting Thor.

"No doubt, Asa Thor, "he said, "you think yourself a good rower and a fine fisher, though you did not catch anything today; but can you break that drinking-cup before you, do you think?" Thor seized the cup, and dashed it against an upright stone. But, lo! the stone was shattered in pieces, and the cup unbroken. Again, with greater strength, he hurled the cup against the pillars in the rock: it was still without a crack.

Now, it happened that the beautiful woman was sitting spinning at her wheel just behind where Thor was standing. From time to time she chanted snatches of old runes and sagas in soft tones; and now, when Thor stood astonished that the cup was not broken, the woman's voice fell on his ear, singing low the following words:—

"Hard the pillar, hard the stone,

Harder yet the giant's bone.

Stones shall break and pillars fall;

Hymir's forehead breaks them all."

Then Thor once more took the cup, and hurled it against the giant's forehead. The cup was this time shivered to pieces; but Hymir himself was unhurt, and cried out, "Well done at last, Ving-Thor; but can you carry that mile-deep kettle out of my hall, think you?" Tyr tried to lift it, and could not even raise the handle. Then Thor grasped it by the rim, and, as he did so, his feet pressed through the floor. With a mighty effort he lifted it; he placed it on his head, while the rings rang at his feet; and so in triumph he bore off the kettle, and set out again for Aegir's Hall.

Part Six

After journeying a little way he chanced to look round, and then he saw that a **host** of many-headed giants, with Hymir for their leader, were thronging after him. From every cavern, and iceberg, and jagged peak some hideous monster grinned and leered as a great wild beast waiting for his prey.

"Treachery!" cried Thor, as he raised Miolnir above his head, and hurled it three times among the giants. In an instant they stood stiff, and cold, and dead, in rugged groups along the shore; one with his arm raised; another with his head stretched out; some upright, some crouching; each in the position he had last assumed. And there still they stand, petrified by ages into giant rocks; and, still pointing their stony fingers at each other, they tell the mighty tale of Thor's achievements, and the wondrous story of their fate.

"Pass round the foaming mead," cried King Aegir, as Thor placed "Mile-deep" on the table; and this time it happened that there was enough for everyone.

[*omission: the end-of-chapter notes*]

Narration and Discussion

Do you think Thor is feeling a little more successful now?

Creative narration #1: What is in the *Asgard Daily News* today? Headlines? Business, sports, jokes? Fishing tips from Thor?

Creative narration #2: News channel K-AESIR has sent out a reporter to speak to Thor about his adventures. How might the conversation go?

Chapter Three: Frey

(Lesson 15) On Tiptoe in Air Throne

Introduction

Frey sits where he should not, and sees something that changes his world.

Vocabulary

descry: pick out, see

Reading

Part One

I told you, some time ago, how Van Frey went away into Alfheim with the light elves, of whom Odin made him king and schoolmaster.
You have heard what Frey was like, and the kind of Lesson s he promised to teach his pupils, so you can imagine what pleasant times they had of it in Alfheim. Wherever Frey came there was summer and sunshine. Flowers sprang up under his footsteps, and bright-winged insects, like flying flowers, hovered round his head. His warm

breath ripened the fruit on the trees, and gave a bright yellow colour to the corn, and purple bloom to the grapes, as he passed through fields and vineyards.

When he rode along in his car, drawn by the stately boar Gullinborsti ("Golden Bristles"), soft winds blew before him, filling the air with fragrance, and spreading abroad the news, "Van Frey is coming!"; and every half-closed flower burst into perfect beauty, and forest, and field, and hill, flushed their richest colours to greet his presence.

Under Frey's care and instruction the pretty little light elves forgot their idle ways, and learned all the pleasant tasks he had promised to teach them. It was the prettiest possible sight to see them in the evening filling their tiny buckets, and running about among the woods and meadows to hang the dew-drops deftly on the slender tips of the grass-blades, or to drop them into the half-closed cups of the sleepy flowers. When this last of their day's tasks was over they used to cluster round their summer-king, like bees about the queen, while he told them stories about the wars between the Aesir and the giants, or of the old time when he lived alone with his father Niord, in Noatun, and listened to the waves singing songs of far distant lands. So pleasantly did they spend their time in Alfheim.

But in the midst of all this work and play Frey had a wish in his mind, of which he could not help often talking to his clear-minded messenger and friend Skirnir. "I have seen many things," he used to say, "and travelled through many lands; but to see all the world at once, as Asa Odin does from Air Throne, *that* must be a splendid sight."

"Only Father Odin may sit on Air Throne," Skirnir would say; and it seemed to Frey that this answer was not so much to the purpose as his friend's sayings generally were.

At length, one very clear summer evening, when Odin was feasting with the other Aesir in Valhalla, Frey could restrain his curiosity no longer. He left Alfheim, where all the little elves were fast asleep, and, without asking any one's advice, climbed into Air Throne, and stood on tiptoe in Odin's very seat. It was a clear evening, and I had, perhaps, better not even try to tell you what Frey saw.

He looked first all round him over Manheim, where the rosy light of the set sun still lingered, and where men, and birds, and flowers were gathering themselves up for their night's repose. Then he glanced towards the heavenly hills where Bifrost rested, and then towards the shadowy land which deepened down into Niflheim.

At length he turned his eyes northward to the misty land of Jotunheim. There the shades of evening had already fallen; but from his high place Frey could still see distinct shapes moving about through the gloom. Strange and monstrous shapes they were, and Frey stood a little higher, on tiptoe, that he might look further after them. In this position he could just **descry** a tall house standing on a hill in the very middle of Jotunheim. While he looked at it a maiden came and lifted up her arms to undo the latch of the door. It was dusk in Jotunheim; but when this maiden lifted up her white arms, such a dazzling reflection came from them, that Jotunheim, and the sky, and all the sea were flooded with clear light. For a moment everything could be distinctly seen; but Frey saw nothing but the face of the maiden with the uplifted arms; and when she had entered the house and shut the door after her, and darkness fell again on earth, and sky, and sea—darkness fell, too, upon Frey's heart.

The next morning, when the little elves awoke up with the dawn, and came thronging round their king to receive his commands, they were surprised to see that he had changed since they last saw him.

"He has grown up in the night," they whispered one to another sorrowfully.

And in truth he was no longer so fit a teacher and playfellow for the merry little people as he had been a few hours before. It was to no purpose that the sweet winds blew, and the flowers opened, when Frey came forth from his chamber. A bright white light still danced before him, and nothing now seemed to him worth looking at.

Narration and Discussion

Was it wrong of Frey to be curious about what could be seen from Odin's throne?

What is going on with Frey now? Do you think it is fixable?

For further thought: In Mark 10, two of Jesus' disciples asked if they could have special "seating" in his kingdom. Can you see any similarities to this story?

(Lesson 16) The Gift

Introduction

Lovesick Frey asks his servant Skirnir to be his messenger to Gerd (whom he has only seen once, and from a great distance). Of course, Skirnir's services come with a price.

Vocabulary

> **recompense:** reward
>
> **pettishly:** rudely and impatiently; showing some attitude
>
> **mantle:** cloak

Reading

That evening when the sun had set, and work was over, there were no stories for the light elves. "Be still," Frey said, when they pressed round. "If you will be still and listen, there are stories enough to be heard better than mine."

I do not know whether the elves heard anything; but to Frey it seemed that flowers, and birds, and winds, and the whispering rivers, united that day in singing one song, which he never wearied of hearing. "We are fair," they said; "but there is nothing in the whole world so fair as Gerda, the giant-maiden whom you saw last night in Jotunheim."

"Frey has dew-drops in his eyes," the little elves said to each other in whispers as they sat round looking up at him, and they felt very much surprised; for only to men and the Aesir is it permitted to be sorrowful and weep.

Soon, however, wiser people noticed the change that had come over the summer king, and his good-natured father, Niord, sent Skirnir one day into Alfheim to inquire into the cause of Frey's sorrow.

He found him walking alone in a shady place, and Frey was glad enough to tell his trouble to his wise friend. When he had related the whole story, he said,—

"And now you will see that there is no use in asking me to be merry as I used to be; for how can I ever be happy in Alfheim, and enjoy the summer and sunshine, while my dear Gerd, whom I love, is living in a dark, cold land, among cruel giants?"

"If she be really as beautiful and beloved as you say," answered Skirnir, "she must be sadly out of place in Jotunheim. Why do not you ask her to be your wife, and live with you in Alfheim?"

"That would I only too gladly do," answered Frey; "but if I were to leave Alfheim only for a few hours, the cruel giant, Ryme [the Frost Giant] would rush in to take my place; all the labours of the year would be undone in a night, and the poor, toiling men, who are watching for the harvest, would wake some morning to find their cornfields and orchards buried in snow."

"Well," said Skirnir, thoughtfully, "I am neither so strong nor so beautiful as you, Frey; but, if you will give me the sword that hangs by your side, I will undertake the journey to Jotunheim; and I will speak in such a way of you, and of Alfheim, to the lovely Gerd, that she will gladly leave her land and the house of her giant-father to come to you."

Now, Frey's sword was a gift, and he knew well enough that he ought not to part with it, or trust it in any hands but his own; and yet how could he expect Skirnir to risk all the dangers of Jotunheim for any less **recompense** than an enchanted sword? and what other hope had he of ever seeing his dear Gerda again?

He did not allow himself a moment to think of the choice he was making. He unbuckled his sword from his side and put it into Skirnir's hands; and then he turned rather **pettishly** away, and threw himself down on a mossy bank under a tree.

"You will be many days in travelling to Jotunheim," he said, "and all that time I shall be miserable."

Skirnir was too sensible to think this speech worth answering. He took a hasty farewell of Frey, and prepared to set off on his journey; but, before he left the hill, he chanced to see the reflection of Frey's face in a little pool of water that lay near. In spite of its sorrowful expression, it was as beautiful as the woods are in full summer, and a clever thought came into Skirnir's mind. He stooped down, without Frey's seeing him, and, with cunning touch, stole the picture out of the water; then he fastened it up carefully in his silver drinking-horn, and, hiding it in his **mantle**, he mounted his horse and rode towards Jotunheim, secure of succeeding in his mission, since he carried a matchless sword to conquer the giant, *and* a matchless picture to win the maiden.

Narration and Discussion

Is Frey making a mistake in giving up his sword?

Should we trust Skirnir? Might he try to win Gerd for himself instead?

Creative narration: Imagine that Frey tries to pass the time by writing some poetry or a song for Gerd. If he sings it for the elves, how might they react?

(Lesson 17) Fairest Gerd

Introduction

Skirnir finds Gerda, and tries to persuade her to come to Asgard and be married to Frey. She is unimpressed by the promise of magic gifts if she accepts, and is unfazed by threats of various evils if she refuses. Skirnir finally plays his last card: will Gerda say yes?

Vocabulary

- **hoar:** probably "ancient"; however, since they are travelling among the frost-giants, it might also be referring to "hoarfrost"

- **stealthy:** in a quiet and cautious manner, so as not to be heard

- **Iduna's grove:** more on this in **Lesson 22**

- **Draupnir:** a ring belonging to Odin, with the magical ability to "multiply itself," or make new rings from the original one. In some versions it is said to be an "armlet" instead of a ring.

- **you shall be doomed to live for ever with the Frost Giant:** In other versions of the story, these threats are enough frighten Gerd into agreement; Frey's picture in the drinking cup seems to be a creative addition.

- **rode from Jotunheim with a glad heart:** Some versions say, however, that Gerda's father insisted on keeping the sword as a "bride price."

Places

- **Hel:** the world of the dead, ruled by Loki's daughter Hela (or Hel)

Barri: a grove of trees with "tranquil path." Some versions say it was a barley field.

Reading

Part One

I told you that the house of Gymir, Gerda's father, stood in the middle of Jotunheim, so it will not be difficult for you to imagine what a toilsome and wondrous journey Skirnir had. He was a brave hero, and he rode a brave horse; but when they came to the barrier of murky flame that surrounds Jotunheim, a shudder came over both.

"Dark it is without," said Skirnir to his horse, "and you and I must leap through flame, and go over **hoar** mountains among Giant Folk. The giants will take us both, or we shall return victorious together." Then he patted his horse's neck, and touched him with his armed heel, and with one bound he cleared the barrier, and his hoofs rang on the frozen land.

Their first day's journey was through the land of the Frost Giants, whose prickly touch kills, and whose breath is sharper than swords. Then they passed through the dwellings of the horse-headed and vulture-headed giants—monsters terrible to see. Skirnir hid his face, and the horse flew along swifter than the wind.

On the evening of the third day they reached Gymir's house. Skirnir rode round it nine times; but though there were twenty doors, he could find no entrance; for fierce three-headed dogs guarded every doorway. At length he saw a herdsman pass near, and he rode up and asked him how it was possible for a stranger to enter Gymir's house, or get a sight of his fair daughter Gerd.

"Are you doomed to death, or are you already a dead man," answered the herdsman, "that you talk of seeing Gymir's fair daughter, or entering a house from which no one ever returns?"

"My death is fixed for one day," said Skirnir, in answer, and his voice, the voice of an Asa, sounded loud and clear through the misty air of Jotunheim. It reached the ears of the fair Gerd as she sat in her chamber with her maidens.

"What is that noise of noises," she said, "that I hear? The earth shakes with it, and all Gymir's halls tremble."

Then one of the maidens got up, and peeped out of the window. "I see a man," she said; "he has dismounted from his horse, and he is fearlessly letting it graze before the door."

"Go out and bring him in stealthily, then," said Gerda; "I must again hear him speak; for his voice is sweeter than the ringing of bells."

So the maiden rose, and opened the house-door softly, lest the grim giant, Gymir, who was drinking mead in the banquet-hall with seven other giants, should hear and come forth.

Part Two

Skirnir heard the door open, and understanding the maiden's sign, he entered with **stealthy** steps, and followed her to Gerda's chamber. As soon as he entered the doorway the light from her face shone upon him, and he no longer wondered that Frey had given up his sword.

"Are you the son of an Asa, or an Alf, or of a wise Van?" asked Gerda; "and why have you come through flame and snow to visit our halls?"

Then Skirnir came forward and knelt at Gerda's feet, and gave his message, and spoke as he had promised to speak of Van Frey and of Alfheim. Gerda listened; and it was pleasant enough to talk to her, looking into her bright face; but she did not seem to understand much of what he said.

He promised to give her eleven golden apples from **Iduna's grove** if she would go with him, and that she should have the magic ring **Draupnir** from which every day a still fairer jewel fell. But he found there was no use in talking of beautiful things to one who had never in all her life anything beautiful. Gerda smiled at him as a child smiles at a fairy tale.

At length he grew angry. "If you are so childish, maiden," he said, "that you can believe only what you have seen, and have no thought of Aesirland or the Aesir, then sorrow and utter darkness shall fall upon you; you shall live alone on the Eagle Mount turned towards **Hel**. Terrors shall beset you; weeping shall be your lot. Men and Aesir will hate you, and **you shall be doomed to live for ever with the Frost Giant**, Ryme, in whose cold arms you will wither away like a thistle on a house-top."

"Gently," said Gerd, turning away her bright head, and sighing. "How am I to blame? You make such a talk of your Aesir and your Aesir; but how can I know about it, when all my life long I have lived with giants?"

At these words, Skirnir rose as if he would have departed, but Gerda called him back. "You must drink a cup of mead," she said, "in return for your sweet-sounding words." Skirnir heard this gladly, for now he knew what he would do. He took the cup from her hand, drank off the mead, and, before he returned it, he contrived cleverly to pour in the water from his drinking-horn, on which Frey's image was painted; then he put the cup into Gerda's hand, and bade her look.

She smiled as she looked; and the longer she looked, the sweeter grew her smile; for she looked for the first time on a face that loved her, and many things became clear to her that she had never understood before. Skirnir's words were no longer like fairy tales. She could now believe in Aesirland, and in all beautiful things.

"Go back to your master," she said, at last, "and tell him that in nine days I will meet him in the warm wood **Barri**."

After hearing these joyful words, Skirnir made haste to take leave, for every moment that he lingered in the giant's house he was in danger. One of Gerda's maidens conducted him to the door, and he mounted his horse again, and **rode from Jotunheim with a glad heart**.

Narration and Discussion

Why did Skirnir's promises and threats have little effect on Gerda?

How did seeing Frey's face make her change her mind?

Creative narration #1: This scene might be a good one to act out; or it could be drawn as a comic strip.

Creative narration #2: Do you know any songs that have similar themes to this story (maybe without the giants)? Here's the beginning of an American folk song:

> I'll give to you this paper of pins
> If that's the way our love begins
> If you will marry me, me, me
> If you will marry me...

(Lesson 18) The Wood Barri

Introduction

This is quite a short reading, about the wedding of Frey and Gerda. However, we also hear some darker notes of things to come, including **Ragnarok**.

Vocabulary

overlooking: overseeing, taking care of

Ragnarok: a series of events that had been prophesied, particularly the Last Great Battle

Names

sons of Muspell: a group of fire-giants led by **Surtr** during the events called **Ragnarok**.

Reading

Part One

When Skirnir got back to Alfheim, and told Gerd's answer to Frey, he was disappointed to find that his master did not immediately look as bright and happy as he expected. "Nine days!" he said; "but how can I wait nine days? One day is long, and three days are very long, but 'nine days' might as well be a whole year."

(I have heard children say such things when one tells them to wait for a new toy.)

Skirnir and old Niord only laughed at it; but Freyja and all the ladies of Asgard made a journey to Alfheim, when they heard the story, to comfort Frey, and hear all the news about the wedding.

"Dear Frey," they said, "it will never do to lie still here, sighing under a tree. You are quite mistaken about the time being long; it is hardly long enough to prepare the marriage presents, and talk over the wedding. You have no idea how busy we are going to be; everything in Alfheim will have to be altered a little."

At these words Frey really did lift up his head, and wake up from his musings. He looked, in truth, a little frightened at the thought; but, when all the Asgard ladies were ready to work for his wedding, how could he make any objection?

Part Two

He was not allowed to have much share in the business himself; but he had little time, during the nine days, to indulge in private thought, for never before was there such a commotion in Alfheim. The ladies found so many things that wanted **overlooking**, and the little light elves were not of the slightest use to any one. They forgot all their usual tasks, and went running about through groves and fields, and by the sedgy banks of rivers, peering into earth-holes, and creeping down into flower-cups and empty snail-shells, every one hoping to find a gift for Gerda. Some stole the light from glow-worms' tails, and wove it into a necklace, and others pulled the ruby spots from cowslip leaves, to set with jewels the acorn cups that Gerda was to drink from; while the swiftest runners chased the butterflies, and pulled feathers from their wings to make fans and bonnet-plumes.

All the work was scarcely finished when the ninth day came, and Frey set out from Alfheim with all his elves, to the warm wood Barri.

The Aesir joined him on the way, and they made, together, something like a wedding procession. First came Frey in his chariot, drawn by [the boar] "Golden Bristles," and carrying in his hand the wedding-ring, which was none other than Draupnir, the magic ring of which so many stories are told.

Odin and Frigga followed with their wedding gift, the Ship Skidbladnir, in which all the Aesir could sit and sail, though it could afterwards be folded up so small, that you might carry it in your hand.

Then came Iduna, with eleven golden apples in a basket on her fair head, and then two and two all the heroes and ladies with their gifts. All round them flocked the elves, toiling under the weight of their offerings. It took twenty little people to carry one gift, and yet there was not one so large as a baby's finger.

Laughing, and singing, and dancing, they entered the warm wood, and every summer flower sent a sweet breath after them. Everything on earth smiled on the wedding-day of Frey and Gerda, only—when it was all over, and every one had gone home, and the moon shone cold into the wood—it seemed as if the Vanir spoke to one another.

"Odin," said one voice, "gave his eye for wisdom, and we have seen that it was well done."

"Frey," answered the other, "has given his sword for happiness. It may be well to be unarmed while the sun shines and bright days last; but when **Ragnarok** has come, and the **sons of Muspell** ride down to the last fight, will not Frey regret his sword?"

[Note: the rest of this chapter has been shortened from the original text.]

Explaining Things

Frey appears as the summer god, and the Boar was sacred to him because, from its tearing up the earth with its tusks, it typified agriculture and return of the seed-sowing time.

Gerda is supposed to represent the frozen earth, which Summer seeing from far off loves and woos to his embrace. The lighting of the sky by the uplifted giant maiden's arms is explained to mean the Northern Lights glancing from one end of heaven to the other.

Narration and Discussion

Why was it so hard for Frey to wait even a few days to be married to Gerda? What do you think is the hardest thing to wait for?

The Vans praise Odin's loss of an eye, but they are not as sure about the wisdom of Frey's sacrifice. Do you think it matters, as long as *somebody* has the sword?

Something else to think about: The "Explaining Things" section gives an extra meaning to the myths. What do you think about having stories unpacked in this way—would you rather the characters just be themselves?

Creative narration: What is in the *Asgard Daily News*? Headlines? Fashion advice, business, sports? Wedding stories?

Chapter Four: The Wanderings of Freyja

(Lesson 19) The Necklace Brisingamen

Introduction

Frey's sister Freyja now has her own adventure, sparked by her quest for something beautiful to wear to a party.

[*For those who want to explore Norse mythology further, please note that there are different versions of this story, some of them less family-friendly than others.*]

Vocabulary

Vana: female Van

Names

Heimdall: the guardian of the bridge Bifrost (mentioned previously)

Aegir: the sea-god (mentioned previously)

Places

Svartheim (or Svartalfheim): an underground realm where the dwarfs live and have their workshop

Reading

Part One

Now, though Frey was made king and schoolmaster of the light elves, and spent the greater part of his time with them in Alfheim, his sister Freyja remained in the city of Asgard, and had a palace built for her named Folkvang. In this palace there was one very beautiful hall, Sessrymnir—the "Roomy Seated"—where Freyja entertained her guests, and she had always plenty of them; for every one liked to look at her beautiful face, and listen to her enchanting music which was quite superior to anybody else's. She had, moreover, a wonderful husband named Odur, who was one of the sons of the immortals, and had come from a long way off on purpose to marry her. Freyja was a little proud of this, and used often to speak of it to Frigga and the other ladies of Asgard. Some of them said she was a very fortunate person; but some were a little jealous of her, whilst Frigga always gravely warned her not to be vain on account of her happiness, lest sorrow should overtake her unawares.

Everything went on quite smoothly, however, for a long time, Freyja leading a very [*omission*] beautiful life in the sunshine of her happiness, and herself a very radiant joy to every one around her. But one day, one unlucky day, Freyja, this fair and sunshiny young **Vana**, went out alone from Asgard to take a walk in Alfheim. She hoped to meet somewhere thereabouts her dear brother Frey, whom she had not seen for a long time, and of whom she wanted to ask a very particular favour. The occasion for it was this: **Heimdall** and **Aegir** were expected to dine at Valhalla the next day, and Freyja and her husband were invited to meet them. All the lords and ladies of Asgard were to be there. Niord, too, was coming, with his new wife, Skadi, the daughter of a giant.

"Every one will be beautifully dressed," said Freyja, "and I have not a single ornament to wear."

"But you are more beautiful than any one, Freyja," said her husband; "for you were born in the spacious Wind-Home."

"All are not so high-minded as you, Odur," answered his wife; "and if I go to Valhalla without an ornament of any kind, I shall certainly be looked down upon."

So saying, Freyja set off, as I told you, to Alfheim, determined to ask of her good-natured brother a garland of flowers at least. But somehow or other she could not find Frey anywhere. She tried to keep in Alfheim—she thought she was there; but all the time she was thinking of her dress and her ornaments, planning what she should wear, and her steps went downward, downward, away from Alfheim, to the cavern of four dwarfs.

Part Two

"Where am I?" said Freyja to herself, as she at last lost the light of day, and went down, wandering on deeper and deeper between the high walls, and under the firm roof of rock. "Why, surely this must be **Svartheim**; and yet it is not unpleasant, nor quite dark here, though the sun is not shining." And in truth it was not dark; for, far on before her, winding in and out through the cavern's inner-most recesses, were groups of little men, who had each a lantern in his cap and a pickaxe in his hand; and they were working hard, digging for diamonds, which they piled up the walls, and hung across the roof in white and rose-coloured coronets, marvellously glittering.

Four clever little dwarf-chiefs were there directing the labours of the rest; but, as soon as they caught sight of Freyja, they sat down in the centre of the cavern, and began to work diligently at something which they held between them, bending over it with strange chattering and grimaces. Freyja felt very curious to see what it was; but her eyes were so dazzled with the blaze of diamonds and lanterns, that she was obliged to go nearer in order to distinguish it clearly. Accordingly, she walked on to where the four dwarfs were sitting, and peeped over their shoulders.

Oh! brilliant! exquisitely worked! bewildering! Freyja drew back again with almost blinded eyes; for she had looked upon the necklace Brisingamen, and at the same moment a passionate wish burst forth in her heart to have it for her own, to wear it in Valhalla, to wear it always round her own fair neck. "Life to me," said Freyja, "is no longer worth having without Brisingamen." Then the dwarfs held it out to her, but also looked cunningly at one another as they did so, and burst into a laugh so loud that it rang through the vaulted caverns, echoed and echoed back again from side to side, from dwarf to dwarf, from depth to depth.

Freyja, however, only turned her head a little on one side, stretched out her hand, grasped the necklace with her small fingers, and then ran out of the cavern as quickly as ever she could, up again to the green hillside. There she sat down and fitted the brilliant ornament about her neck, after which she looked a little shyly at the reflection of herself in a still pool that was near, and turned homewards with an exulting heart. She felt certain that all was well with her; nevertheless, all was not well, but very miserable indeed.

[*In another version, Freyja must pay for the necklace by being married to the four dwarfs, each for just one day, before she returns to Asgard. This may help the rest of the story make more sense.*]

Part Three

When Freyja was come back to Asgard again, and to her palace of Folkvang, she sought her own private apartments, that she might see Odur alone, and make him admire her necklace Brisingamen. But Odur was not there. She searched in every room, hither and thither; but alas! he was not to be found in any room or any hall in all the palace of Folkvang. Freyja searched for him in every place; she walked restlessly about, in and out, among the places of the "Roomy Seated." She peered wistfully, with sad eyes, in the face of every guest; but the only face she cared to see, she never saw. Odur was gone, gone back for ever to the home of the Immortals. Brisingamen and Odur could not live together in the palace of Folkvang. But Freyja did not know this; she did not know why Odur was gone, nor where he was gone; she only saw he was not there, and she wrung her hands sadly, and watered her jewels with salt, warm tears.

As she sat thus and mourned in the entrance of her palace, all the ladies of Asgard passed by on their way to Valhalla, and looked at her. Some said one thing, some another; but no one said anything at all encouraging, or much to the purpose.

Frigga passed by last of all, and she raised her head with a little severe shake, saying something about beauty, and pride, and punishment, which sank down so deeply into the heart of the sorrow-stricken young Vana that she got up with a desperate resolution, and, presenting herself before the throne of Asa Odin, spoke to him thus: "Father of Aesir, listen to my weeping, and do not turn away from me with a cruel frown. I have searched through my palace of Folkvang, and all through the city of Asgard, but nowhere is Odir the Immortal to be found. Let me go, Father Odin, I beseech you, and seek him far and near, across the earth, through the air, over the sea, even to the borders of Jotunheim."

And Odin answered, "Go, Freyja, and good fortune go with you."

Then Freyja sprang into her swift, softly-rolling chariot, which was drawn by two cats, waved her hand as she rose over the city, and was gone.

Narration and Discussion

Do you think Brisingamen is a magic necklace, or has all the trouble been caused (as Frigga says) by Freyja's vanity and pride?

How do you know that Freyja has already had a change of heart?

Creative narration: Retell the story so far in any way you like.

Something to think about: Do you know any other stories where someone's desire for beauty (or beautiful things) caused trouble?

> She was so absorbed in these reflections that it came as a frightful shock when Miss Pearl gave her back one of her hands to look at. All five nails had been painted red as blood! Mona was horrified and fascinated at the same time. Cuffy would faint dead away if she ever saw them, but they were so beautiful! Like little red shells, or curved rubies, or even drops of sealing wax, but nothing at all like fingernails. After all, I can take it off when I get home, Mona told herself. I'll just keep them this way till I get back and look at them once in a while. (Elizabeth Enright, *The Saturdays*)

(Lesson 20) Loki—The Iron Wood—A Boundless Waste

Introduction

Freyja continues her search for Odur, but without much success.

Vocabulary

champed: bit down, chomped

bits: the parts of a harness that go in the mouth

Reading

Part One

The cats **champed** their bright **bits**, and skimmed alike over earth and air with swift, clinging steps, eager and noiseless. The chariot rolled on, and Freyja was carried away up and down into every part of the world, weeping golden tears wherever she went; they fell down from her pale cheeks, and rippled away behind her in little sunshiny rivers, that carried beauty and weeping to every land.

She came to the greatest city in the world, and drove down its wide streets. "But none of the houses here are good enough for Odur," said Freyja to herself. "I will not ask for him at such doors as these."

So she went straight on to the palace of the king. "Is Odur in this palace?" she asked of the gate-keeper. "Is Odur, the Immortal, living with the king?" But the gate-keeper shook his head, and assured her that his master had never even heard of such a person.

Then Freyja turned away, and knocked at many other stately doors, asking for Odur; but no one in all that great city so much as knew her husband's name. [She] went into the long, narrow lanes and shabby streets, where the poor people lived, but there it was all the same; every one said only, "No—not here," and stared at her.

Part Two

In the night-time Freyja went quite away from the city, and the lanes, and the cottages, far off to the side of a lake, where she lay down and looked over into the water. By and by the moon came and looked there too, and the Queen of Night saw a calm face in the water, serene and high; but the Queen of Beauty saw a troubled face, frail and fair. Brisingamen was reflected in the water too, and its rare colours flashed from the little waves. Freyja was pleased at the sight of her favourite ornament, and smiled even in the midst of her tears; but as for the moon, instead of Brisingamen, the deep sky and the stars were around her.

At last Freyja slept by the side of the lake, and then a dark shape crept up the bank on which she was lying, sat down beside her, and took her fair head between its hands. It was Loki, and he began to whisper into Freyja's ear as she slept. "You were quite right, Freyja, "he said, "to go out and try to get something for yourself in Svartheim, instead of staying at home with your husband. It was very wise of you to care more for your dress and your beauty than for Odur. You went down into Svartheim, and found Brisingamen. Then the Immortal went away; but is not Brisingamen better then he? Why do you cry, Freyja? Why do you start so?"

Freyja turned, moaning, and tried to lift her head from between his hands; but she could not, and it seemed in her dream as if a terrible nightmare brooded over her. "Brisingamen is dragging me down," she cried in her sleep, and laid her little hand upon the clasp without knowing what she was doing.

Then a great laugh burst forth in Svartheim, and came shuddering up through the vaulted caverns until it shook the ground upon which she lay. Loki started up, and was gone before Freyja had time to open her eyes.

Part Three

It was morning, and the young Vana prepared to set out on her journey. "Brisingamen is fair," she said, as she bade farewell to her image in the lake. "Brisingamen is fair; but I find it heavy sometimes."

After this, Freyja went to many cities, and towns, and villages, asking everywhere for Odur; but there was not one in all the world who could tell her where he was gone, and at last her chariot rolled eastward and northward to the very borders of Jotunheim. There Freyja stopped; for before her lay Jarnvid, the Iron Wood, which was one road from earth to the abode of the giants, and whose tall trees, black and hard, were trying to pull down the sky with their iron claws. In the entrance sat an Iron Witch, with her back to the forest and her face towards the Vana. Jarnvid was full of the sons and daughters of this Iron Witch; they were wolves, and bears, and foxes, and many-headed ravenous birds.

"Eastward," croaked a raven as Freyja drew near—

"Eastward in the Iron Wood

The old one sitteth";

—and there she did sit, talking in quarrelsome tones to her wolf-sons and vulture-daughters, who answered from the wood behind her, howling, screeching, and screaming all at the same time. There was a horrible din, and Freyja began to fear that her low voice would never be heard. She was obliged to get out of her chariot, and walk close up to the old witch, so that she might whisper in her ear. "Can you tell me, old mother," she said, "where Odur is? Have you seen him pass this way? "

"I don't understand one word of what you are saying," answered the iron woman; "and if I did, I have no time to waste in answering foolish questions." Now, the witch's words struck like daggers into Freyja's heart, and she was not strong enough to pull them out again; so she stood there a long time, not knowing what she should do.

"You had better go," said the crone to her at last; "there's no use in standing there crying." For this was the grandmother of strong-minded women, and she hated tears.

Part Four

Then Freyja got into her chariot again, and went westward a long way to the wide, boundless land where impenetrable forests were growing, and undying nature reigned in silence. She knew that the silent Vidar was living there; for, not finding any pleasure in the [lively company] of Asgard, he had obtained permission from Father Odin to retire to this place. "He is one of the Aesir, and perhaps he will be able to help me," said the sad-hearted young Vana, as her chariot rolled on through empty moor-lands and forests, always in twilight. Her ear heard no sound, her eye saw no living shape; but still she went on with a trembling hope till she came to the spot,

"Begrown with branches

And high grass,

Which was Vidar's dwelling."

Vidar was sitting there firm as an oak, and as silent as night. Long grass grew up through his long hair, and the branches of trees crossed each other over his eyes; his ears were covered with moss, and dewdrops glistened upon his beard. "It is almost impossible to get to him," sighed Freyja, "through all these wet leaves, and I am afraid his moss-covered ears are very deaf." But she threw herself down on the ground before him, and said, "Tell me, Vidar, does Odur hide among thick trees? Or is he wandering over the broad west lands?"

Vidar did not answer her—only a pale gleam shot over his face, as if reflected from that of Freyja, like sunshine breaking through a wood.

"He does not hear me," said Freyja to herself; and she crushed nearer to him through the branches. "Only tell me, Vidar," she said, "is Odur here?" But Vidar said nothing, for he had no voice.

Then Freyja hid her face in her lap, and wept bitterly for a long time. "An Asa," she said, at last, looking up, "is no better to one than an Iron Witch when one is really in trouble." And then she gathered her disordered dress about her, threw back her long bright hair, and, springing into her chariot, once again went wearily on her way.

Narration and Discussion

Why do you think everyone is being so unhelpful to Freyja?

Something to think about: *"An Asa," she said, at last, looking up, "is no better to one than an Iron Witch when one is really in trouble."* Is Freyja right? If you were travelling with her, would you have any suggestions?

(Lesson 21) The King of the Sea and his Daughters

Introduction

In this short ending to Freyja's tale, we hear a poetic "narration" of the story.

Names

Siofna (Sjofn): a goddess of love

Reading

At last she came to the wide sea-coast, and there everything was gloriously beautiful. It was evening, and the western sky looked like a broad crimson flower. No wind stirred the ocean, but the small waves rippled in rose-coloured froth on the shore, like the smiles of a giant at play.

Aegir, the old sea-king, supported himself on the sand, whilst the cool waters were [lapping over him], and his ears drank their sweet murmur; for nine waves were his beautiful daughters, and they and their father were talking together. Now, though Aegir looked so stormy and old, he was really as gentle as a child, and no mischief would ever have happened in his kingdom if he had been left to himself. But he had a cruel wife, called Ran, who was the daughter of a giant, and so eagerly fond of fishing that, whenever any of the rough winds came to call upon her husband, she used to steal out of the deep sea-caves where she lived, and follow ships for miles under the water, dragging her net after her, so that she might catch any one who fell overboard.

Freyja wandered along the shore towards the place where the Sea King was lying, and as she went she heard him speaking to his daughters.

"What is the history of Freyja?" he asked.

And the first wave answered,— "Freyja is a fair young Vana, who once was happy in Asgard. "

Then the second wave said,— "But she left her fair palace there, and Odur, her Immortal Love."

Third wave,— "She went down to the cavern of dwarfs."

Fourth wave,— "She found Brisingamen there, and carried it away with her."

Fifth wave,— "But when she got back to Folkvang she found that Odur was gone."

Sixth wave,— "Because the Vana had loved herself more than Immortal Love."

Seventh wave,— "Freyja will never be happy again, for Odur will never come back."

Eighth wave,— "Odur will never come back as long as the world shall last"

Ninth wave,— "Odur will never return, nor Freyja forget to weep."

Freyja stood still, spell-bound, listening, and when she heard the last words, that Odur would never come back, she wrung her hands, and cried, "O, Father Aegir! trouble comes, comes surging up from a wide sea, wave over wave, into my soul."

And in truth it seemed as if her words had power to change the whole surface of the ocean—wave over wave rose higher and spoke louder. Ran was seen dragging her net in the distance—old Aegir shouted, and dashed into the deep—[the] sea and sky mixed in confusion, and night fell upon the storm. Then Freyja sank down exhausted on the sand, where she lay until her kind daughter, the sleepy little **Siofna**, came and carried her home again in her arms.

After this the beautiful Vana lived in her palace of Folkvang, with friends and sisters, Aesir and Asyniur; but Odur did not return, nor Freyja forget to weep.

[*Note: the rest of this chapter is shortened from the original text.*]

Explaining Things

Supposing [Freyja] to have been the beautiful year, or rather the earth during the beautiful part of the year, Odur leaving her would imply the beginning of the shortening of the days at midsummer. The source of summer flies, [and] Summer seeks him, weeping golden tears…

A German scholar named [Karl Joseph] Simrock wrote, "Every mythology tells us of the death of the beautiful part of the year, like the flight of a god, who is mourned by his wife or his beloved." Looked at from this point of view, we see the summerly earth vaunting and decking herself with her richest jewels in the deepest pride of her delight at the very moment when the spirit of her existence is stealing away from her.

Narration and Discussion

Why do you think Freyja's lament "changed the whole surface of the ocean?"
Does Freyja ever find her husband? There are some versions of the story that say she did, that the golden tears are the autumn leaves falling, and that finding him represents the coming of spring. Other storytellers say that she continues to search for him.

> Tears, idle tears, I know not what they mean,
> Tears from the depth of some divine despair
> Rise in the heart, and gather to the eyes,
> In looking on the happy Autumn-fields,
> And thinking of the days that are no more.
>
> (Alfred, Lord Tennyson, from "The Princess")

Creative narration: What is in the *Asgard Daily News*? News on the street, recipes, business, sports? A classified ad selling jewelry?

Something to think about: Christians believe that the Bible tells us where to turn when there is no other help or answer. "In my distress I cried unto the LORD, and he heard me." (Psalm 120:1)

Chapter Five: Iduna's Apples

(Lesson 22) Reflections in the Water

Introduction

We now meet Iduna, the grower of life-giving apples, and wife of the poetic god Bragi. Like Freyja, Iduna has a happy life and home; but, also like Freyja, there are threats to her happiness.

Vocabulary

> **bower:** A bower can mean a lady's private room; but it also means a pleasant, shady place under trees, which makes more sense here.

casket: ornamental box or chest

solitary: deserted, lonely

Names

Iduna (Idunn): a goddess associated with apples and with youth

Bragi: the god of poetry

a strange form was reflected up to her from the water: This, though not explained yet, is the jotun Thiassi, in the form of a bird, who is already planning to capture Iduna (more on that later). The insects are formed from his feathers as they drop, and their mission is apparently to weaken Iduna, although (as we will see) she seems to be more vulnerable to Loki's trickery than to these **Nervous Apprehensions** (worries and anxieties). Or perhaps they are what make her listen to Loki at all. We shall see…

Reading

Part One

Of all the groves and gardens round the city of Asgard—and they were many and beautiful—there was none so beautiful as the one where **Iduna**, the wife of **Bragi**, lived. It stood on the south side of the hill, not far from Gladsheim, and it was called "Always Young," because nothing that grew there could ever decay, or become the least bit older than it was on the day when Iduna entered it. The trees wore always a tender, light green colour, as the hedges do in spring. The flowers were mostly half-opened, and every blade of grass bore always a trembling, glittering drop of early dew. Brisk little winds wandered about the grove, making the leaves dance from morning till night and swaying backwards and forwards the heads of the flowers.

"Blow away!" said the leaves to the wind, "for we shall never be tired."

"And you will never be old," said the winds in answer. And then the birds took up the chorus and sang, "Never tired and never old."

Iduna, the mistress of the grove, was fit to live among young birds, and tender leaves, and spring flowers. She was so fair that when she bent over the river to entice her swans to come to her, even the stupid fish stood still in the water, afraid to destroy so beautiful an image by swimming over it; and when she held out her hand with bread for the swans to eat, you would not have known it from a water-lily—it was so wonderfully white.

Iduna never left her grove even to pay a visit to her nearest neighbour, and yet she did not lead by any means a dull life; for–besides having the company of her husband, Bragi, who must have been an entertaining person to live with, for he is said to have known a story which never came to an end, and yet which never grew wearisome–all the heroes of Asgard made a point of coming to call upon her every day. It was natural enough that they should like to visit so beautiful a grove and so fair a lady; and yet, to confess the truth, it was not quite to see either the grove or Iduna that they came.

Iduna herself was well aware of this, and when her visitors had chatted a short time with her, she never failed to bring out from the innermost recess of her **bower** a certain golden **casket**, and to request, as a favour, that her guests would not think of going away till they had tasted her apples, which, she flattered herself, had a better flavour than any other fruit in the world.

It would have been quite unlike a hero of Asgard to have refused such courtesy; and, besides, Iduna was not as far wrong about her apples as hostesses generally are, when they boast of the good things on their tables. There is no doubt, her apples *had* a peculiar flavour; and if any one of the heroes happened to be a little tired, or a little out of spirits, or a little cross, when he came into the bower, it always followed that, as soon as he had eaten one apple, he found himself as fresh, and vigorous, and happy as he had ever been in his life.

So fond were the heroes of these apples, and so necessary did they think them to their daily comfort, that they never went on a journey without requesting Iduna to give them one or two, to fortify them against the fatigues of the way. Iduna had no difficulty in complying with this request; she had no fear of her store ever failing, for as surely as she took an apple from her casket, another fell in; but where it came from Iduna could never discover. She never saw it till it was close to the bottom of the casket; but she always heard the sweet tinkling sound it made when it touched the golden rim. It was as good as play to Iduna to stand by her casket, taking the apples out, and watching the fresh rosy ones come tumbling in, without knowing who threw them.

One spring morning, Iduna was very busy taking apples out of her casket; for several of the heroes were taking advantage of the fine weather to journey out into the world. Bragi was going from home for a time; perhaps he was tired of telling his story only to Iduna, and perhaps she was beginning to know it by heart. And Odin, Loki, and Hoenir had agreed to take a little tour in the direction of Jotunheim, just to see if any entertaining adventure would befall them. When they had all received their apples, and taken a tender farewell of Iduna, the grove—green and fair as it was—looked, perhaps, a little **solitary**.

Part Two

Iduna stood by her fountain, watching the bright water as it danced up into the air and quivered, and turned, and fell back, making a hundred little flashing circles in the river; and then she grew tired, for once, of the light and the noise, and wandered down to a still place, where the river was shaded by low bushes on each side, and reflected clearly the blue sky overhead. Iduna sat down and looked into the deep water. Besides her own fair face there were little, wandering, white clouds to be seen reflected there. She counted them as they sailed past.

At length **a strange form was reflected up to her from the water**—large, dark, lowering wings, pointed claws, a head with fierce eyes—looking at her. Iduna started and raised her head. It was above as well as below; the same wings—the same eyes—the same head—looking down from the blue sky, as well as up from the water. Such a sight had never been seen near Asgard before; and, while Iduna looked, the thing waved its wings, and went up, up, up, till it lessened to a dark spot in the clouds and on the river. It was no longer terrible to look at; but, as it shook its wings a number of little black feathers fell from them, and flew down towards the grove.

As they neared the trees, they no longer looked like feathers—each had two independent wings and a head of its own. They were, in fact, a swarm of **Nervous Apprehensions**; troublesome little insects enough, and well-known elsewhere, but which now, for the first time, found their way into the grove.

Iduna ran away from them; she shook them off; she fought quite bravely against them; but they are by no means easy to get rid of; and when, at last, one crept within the folds of her dress, and twisted itself down to her heart, a new, strange feeling thrilled there—a feeling never yet known to any dweller in Asgard. Iduna did not know what to make of it.

Narration and Discussion

Make a list of things Iduna enjoys about being the apple goddess. Is there anything she doesn't like as much?

What do you think this new feeling might be inside Iduna?

Creative narration: Since Iduna's husband Bragi is a poet, what poem or song might he write about his wife?

Something to think about: Do you know any other stories about people living without trouble or anxiety in a garden?

(Lesson 23) The Winged-Giant (First Half)

Introduction

The Aesir men are off on a camping trip; but their attempt to cook dinner does not end well.

Vocabulary

 comporting: behaving

 deal-board: kitchen table, usually made of pine or fir

provisions: food

She kept her own counsel about it: She didn't talk about it

an enormous human-headed eagle: Thiassi, again

Reading

Part One

In the meantime Odin, Loki, and Hoenir proceeded on their journey. They were not bound on any particular quest. They strayed hither and thither that Odin might see that things were going on well in the world, and his subjects **comporting** themselves in a becoming manner. Every now and then they halted while Odin inspected the thatching of a barn, or stood at the smithy to see how the smith wielded his hammer, or in a furrow to observe if the ploughman guided his plough-share evenly through the soil. "Well done," he said if the workman was working with all his might; and he turned away, leaving something behind him, a straw in the barn, a piece of old iron at the forge-door, a grain in the furrow—nothing to look at; but ever after the barn was always full, the forge-fire never went out, the field yielded bountifully.

Towards noon the Aesir reached a shady valley, and, feeling tired and hungry, Odin proposed to sit down under a tree, and while he rested and studied a book of runes which he had with him, he requested Loki and Hoenir to prepare some dinner.

"I will undertake the meat and the fire," said Hoenir. "You, Loki, will like nothing better than foraging about for what good things you can pick up."

"That is precisely what I mean to do," said Loki. "There is a farmhouse near here, from which I can perceive a savoury smell. It will be strange, with my cunning, if I do not contrive to have the best of all the dishes under this tree before your fire is burnt up."

As Loki spoke he turned a stone in his hand, and immediately he assumed the shape of a large black cat. In this form he stole in at the kitchen-window of a farmhouse, where a busy housewife was intent on taking pies and cakes from a deep oven, and ranging them on a dresser under the window. Loki watched his opportunity, and whenever the mistress's back was turned he whisked a cake or a pie out of the window.

"One, two, three. Why, there are fewer every time I bring a fresh one from the oven!" cried the bewildered housewife. "It's that thieving cat. I see the end of her tail on the windowsill." Out of the window leant the housewife to throw a stone at the cat, but she could see nothing but a thin cow trespassing in her garden; and when she ran out with a stick to drive away the cow, it, too, had vanished, and an old raven, with six young ones, was flying over the garden-hedge.

The raven was Loki, the little ones were the pies; and when he reached the valley, and changed himself and them into their proper shapes, he had a hearty laugh at his own cleverness, and at the old woman's dismay.

"Well done, Loki, king of thieves," said a chorus of foxes, who peeped out of their holes to see the only one of the Aesir whose conduct they could appreciate; but Odin, when he heard of it, was very far from thinking it well done. He was extremely displeased with Loki for having disgraced himself by such mean tricks.

"It is true," he said, "that my subjects may well be glad to furnish me with all I require, but it should be done knowingly. Return to the farmhouse, and place these three black stones on the table from whence you stole the provisions."

Part Two

Loki—unwilling as he was to do anything he believed likely to bring good to others—was obliged to obey. He made himself into the shape of a white owl, flew once more through the window, and dropped the stones out of his beak; they sank deep into the table, and looked like three black stains on the white **deal-board**.

From that time the housewife led an easy life; there was no need for her to grind corn, or mix dough, or prepare meat. Let her enter her kitchen at what time of day she would, stores of **provisions** stood smoking hot on the table. **She kept her own counsel about it**, and enjoyed the reputation of being the most economical housekeeper in the whole countryside; but one thing disturbed her mind, and prevented her thoroughly enjoying the envy and wonder of the neighbouring wives. All the rubbing, and brushing, and cleaning in the world would not remove the three black stains from her kitchen table, and as she had no cooking to do, she spent the greater part of her time in looking at them.

"If they were but gone," she said, a hundred times every day, "I should be content; but how is one to enjoy one's life when one cannot rub the stains off one's own table?"

Part Three

Perhaps Loki foresaw how the good wife would use her gift; for he came back from the farmhouse in the best spirits. "We will now, with Father Odin's permission, sit down to dinner," he said; "for surely, brother Hoenir, while I have been making so many journeys to and fro, you have been doing something with that fire which I see blazing so fiercely, and with that old iron pot smoking over it."

"The meat will be by this time ready, no doubt," said Hoenir. "I killed a wild ox while you were away, and part of it has been now for some time stewing in the pot." The Aesir now seated themselves near the fire, and Hoenir lifted up the lid of the pot. A thick steam rose up from it; but when he took out the meat it was as red and uncooked as when he first put it into the pot.

"Patience," said Hoenir; and Odin again took out his book of Runes. Another hour passed, and Hoenir again took off the lid, and looked at the meat; but it was in precisely the same state as before. This happened several times, and even the cunning Loki was puzzled; when, suddenly, a strange noise was heard coming from a tree near, and, looking up, they saw **an enormous human-headed eagle** seated on one of the branches, and looking at them with two fierce eyes. While they looked it spoke.

"Give me my share of the feast," it said, "and the meat shall presently be done."

"Come down and take it—it lies before you," said Loki, while Odin looked on with thoughtful eyes; for he saw plainly that it was no mortal bird who had the boldness to claim a share in the Aesir's food.

Undaunted by Odin's majestic looks, the eagle flew down, and, seizing a large piece of meat, was going to fly away with it, when Loki, thinking he had now got the bird in his power, took up a stick that lay near, and struck a hard blow on the eagle's back. The stick made a ringing sound as it fell; but, when Loki tried to draw it back, he found that it stuck with extraordinary force to the eagle's back; neither could he withdraw his own hands from the other end. Something like a laugh came from the creature's half-human, half-bird-like mouth; and then it spread its dark wings and rose up into the air, dragging Loki after.

Narration and Discussion

Why was Odin not pleased with Loki's food contributions?

Do you think the bird came to find Loki, or was it just bad luck that he got caught?

Creative narration: Have someone interview the farm wife; or, imagine a conversation she might have with a curious neighbour.

(Lesson 24) The Winged-Giant (Second Half)

Introduction

Loki appears back at home, apparently unharmed by Thiassi. However, he definitely seems to have something on his mind.

Vocabulary

forbore: restrained himself; kept himself from doing it

with a contemptuous air: scornfully, as if he did not think much of it

sumptuously: richly

Names

Thiassi: In D'Aulaires' *Norse Gods and Giants*, he is called Tjasse.

Hela: As told in "Loki's children," Hela rules in the underworld and represents death.

Reading

Part One

"It is as I thought," said Odin, as he saw the eagle's enormous bulk brought out against the sky; "it is **Thiassi**, the strongest giant in Jotunheim, who has presumed to show himself in our presence. Loki has only received the reward of his treachery, and it would ill-become us to interfere in his behalf; but, as the monster is near, it will be well for us to return to Asgard, lest any misfortune should befall the city in our absence." While Odin spoke, the winged creature had risen up so high as to be invisible even to the eyes of the Aesir; and, during their return to Asgard, he did not again appear before them.

But, as they approached the gates of the city, they were surprised to see Loki coming to meet them. He had a crest-fallen and bewildered look; and when they questioned him as to what had happened to him since they parted in such a strange way, he declared himself to be quite unable to give any further account of his adventures than that he had been carried rapidly through the air by the giant, and, at last, thrown down from a great height near the place where the Aesir met him.

Odin looked steadfastly at him as he spoke, but he **forbore** to question him further: for he knew well that there was no hope of hearing the truth from Loki, and he kept within his own mind the conviction he felt that some disastrous result must follow a meeting between two such evildoers as Loki and the giant Thiassi.

Part Two

That evening, when the Aesir were all feasting and telling stories to each other in the great hall of Valhalla, Loki stole out from Gladsheim, and went alone to visit Iduna in her grove. It was a still, bright evening. The leaves of the trees moved softly up and down, whispering sweet words to each other; the flowers, with half-shut eyes, nodded sleepily to their own reflections in the water, and Iduna sat by the fountain, with her head resting in one hand, thinking of pleasant things.

"It is all very well," thought Loki; "but I am not the happier because people can here live such pleasant lives. It does not do me any good, or cure the pain I have had so long in my heart."

Loki's long shadow—for the sun was setting—fell on the water as he approached, and made Iduna start. She remembered the sight that had disturbed her so much in the morning; but when she saw only Loki, she looked up and smiled kindly; for he had often accompanied the other Aesir in their visits to her grove.

"I am wearied with a long journey," said Loki abruptly, "and I would eat one of your apples to refresh me after my fatigue." The casket stood by Iduna's side, and she immediately put in her hand and gave Loki an apple. To her surprise, instead of thanking her warmly, or beginning to eat it, he turned it round and round in his hand **with a contemptuous air**.

"It is true then," he said, after looking intently at the apple for some time, "your apples are but small and withered in comparison. I was unwilling to believe it at first, but now I can doubt no longer."

"Small and withered!" said Iduna, rising hastily. "Nay, Asa Odin himself, who has traversed the whole world, assures me that he has never seen any to be compared to them."

"That will never be said again," returned Loki; "for this very afternoon I have discovered a tree, in a grove not far from Asgard, on which grow apples so beautiful that no one who has seen them will ever care again for yours."

"I do not wish to see or hear of them," said Iduna, trying to turn away with an indifferent air; but Loki followed her, and continued to speak more and more strongly of the beauty of this new fruit, hinting that Iduna would be sorry that she had refused to listen when she found all her guests deserting her for the new grove, and when even Bragi began to think lightly of her and of her gifts. At this Iduna sighed, and Loki came up close to her, and whispered in her ear, "It is but a short way from Asgard, and the sun has not yet set. Come out with me, and, before any one else has seen the apples, you shall gather them, and put them in your casket, and no woman shall ever have it in her power to boast that she can feast the Aesir more **sumptuously** than Iduna."

Now Iduna had often been cautioned by her husband never to let anything tempt her to leave the grove, and she had always been so happy here, that she thought there was no use in his telling her the same thing so often over; but now her mind was so full of the wonderfully beautiful fruit, and she felt such a burning wish to get it for herself, that she quite forgot her husband's commands. "It is only a little way," she said to herself; "there can be no harm in going out just this once." And, as Loki went on urging her, she took up her casket from the ground hastily, and begged him to show her the way to this other grove.

Part Three

Loki walked very quickly, and Iduna had not time to collect her thoughts before she found herself at the entrance of "Always Young." At the gate she would gladly have stopped a minute to take breath; but Loki took hold of her hand, and forced her to pass through, though, at the very moment of passing, she half drew back; for it seemed to her as if all the trees in the grove suddenly called out in alarm, "Come back, come back, oh, come back, Iduna!" She half drew back her hand, but it was too late; the gate fell behind her, and she and Loki stood together [outside] the grove.

The trees rose up between them and the setting sun, and cast a deep shadow on the place where they stood; a cold, night air blew on Iduna's cheek, and made her shiver. "Let us hasten on," she said to Loki; "let us hasten on, and soon come back again."

But Loki was not looking on, he was looking up. Iduna raised her eyes in the direction of his, and her heart died within her; for there, high up over her head, just as she had seen it in the morning, hung the lowering, dark wings—the sharp talons—the fierce head, looking at her. For one moment it stood still above her head, and then lower, lower, lower, the huge shadow fell; and, before Iduna found breath to speak, the dark wings were folded round her, and she was borne high up in the air, northwards, towards the grey mist that hangs over Jotunheim.

Part Four

Loki watched till she was out of sight, and then returned to Asgard. The presence of the giant was no wonder to him; for he had, in truth, purchased his own release by promising to deliver up Iduna and her casket into his power; but, as he returned alone through the grove, a foreboding fear pressed on his mind.

"If it should be true," he thought, "that Iduna's apples have the wonderful power Odin attributes to them! If I among the rest should suffer from the loss!" Occupied with these thoughts, he passed quickly among the trees, keeping his eyes resolutely fixed on the ground. He dare not trust himself to look around; for once, when he had raised his head, he fancied that, gliding through the brushwood, he had seen the dark robes and pale face of his daughter **Hela**.

Narration and Discussion

How did Loki convince Iduna to follow him outside her grove?

What is Loki worried about at the end? What does this say about his character?

Creative narration: What is in the *Asgard Daily News* today? Headlines? Music reviews, business, sports? Apple recipes?

(Lesson 25) Hela

Introduction

The absence of Iduna, and the lack of her apples, mean rapid aging—perhaps even death—for the Aesir. Her husband Bragi finally realizes that mourning alone is not enough, and perhaps it is not too late to *do* something.

Vocabulary

somber: dark, gloomy

languidly: slowly, weakly

humour: mood

Reading

Part One

When it was known that Iduna had disappeared from her grove, there were many sorrowful faces in Asgard, and anxious voices were heard inquiring for her. Loki walked about with as grave a face, and asked as many questions, as anyone else; but he had a secret fear that became stronger every day, that now, at last, the consequence of his evil ways would find him out.

Days passed on, and the looks of care, instead of wearing away, deepened on the faces of the Aesir. They met, and looked at each other, and turned away sighing; each saw that some strange change was creeping over all the others, and none liked to be the first to speak of it. It came on very gradually—a little change every day, and no day ever passing without the change. The leaves of the trees in Iduna's grove deepened in colour. They first became a **somber** green, then a glowing red, and, at last, a pale brown; and when the brisk winds came and blew them about, they moved every day more **languidly**. "Let us alone," they said at length. "We are tired, tired, tired."

The winds, surprised, carried the new sound to Gladsheim, and whispered it all round the banquet-hall where the Aesir sat, and then they rushed back again, and blew all through the grove.

"We are tired," said the leaves again; "we are tired, we are old; we are going to die"; and at the word they broke from the trees one by one, and fluttered to the ground, glad to rest anywhere; and the winds, having nothing else to do, went back to Gladsheim with the last strange word they had learned.

The Aesir were all assembled in Valhalla; but there were no stories told, and no songs sung. No one spoke much but Loki, and he was that day in a talking **humour**. He moved from one to another, whispering an unwelcome word in every ear.

"Have you noticed your mother, Frigga?" he said to Baldur. "Do you see how white her hair is growing, and what a number of deep lines are printed on her face?" Then he turned to Frey. "Look at your sister Freyja and your friend Baldur," he said, "as they sit opposite to us. What a change has come over them lately! Who would think that that pale man and that faded woman were Baldur the beautiful and Freyja the fair?"

"You are tired—you are old—you are going to die,"—moaned the winds, wandering all round the great halls, and coming in and out of the hundred doorways, and all the Aesir looked up at the sad sound. Then they saw, for the first time, that a new guest had seated herself that day at the table of the Aesir. There could be no question of her fitness on the score of royalty, for a crown rested on her brow, and in her hand she held a scepter; but the fingers that grasped the scepter were white and fleshless, and under the crown looked the threatening face of Hela, half corpse, half queen.

Part Two

A great fear fell on all the Aesir as they looked, and only Odin found voice to speak to her. "Dreadful daughter of Loki!" he said, "by what warrant do you dare to leave the kingdom where I permit you to reign, and come to take your place among the Aesir, who are no mates for such as you?"

Then Hela raised her bony finger, and pointed, one by one, to the guests that sat round. "White hair," she said, "wrinkled faces, weary limbs, dull eyes—these are the warrants which have summoned me from the land of shadows to sit among the Aesir. I have come to claim you, by these signs, as my future guests, and to tell you that I am preparing a place for you in my kingdom." At every word she spoke a gust of icy wind came from her mouth and froze the blood in the listeners' veins. If she had stayed a moment longer they would have stiffened into stone; but when she had spoken thus, she rose and left the hall, and the sighing winds went out with her.

Part Three

Then, after a long silence, Bragi stood up and spoke. "Aesir," he said, "*We* are to blame. It is now many months since Iduna was carried away from us; we have mourned for her, but we have not yet avenged her loss. Since she left us a strange weariness and despair have come over us, and we sit looking on each other as if we had ceased to be warriors and Aesir. It is plain that, unless Iduna returns, we are lost. Let two of us journey to the Urda fount, which we have so long neglected to visit, and enquire of her from the Norns—for they know all things—and then, when we have learnt where she is, we will fight for her liberty, if need be, till we die; for that will be an end more fitting for us than to sit here and wither away under the breath of Hela."

At these words of Bragi, the Aesir felt a revival of their old strength and courage. Odin approved of Bragi's proposal, and decreed that he [Bragi] and Baldur should undertake the journey to the dwelling-place of the Norns. That very evening they set forth; for Hela's visit showed them that they had no time to lose.

Narration and Discussion

How did Bragi's words restore courage to the Aesir?

What do you think has happened to Iduna?

Something to think about: Was it just the lack of apples that sickened the Aesir, or was it also Hela's and Loki's taunts? What does the Bible say about the power of words to harm or to heal? Here's one verse to start with: Proverbs 17:22, "A merry heart doeth good like a medicine: but a broken spirit drieth the bones."

Creative narration: Imagine a conversation between the leaves on Iduna's apple trees.

What might they say besides "We are tired?"

(Lesson 26) Through Flood and Fire

Introduction

The Norns say that since Loki began this trouble, he has to be the one to end it.

Vocabulary

treacherous: deceptive, false

fair: pretty

changed into a sparrow: Other versions of the story say that Loki turned Iduna into a hazelnut, which he (in the form of a falcon) held in his talons as he flew home.

Names

Ellewomen: beings who do their tasks but have no feelings

Reading

Part One

It was a weary time to the dwellers in Asgard while [Bragi and Baldur] were absent. Two new citizens had taken up their abode in the city, Age and Pain. They walked the streets hand-in-hand, and there was no use in shutting the doors against them; for however closely the entrance was barred, the dwellers in the houses felt them as they passed.

At length, Baldur and Bragi returned with the answer of the Norns, couched in mystic words which Odin alone could understand. It revealed Loki's **treacherous** conduct to the Aesir, and declared that Iduna could only be brought back by Loki, who must go in search of her, clothed in Freyja's garments of falcon feathers.

Loki was very unwilling to venture on such a search; but Thor threatened him with instant death if he refused to obey Odin's commands, or failed to bring back Iduna; and, for his own safety, he was obliged to allow Freyja to fasten the falcon wings to his shoulders, and to set off towards Thiassi's castle in Jotunheim, where he well knew that Iduna was imprisoned.

Part Two

It was called a castle; but it was, in reality, a hollow in a dark rock; the sea broke against two sides of it; and, above, the sea-birds clamoured day and night

There the giant had taken Iduna on the night on which she had left her grove; and, fearing lest Odin should spy her from Air Throne, he had shut her up in a gloomy chamber, and strictly forbidden her ever to come out It was hard to be shut up from the fresh air and sunshine; and yet, perhaps, it was safer for Iduna than if she had been allowed to wander about Jotunheim, and see the monstrous sights that would have met her there. She saw nothing but Thiassi himself and his servants, whom he had commanded to attend upon her; and they, being curious to see a stranger from a distant land, came in and out many times every day. They were **fair**, Iduna saw—fair and smiling; and, at first, it relieved her to see such pleasant faces round her, when she had expected something horrible. "Pity me!" she used to say to them; "pity me! I have been torn away from my home and my husband, and I see no hope of ever getting back." And she looked earnestly at them; but their pleasant faces never changed, and there was always—however bitterly Iduna might be weeping—the same smile on their lips.

At length Iduna, looking more narrowly at them, saw, when they turned their backs to her, that they were hollow behind; they were, in truth, **Ellewomen**, who have no hearts, and can never pity any one. After Iduna saw this she looked no more at their smiling faces, but turned away her head and wept silently. It is very sad to live among Ellewomen when one is in trouble.

Every day the giant came and thundered at Iduna's door. "Have you made up your mind yet," he used to say, "to give me the apples? Something dreadful will happen to you if you take much longer to think of it." Iduna trembled very much every day, but still she had strength to say, "No"; for she knew that the most dreadful thing would be for her to give to a wicked giant the gifts that had been entrusted to her for the use of the Aesir.

The giant would have taken the apples by force if he could; but, whenever he put his hand into the casket, the fruit slipped from beneath his fingers, shrivelled into the size of a pea, and hid itself in crevices of the casket where his great fingers could not come—only when Iduna's little white hand touched it, it swelled again to its own size, and this she would never do while the giant was with her. So the days passed on, and Iduna would have died of grief among the smiling Ellewomen if it had not been for the moaning sound of the sea and the wild cry of the birds; "for, however others may smile, these pity me," she used to say, and it was like music to her.

Part Three

One morning when she knew that the giant had gone out, and when the Ellewomen had left her alone, she stood for a long time at her window by the sea, watching the mermaids floating up and down on the waves, and looking at heaven with their sad blue eyes. She knew that they were mourning because they had no souls, and she thought within herself that even in prison it was better to belong to the Aesir than to be a mermaid or an Ellewoman, were they ever so free or happy.

While she was still occupied with these thoughts she heard her name spoken, and a bird with large wings flew in at the window, and, smoothing its feathers, stood upright before her. It was Loki in Freyja's garment of feathers, and he made her understand in a moment that he had come to set her free, and that there was no time to lose. He [omission] said a few words over her, and she found herself **changed into a sparrow**, with the casket fastened among [her] feathers. Then Loki spread his wings once more, and flew out of the window, and Iduna followed him.

The sea-wind blew cold and rough, and her little wings fluttered with fear; but she struck them bravely out into the air and flew like an arrow over the water. "This way lies Asgard," cried Loki, and the word gave her strength. But they had not gone far when a sound was heard above the sea, and the wind, and the call of the sea-birds. Thiassi had put on his eagle plumage, and was flying after them.

For five days and five nights the three flew over the water that divides Jotunheim from Asgard, and, at the end of every day, they were closer together, for the giant was gaining on the other two. All the five days the dwellers in Asgard stood on the walls of the city, watching. On the sixth evening they saw a falcon and a sparrow, closely pursued by an eagle, flying towards Asgard.

"There will not be time," said Bragi, who had been calculating the speed at which they flew. "The eagle will reach them before they can get into the city."

But Odin [ordered] a fire to be lighted upon the walls; and Thor and Tyr, with what strength remained to them, tore up the trees from the groves and gardens, and made a rampart of fire all round the city. The light of the fire showed Iduna her husband and her friends waiting for her. She made one last effort, and, rising high up in the air above the flames and smoke, she passed the walls, and dropped down safely at the foot of Odin's throne. The giant tried to follow; but, wearied with his long flight, he was unable to raise his enormous bulk sufficiently high in the air. The flames scorched his wings as he flew through them, and he fell among the flaming piles of wood, and was burnt to death.

How Iduna feasted the Aesir on her apples, how they grew young and beautiful again, and how spring, and green leaves, and music came back to the grove, I must leave you to imagine, for I have made my story long enough already; and if I say any more you will fancy that it is Bragi who has come among you, and that he has entered on his endless story.

[*Note: the rest of this chapter has been shortened from the original text.*]

Explaining Things

Iduna is supposed to typify the Spring, and her falling into captivity for a time to the giant Thiassi corresponds to the falling of the leaf in Autumn.

The union of Poetry with Spring seems very appropriate, and we must not forget to mention that Bragi's name calls to mind the old story of the Bragarfull. At feasts, in old times, it was the custom to drink from cups of mead. One to Odin for victory, one to Frey and one to Niord for a good year and peace, and the fourth to Bragi. It was called the "Cup of Vows," and the drinker vowed over it to perform some great deed worthy of the song of a skald.

Narration and Discussion

Do you think the Aesir will trust Loki more after his rescue of Iduna?

Why did the smiles of the Ellewomen give no comfort to Iduna? How did the wild sounds outside help her instead? American poet Wendell Berry says that he does something similar when he feels "despair":

> I go and lie down where the wood drake
> rests in his beauty on the water, and the great heron feeds.
> I come into the peace of wild things
> who do not tax their lives with forethought
> of grief.
>
> (from "The Peace of Wild Things")

Creative narration: What is in the *Asgard Daily News* today? (Maybe a special apple edition for the return of Iduna?)

Chapter Six: Baldur

(Lesson 27) The Dream

Introduction

> "...dreams know more than they reveal, even to the wisest of the gods." (Neil Gaiman, *Norse Mythology*)

This story is the start of a very important chain of events. It begins with Baldur's dream which seems to foretell his death. His father, Odin, goes off to ask for magic advice (because that's what wise Aesir fathers do). His mother, Frigga, makes everything she can think of promise to leave Baldur alone (because that's what powerful goddess mothers do). But can all their best efforts save Baldur?

Vocabulary

Sleipnir, his eight-footed steed: The eight-legged horse has his own story, but it is not told in this book.

defile: passage, opening

Names

Vala: a prophetess who had died and must be awakened to ask for advice. (Not to be confused with a Vana.)

Places

Broadblink (or Breidablik): Baldur's palace. Can be translated as "Broad-Gleaming."

Reading

Part One

Upon a summer's afternoon it happened that Baldur the Bright and Bold, beloved of men and Aesir, found himself alone in his palace of **Broadblink**. Thor was walking low down among the valleys, his brow heavy with summer heat; Frey and Gerda sported on still waters in their cloud-leaf ship; Odin, for once, slept on the top of Air Throne; a noonday stillness pervaded the whole earth; and Baldur in Broadblink, the wide-glancing most sunlit of palaces, dreamed a dream.

Now the dream of Baldur was troubled. He knew not whence nor why; but when he awoke he found that a most new and weighty care was within him. It was so heavy that Baldur could scarcely carry it, and yet he pressed it closely to his heart, and said, "Lie there, and do not fall on any one but me." Then he rose up, and walked out from the expanded splendour of his hall, that he might seek his own mother, Frigga, and tell her what had happened to him. He found her in her crystal [hall], calm and kind, waiting to listen, and ready to sympathise; so he walked up to her, his hands pressed closely on his heart, and lay down at her feet sighing.

"What is the matter, dear Baldur?" asked Frigga, gently.

"I do not know, mother," answered he. "I do not know what the matter is; but I have a shadow in my heart."

"Take it out, then, my son, and let me look at it," replied Frigg.

"But I fear, mother, that if I do it will cover the whole earth."

Then Frigga laid her hand upon the heart of her son that she might feel the shadow's shape. Her brow became clouded as she felt it; her parted lips grew pale, and she cried out, "Oh! Baldur, my beloved son! the shadow is the shadow of death!"

Then said Baldur, "I will die bravely, my mother."

But Frigga answered, "You shall not die at all; for I will not sleep to-night until everything on earth has sworn to me that it will neither kill nor harm you."

So Frigga stood up, and called to her everything on earth that had power to hurt or slay. First she called all metals to her; and heavy iron-ore came lumbering up the hill into the crystal hall, brass and gold, copper, silver, lead, and steel, and stood before the

Queen, who lifted her right-hand high in the air, saying, "Swear to me that you will not injure Baldur;" and they all swore, and went.

Then she called to her all stones; and huge granite came with crumbling sandstone, and white lime, and the round, smooth stones of the seashore, and Frigga raised her arm, saying, "Swear that you will not injure Baldur"; and they swore, and went.

Then Frigga called to her the trees; and wide-spreading oak-trees, with tall ash and sombre firs came rushing up the hill, with long branches, from which green leaves like flags were waving, and Frigga raised her hand, and said, "Swear that you will not hurt Baldur"; and they said, "We swear," and went.

After this Frigga called to her the diseases, who came blown thitherward by poisonous winds on wings of pain, and to the sound of moaning. Frigga said to them, "Swear"; and they sighed, "We swear," then flew away. Then Frigga called to her all beasts, birds, and venomous snakes, who came to her and swore, and disappeared. After this she stretched out her hand to Baldur, whilst a smile spread over her face, saying, "And now, my son, you cannot die."

But just then Odin came in, and when he had heard from Frigga the whole story, he looked even more mournful than she had done; neither did the cloud pass from his face when he was told of the oaths that had been taken.

"Why do you still look so grave, my lord?" demanded Frigg, at last. "Baldur cannot now die."

But Odin asked very gravely, "Is the shadow gone out of our son's heart, or is it still there?"

"It cannot be there," said Frigg, turning away her head resolutely, and folding her hands before her.

But Odin looked at Baldur, and saw how it was. The hands pressed to the heavy heart, the beautiful brow grown dim. Then immediately he arose, saddled **Sleipnir, his eight-footed steed**, mounted him, and, turning to Frigga, said, "I know of a dead wise woman, a **Vala**, who, when she was alive, could tell what was going to happen; her grave lies on the east side of Helheim, and I am going there to awake her, and ask whether any terrible grief is really coming upon us."

So saying, Odin shook the bridle in his hand, and the Eight-footed, with a bound, leapt forth, rushed like a whirlwind down the mountain of Asgard, and then dashed into a narrow **defile** between rocks.

Part Two

Sleipnir went on through the defile a long way, until he came to a place where the earth opened her mouth. There Odin rode in and down a broad, steep, slanting road which led him to the cavern Gnipa, and the mouth of the cavern Gnipa yawned upon Niflheim. Then thought Odin to himself, "My journey is already done." But just as Sleipnir was about to leap through the jaws of the pit, Garm, the voracious dog who was chained to the rock, sprang forward, and tried to fasten himself upon Odin. Three times Odin shook him off, and still Garm, as fierce as ever, went on with the fight At last Sleipnir leapt, and Odin thrust just at the same moment; then horse and rider cleared the entrance, and turned eastward toward the dead Vala's grave, dripping blood along the road as they went; while the beaten Garm stood baying in the cavern's mouth.

Part Three

When Odin came to the grave he got off his horse, and stood with his face northwards looking through barred enclosures into the city of Helheim itself. The servants of Hela were very busy there making preparations for some new guest— hanging gilded couches with curtains of anguish and splendid misery upon the walls. Then Odin's heart died within him and he began to repeat mournful runes in a low tone to himself.

The dead Vala turned heavily in her grave at the sound of his voice, and, as he went on, sat bolt upright. "What man is this," she asked, "who dares disturb my sleep?"

Then Odin, for the first time in his life, said what was not true; the shadow of Baldur dead fell upon his lips, and he made answer, "My name is Vegtam, the son of Valtam."

"And what do you want from me?" asked the Vala.

"I want to know," replied Odin, "for whom Hela is making ready that gilded couch in Helheim?"

"That is for Baldur the Beloved," answered the dead Vala. "Now go away, and let me sleep again, for my eyes are heavy."

But Odin said, "Only one word more. Is Baldur going to Helheim?"

"Yes, I've told you that he is," answered the Vala.

"Will he never come back to Asgard again?"

"If everything on earth should weep for him," answered she, "he will go back; if not, he will remain in Helheim."

Then Odin covered his face with his hands, and looked into darkness.

"Do go away," said the Vala, "I'm so sleepy; I cannot keep my eyes open any longer."

But Odin raised his head, and said again, "Only tell me this one thing. Just now, as I looked into darkness, it seemed to me as if I saw one on earth who would not weep for Baldur. Who was it?"

At this the Vala grew very angry and said, "How couldst thou see in darkness? I know of only one who, by giving away his eye, gained light. No Vegtam art thou, but Odin, chief of men."

At her angry words Odin became angry too, and called out as loudly as ever he could, "No Vala art thou, nor wise-woman, but rather the mother of three giants."

"Go, go!" answered the Vala, falling back in her grave; "no man shall waken me again until Loki have burst his chains and Ragnarok be come."

After this Odin mounted the Eight-footed once more, and rode thoughtfully towards home.

Narration and Discussion

Why do Odin and Frigga think that Baldur's dream should be taken seriously? After all, they are "gods" who live in a world where even the animals eaten for dinner come back to life the next day; so death should probably not be a great concern for them.

Do you think Baldur should put those promises to the test?

Something to think about: Frigga uses the phrase "the shadow of death." Where else might you have heard those words? Here is one example (which itself is said to come from a dream). Note what Christian does in response.

> Chris. "But what have you seen?" said Christian.
>
> Men. Seen! why, the valley itself, which is as dark as pitch: we also saw there the hobgoblins, satyrs, and dragons of the pit; we heard also in that valley a continual howling and yelling, as of a people under unutterable misery, who there sat bound in affliction and irons; and over that hung the discouraging clouds of confusion; Death also does always spread his wings over it. In a word, it is every whit dreadful, being utterly without order.
>
> ...So they parted, and Christian went on his way, but still with his sword drawn in his hand, for fear lest he should be attacked.
>
> (John Bunyan, *The Pilgrim's Progress*)

(Lesson 28) The Peacestead

Introduction

All seems to be going well, and Baldur is enjoying his new immunity to danger—until Loki arrives.

Vocabulary

sham: pretend, practice

clave: cut

tremulous: trembling, shaky

Names

Hermod: Odin's son who acts as his messenger (last seen in **Lesson 3**)

Reading

Part One

When Odin came back to Asgard, **Hermod** took the bridle from his father's hand, and told him that the rest of the Aesir were gone to the Peacestead—a broad, green plain which lay just outside the city. Now this was, in fact, the playground of the Aesir, where they practised trials of skill one with another, and held tournaments and **sham** fights. These last were always conducted in the gentlest and most honourable manner; for the strongest law of the Peacestead was, that no angry blow should be struck, or spiteful word spoken, upon the sacred field; and for this reason some have thought it might be well if children also had a Peacestead to play in.

Odin was too much tired by his journey from Helheim to go to the Peacestead that afternoon; so he turned away, and shut himself up in his palace of Gladsheim. But when he was gone, Loki came into the city by another way, and hearing from Hermod where the Aesir were, set off to join them.

When he got to the Peacestead, Loki found that the Aesir were standing round in a circle shooting at something, and he peeped between the shoulders of two of them to find out what it was. To his surprise he saw Baldur standing in the midst, erect and calm, whilst his friends and brothers were aiming their weapons at him. Some hewed at him with their swords—others threw stones at him—some shot arrows pointed with steel, and Thor continually swung Miolnir at his head. "Well," said Loki to himself, "if this is the sport of Asgard, what must that of Jotunheim be? I wonder what Father Odin and Mother Frigg would say if they were here?" But as Loki still looked, he became even more surprised, for the sport went on, and Baldur was not hurt Arrows aimed at his very heart glanced back again untinged with blood. The stones fell down from his broad bright brow, and left no bruises there. Swords **clave**, but did not wound him; Miolnir struck him, and he was not crushed. At this Loki grew perfectly furious with envy and hatred. "And why is Baldur to be so honoured," said he, "that even steel and stone shall not hurt him?"

Part Two

Then Loki changed himself into a little, dark, bent, old woman, with a stick in his hand, and hobbled away from the Peacestead to Frigga's cool [salon]. At the door he knocked with his stick. "Come in!" said the kind voice of Frigg, and Loki lifted the latch.

Now when Frigga saw, from the other end of the hall, a little, bent, crippled, old woman, come hobbling up her crystal floor, she got up with true queenliness, and met her half way, holding out her hand, and saying in the kindest manner, "Pray sit down, my poor old friend; for it seems to me that you have come from a great way off."

"That I have, indeed," answered Loki in a **tremulous**, squeaking voice.

"And did you happen to see anything of the Aesir," asked Frigg, "as you came? "

"Just now I passed by the Peacestead, and saw them at play."

"What were they doing?"

"Shooting at Baldur."

Then Frigg bent over her work with a pleased smile on her face. "And nothing hurt him?" she said.

"Nothing," answered Loki, looking keenly at her.

"No, nothing," murmured Frigg, still looking down and speaking half musingly to herself; "for all things have sworn to me that they will not."

"Sworn!" exclaimed Loki, eagerly; "what is that you say? Has everything sworn then?"

"Everything," answered she, "excepting, indeed, the little shrub mistletoe, which grows, you know, on the west side of Valhalla, and to which I said nothing, because I thought it was too young to swear."

"Excellent!" thought Loki; and then he got up.

"You're not going yet, are you?" said Frigg, stretching out her hand and looking up at last into the eyes of the old woman.

"I'm quite rested now, thank you," answered Loki in his squeaky voice, and then he hobbled out at the door, which clapped after him, and sent a cold gust into the room. Frigga shuddered, and thought that a serpent was gliding down the back of her neck.

Part Three

When Loki had left the presence of Frigg, he changed himself back to his proper shape, and went straight to the west side of Valhalla, where the mistletoe grew. Then he opened his knife, and cut off a large branch, saying these words, "Too young for Frigga's oaths, but not too weak for Loki's work." After which he set off for the Peacestead once more, the mistletoe in his hand. When he got there he found that the Aesir were still at their sport, standing round, taking aim, and talking eagerly, and Baldur did not seem tired.

But there was one who stood alone, leaning against a tree, and who took no part in what was going on. This was Hodur, Baldur's blind twin-brother; he stood with his head bent downwards, silent, whilst the others were speaking, doing nothing when they were most eager; and Loki thought that there was a discontented expression on his face, just as if he were saying to himself, "Nobody takes any notice of me." So Loki went up to him, and put his hand upon his shoulder.

"And why are you standing here all alone, my brave friend?" said he. "Why don't you throw something at Baldur? Hew at him with a sword, or show him some attention of that sort."

"I haven't got a sword," answered Hodur, with an impatient gesture; "and you know as well as I do, Loki, that Father Odin does not approve of my wearing warlike weapons, or joining in sham fights, because I am blind."

"Oh! is that it?" said Loki. "Well, I only know I shouldn't like to be left out of everything. However, I've got a twig of mistletoe here which I'll lend you if you like; a harmless little twig enough, but I shall be happy to guide your arm if you would like to throw it, and Baldur might take it as a compliment from his twin-brother."

"Let me feel it," said Hodur, stretching out his uncertain hands.

"This way, this way, my dear friend," said Loki, giving him the twig. "Now, as hard as ever you can, to do him honour; throw!"

Hodur threw—Baldur fell, and the shadow of death covered the whole earth.

Narration and Discussion

What just happened here? Who is to blame?

Something to think about: Is it true that the tiniest, most overlooked or underestimated things can cause the most trouble? Give an example.

Creative narration: This story, or parts of it, might lend itself to drama. (Please be careful about throwing things at Baldur. Perhaps a drawn narration would be safer.)

(Lesson 29) Baldur Dead

Introduction

This short reading tells about the Aesirs' reaction to Baldur's death, and his funeral. (If you prefer, this reading can be combined with **Lesson 30**.)

Vocabulary

a ring: believed to be Draupnir (see **Lesson 17**)

Reading

Part One

One after another they turned and left the Peacestead, those friends and brothers of the slain.

One after another they turned and went towards the city; crushed hearts, heavy footsteps, no word amongst them, a shadow upon all.

The shadow was in Asgard too—had walked through Frigga's hall, and seated itself upon the threshold of Gladsheim. Odin had just come out to look at it, and Frigg stood by in mute despair as the Aesir came up. "Loki did it! Loki did it!" they said at last in confused, hoarse whispers, and they looked from one to another, upon Odin, upon Frigg, upon the shadow which they saw before them, and which they felt within. "Loki did it! Loki, Loki!" they went on saying; but it was no use repeating the name of Loki over and over again when there was another name they were too sad to utter which yet filled all their hearts—Baldur.

Frigga said it first, and then they all went to look at him lying down so peacefully on the grass—dead, dead.

"Carry him to the funeral pyre!" said Odin, at length; and four of the Aesir stooped down, and lifted their dead brother.

With scarcely any sound they carried the body tenderly to the sea-shore, and laid it upon the deck of that majestic ship called Ringhorn, which had been his. Then they stood round waiting to see who would come to the funeral.

Part Two

Odin came, and on his shoulders sat his two ravens, whose croaking drew clouds down over the Asa's face, for Thought and Memory sang one sad song that day.

Frigga came—[and] Frey, Gerda, Freyja, Thor, Hoenir, Bragi, and Iduna.

Heimdall came sweeping over the tops of the mountains on Golden Mane, his swift, bright steed.

Aegir the Old groaned from under the deep, and sent his daughters up to mourn around the dead.

Frost-giants and mountain-giants came crowding round the rimy shores of Jotunheim to look across the sea upon the funeral of an Asa.

Nanna came, Baldur's fair young wife; but when she saw the dead body of her husband her own heart broke with grief, and the Aesir laid her beside him on the stately ship.

After this Odin stepped forward, and placed **a ring** on the breast of his son, whispering something at the same time in his ear; but when he and the rest of the Aesir tried to push Ringhorn into the sea before setting fire to it, they found that their hearts were so heavy they could lift nothing. So they beckoned to the giantess Hyrrokin to come over from Jotunheim and help them. She, with a single push, set the ship floating, and then, whilst Thor stood up holding Miolnir high in the air, Odin lighted the funeral pile of Baldur and of Nanna.

So Ringhorn went out floating towards the deep, and the funeral fire burnt on. Its broad red flame burst forth towards heaven; but when the smoke would have gone upward too, the winds came sobbing and carried it away.

Narration and Discussion

How do the gods show their grief? Choose one phrase or line from the reading that seems to sum up their sorrow.

Creative narration: This might be a good day to put out a special edition of the Aesir newspaper. What would the headlines say? Might Bragi compose some poetry?

(Lesson 30) Helheim

Introduction

When Odin spoke to the Vala, she told him that Baldur would be arriving in Hela's underworld realm. The response seems obvious: somebody has to go and get him out.

(As noted, this Lesson can be combined with **Lesson 29**).

Vocabulary

alighted: got off the horse

man: waiter

Reading

Part One

When at last the ship Ringhorn had floated out so far to sea that it looked like a dull, red lamp on the horizon, Frigga turned round and said, "Does any one of you, my children, wish to perform a noble action, and win my love for ever?"

"I do," cried Hermod, before any one else had time to open his lips.

"Go, then, Hermod," answered Frigg, "saddle Sleipnir with all speed, and ride down to Helheim; there seek out Hela, the stern mistress of the dead, and entreat her to send our beloved back to us once more."

Hermod was gone in the twinkling of an eye, not in at the mouth of the earth and through the steep cavern down which Odin went to the dead Vala's grave. He chose another way, though not a better one; for, go to Helheim how you will, the best is but a downward road, and so Hermod found it—downward, slanting, slippery, dark and very cold. At last he came to the Giallar Bru—that sounding river which flows between the living and the dead, and the bridge over which is paved with stones of glittering gold. Hermod was surprised to see gold in such a place; but as he rode over the bridge, and looked down carefully at the stones, he saw that they were only tears which had been shed round the beds of the dying—only tears, and yet they made the way seem brighter. But when Hermod reached the other end of the bridge, he found the courageous woman who, for ages and ages, had been sitting there to watch the dead go by, and she stopped him saying,—

"What a noise you make. Who are you? Yesterday five troops of dead men went over the Giallar Bridge, and did not shake it so much as you have done. Besides," she added, looking more closely at Hermod, "you are not a dead man at all. Your lips are neither cold nor blue. Why, then, do you ride on the way to Helheim?"

"I seek Baldur," answered Hermod. "Tell me, have you seen him pass?"

"Baldur," she said, "has ridden over the bridge; but there below, towards the north, lies the way to the Abodes of Death."

Part Two

So Hermod went on the way until he came to the barred gates of Helheim itself. There he **alighted**, tightened his saddle-girths, remounted, clapped both spurs to his horse, and cleared the gate by one tremendous leap. Then Hermod found himself in a place where no living man had ever been before—the City of the Dead.

Perhaps you think there is a great silence there, but you are mistaken. Hermod thought he had never in his life heard so much noise; for the echoes of all words were speaking together—words, some newly uttered and some ages old; but the dead men did not hear who flitted up and down the dark streets, for their ears had been stunned and become cold long since.

Hermod rode on through the city until he came to the palace of Hela, which stood in the midst. Precipice was its threshold, the entrance-hall, Wide-Storm, and yet Hermod was not too much afraid to seek the innermost rooms; so he went on to the banqueting-hall, where Hela sat at the head of her table, and served her newest guests. Baldur, alas! sat at her right-hand, and on her left his pale young wife. When Hela saw Hermod coming up the hall she smiled grimly, but beckoned to him at the same time to sit down, and told him that he might sup that night with her.

It was a strange supper for a living man to sit down to. Hunger was the table; Starvation, Hela's knife; Delay her **man**; Slowness, her maid; and Burning Thirst, her wine. After supper Hela led the way to the sleeping apartments. "You see," she said, turning to Hermod, "I am very anxious about the comfort of my guests. Here are beds of Unrest provided for all, hung with curtains of Weariness, and look how all the walls are furnished with Despair."

So saying she strode away, leaving Hermod and Baldur together. The whole night they sat on those unquiet couches and talked. Hermod could speak of nothing but the past, and as he looked anxiously round the room his eyes became dim with tears. But Baldur seemed to see a light far off, and he spoke of what was to come.

Part Three

The next morning Hermod went to Hela, and entreated her to let Baldur return to Asgard. He even offered to take his place in Helheim if she pleased; but Hela only laughed at this, and said, "You talk a great deal about Baldur, and boast how much every one loves him; I will prove now if what you have told me be true. Let everything on earth, living or dead, weep for Baldur and he shall go home again; but if one thing only refuse to weep, then let Helheim hold its own; he shall *not* go."

"Every one will weep willingly," said Hermod, as he mounted Sleipnir, and rode towards the entrance of the city. Baldur went with him as far as the gate, and began to send messages to all his friends in Asgard, but Hermod would not listen to many of them. "You will so soon come back to us," he said, "there is no use in sending messages."

So Hermod darted homewards, and Baldur watched him through the bars of Helheim's gateway as he flew along. "Not soon, not soon," said the dead Asa; but still he saw the light far off, and thought of what was to come.

Narration and Discussion

Why do you think Hela did not accept Hermod's offer to take Baldur's place?

When Frigga made everything on earth swear not to harm Baldur, she overlooked one small thing that was then used for evil. Similarly, everything and everyone must now weep for him, without even one small exception. Do you think his friends can make that happen?

Something to think about: Hela's palace is furnished with Weariness and Despair. What words should characterize the homes of Christians? What are some ways we might do that, so that those who enter can see what we believe?

(Lesson 31) Weeping

Introduction

In this last reading of the chapter "Baldur," the gods ask the world to weep for him.

Vocabulary

machinations: schemes

Names

Thaukt: also spelled Thokk

Reading

Part One

"Well, Hermod, what did she say?" asked the Aesir from the top of the hill, as they saw him coming; "make haste and tell us what she said." And Hermod came up.

"Oh! is that all?" they cried, as soon as he had delivered his message. "Nothing can be more easy"; and then they all hurried off to tell Frigga. She was weeping already, and in five minutes there was not a tearless eye in Asgard.

"But this is not enough," said Odin; "the whole earth must know of our grief that it may weep with us."

Then the father of the Aesir called to him his messenger maidens—the beautiful Valkyrior—and sent them out into all worlds with these three words on their lips, "Baldur is dead!" But the words were so dreadful that at first the messenger maidens could only whisper them in low tones as they went along, "Baldur is dead!" The dull, sad sounds flowed back on Asgard like a new river of grief, and it seemed to the Aesir as if they now wept for the first time— "Baldur is dead! "

"What is that the Valkyrior are saying?" asked the men and women in all the country round, and when they heard rightly, men left their labour and lay down to weep— women dropped the buckets they were carrying to the well, and, leaning their faces over them, filled them with tears. The children crowded upon the doorsteps, or sat down at the corners of the streets, crying as if their own mothers were dead.

The Valkyrior passed on. "Baldur is dead!" they said to the empty fields; and straightway the grass and the wild field-flowers shed tears. "Baldur is dead!" said the messenger maidens to the rocks and the stones; and the very stones began to weep. "Baldur is dead!" the Valkyrior cried; and even the old mammoth's bones, which had lain for centuries under the hills, burst into tears, so that small rivers gushed forth from every mountain's side. "Baldur is dead!" said the messenger maidens as they swept over silent sands; and all the shells wept pearls. "Baldur is dead!" they cried to the sea, and to Jotunheim across the sea; and when the giants understood it, even they wept, whilst the sea rained spray to heaven.

After this the Valkyrior stepped from one stone to another until they reached a rock that stood alone in the middle of the sea; then, all together, they bent forward over the edge of it, stooped down and peeped over, that they might tell the monsters of the deep. "Baldur is dead!" they said; and, the sea monsters and the fish wept. Then the messenger maidens looked at one another, and said, "Surely our work is done." So they twined their arms round one another's waists, and set forth on the downward road to Helheim, there to claim Baldur from among the dead.

Part Two

Now after he had sent forth his messenger maidens, Odin had seated himself on the top of Air Throne that he might see how the earth received his message. At first he watched the Valkyrior as they stepped forth north and south, and east and west; but soon the whole earth's steaming tears rose up like a great cloud, and hid everything from him. Then he looked down through the cloud, and said, "Are you all weeping?" The Valkyrior heard the sound of his voice as they went all together down the slippery road, and they turned round, stretching out their arms towards Air Throne, their long hair falling back, whilst, with choked voices and streaming eyes, they answered, "The world weeps, Father Odin; the world and we."

After this they went on their way until they came to the end of the cave Gnipa, where Garm was chained, and which yawned over Niflheim. "The world weeps," they said one to another by way of encouragement, for here the road was so dreadful; but just as they were about to pass through the mouth of Gnipa they came upon a haggard witch named **Thaukt**, who sat in the entrance with her back to them, and her face towards the abyss. "Baldur is dead! Weep, weep!" said the messenger maidens, as they tried to pass her; but Thaukt made answer—

"What she doth hold,
    Let Hela keep;
For naught care I,
    Though the world weep,
        O'er Baldur's bale.
Live he or die
With tearless eye
    Old Thaukt shall wail."

And with these words [she] leaped into Niflheim with a yell of triumph.

"Surely that cry was the cry of Loki," said one of the maidens; but another pointed towards the city of Helheim, and there they saw the stern face of Hela looking over the wall. "One has not wept," said the grim Queen, "and Helheim holds its own." So saying she motioned the maidens away with her long, cold hand. Then the Valkyrior turned and fled up the steep way to the foot of Odin's throne, like a pale snow-drift that flies before the storm.

After this a strong child, called Vali, was born in the city of Asgard. He was the youngest of Odin's sons—strong and cold as the icy January blast; but full, also, as it is of the hope of the new year. When only a day old he slew the blind Hodur by a single blow, and then spent the rest of his life in trying to lift the shadow of death from the face of the weeping earth.

Explaining Things

The death of Baldur was probably in the first place an expression of the decline of the Summer sun. At midsummer Freyja's husband forsook her, at midsummer also the bright god begins to turn his face Helheim-wards. Midsummer day is observed in the North of Europe under the name of Beltan, and fires are lighted upon the hills, a custom which evidently had its origin in a commemoration of Baldur's death.

Some think that Baldur and Hodur typify the two halves of the year. At the turn of the day in Summer Hod kills Baldur, at the turn of the day in Winter Vali kills Hodur. Vali was the son of Odin and Rind, a giantess, whose name means the winterly earth, so that clearly Vali comes at midwinter. Why the mistletoe should be used to kill Baldur it is difficult to say. Might its being so weak and small imply the very small beginning of the day's decline?

But Baldur, from the description given of him in the *Edda*, must surely be a personification of goodness morally, as well as the sun of the outward year, and his not returning from Helheim, being retained there through the **machinations** of Loki, seems to be a sort of connecting link between the first sorrow of the gods, the beginning of evil and their final defeat by the evil powers at Ragnarok—the giants have already one foot upon the gods.

Narration and Discussion

Why did Thaukt refuse to weep for Baldur?

Something to think about: We are told that Odin's son Vali "spent the rest of his life in trying to lift the shadow of death from the face of the weeping earth." Whose Son has truly defeated Death? (Romans 8:2-4, 37-39.)

Creative narration: At the end of each chapter, we suggest creating a new edition (or just the first page) of the *Asgard Daily News*. What are some of the recent headlines?

Chapter Seven: The Binding of Fenrir

(Lesson 32) The Might of Asgard

Introduction

The Aesir now sense increasing danger to their world and to themselves. The place where they see it most literally is in Loki's wolf-son Fenrir, who grows "a little stronger and a little fiercer every day." But what is to be done with him?

Vocabulary

uncouth: ill-mannered

placid: calm

prowess: skill

ponderous: heavy, clumsy

dilate: become larger and wider

Reading

Part One

I hope you have not forgotten what I told you of Fenrir, Loki's fierce wolf-son, whom Odin brought home with him to Asgard, and of whose reformation, **uncouth** and wolfish as he was, All-father entertained some hope, thinking that the wholesome, bright air of Gladsheim, the sight of the fair faces of the Asyniur and the hearing of the brave words which day by day fell from the lips of heroes, would, perhaps, have power to change the cruel nature he had inherited from his father, and make him worthy of his place as a dweller in the City of Lords.

To Tyr, the brave and strong-handed, Odin assigned the task of feeding Fenrir, and watching him, lest, in his cruel strength, he should injure any who were unable to defend themselves. And truly it was a grand sight, and one that Asa Odin loved, to see the two together, when, in the evening after the feast was over in Valhalla, Fenrir came prowling to Tyr's feet to receive his food from the one hand strong enough to quell him. Tyr stood up in his calm strength like a tall, sheltering rock in which the timid sea-birds find a home; and Fenrir roared and howled round him like the bitter, destroying wave that slowly undermines its base.

Time passed on. Tyr had reached the prime of his strength; but Fenrir went on growing, not so rapidly as to awaken fear, as his brother Jormungand had done, but slowly, surely, continually—a little stronger and a little fiercer every day.

The Aesir and the Asyniur had become accustomed to his presence; the gentlest lady in Asgard no longer turned away from the sight of his fierce mouth and fiery eye; they talked to each other about the smallest things, and every daily event was commented on and wondered about; but no one said anything of Fenrir, or noticed how gradually he grew, or how the glad air and the strong food, which gave valour and strength to an Asa, could only develop with greater rapidity fierceness and cruelty in a wolf. And they would have gone on living securely together while the monster grew and grew, if it had not been that Asa Odin's one eye, enlightened as it was by the upspringing well of wisdom within, saw more clearly than the eyes of his brothers and children.

One evening, as he stood in the court of Valhalla watching Tyr as he gave Fenrir his evening meal, a sudden cloud of care fell on the **placid** face of All-father. And when the wolf, having satisfied his hunger, crouched back to his lair, he called together a council of the heads of the Aesir—Thor, Tyr, Bragi, Hoenir, Frey, and Niord; and, after pointing out to them the evil which they had allowed to grow up among them unnoticed, he asked their counsel as to the best way of overcoming it before it became too strong to withstand.

Thor, always ready, was the first to answer. "One would think," he said, "to hear the grave way in which you speak, Father Odin, that there was no such thing as a smithy near Asgard, or that I, Asa Thor, had no power to forge mighty weapons, and had never made my name known in Jotunheim as the conqueror and binder of monsters. Set your mind at rest. Before tomorrow evening at this time I will have forged a chain with which you shall bind Fenrir; and, once bound in a chain of my workmanship, there will be nothing further to fear from him."

The assembled Aesir applauded Thor's speech; but the cloud did not pass away from Odin's brow. "You have done many mighty deeds, Son Thor," he said; "but, if I mistake not, this binding of Fenrir will prove a task too difficult even for you."

Thor made no answer; but he seized Miolnir, and, with sounding steps, strode to the smithy. All night long the mighty blows of Miolnir rang on the anvil, and the roaring bellows breathed a hot blast over all the hill of Asgard. None of the Aesir slept that night; but every now and then one or other of them came to cheer Thor at his work. Sometimes Frey brought his bright face into the dusky smithy; sometimes Tyr entreated permission to strike a stout blow; sometimes Bragi seated himself among the workers, and, with his eyes fixed on the glowing iron, poured forth a hero song, to which the ringing blows kept time.

There was also another guest, who, at intervals, made his presence known. By the light of the fire the evil form of Fenrir was seen prowling round in the darkness, and every now and then a fiendish, mocking laugh filled the pauses of the song, and the wind, and the ringing hammer.

Part Two

All that night and the next day Thor laboured and Fenrir watched, and, at the time of the evening meal, Thor strode triumphantly into Father Odin's presence, and laid before him Laeding, the strongest chain that had ever yet been forged on earth. The Aesir passed it from one to another, and wondered at its immense length, and at the ponderous moulding of its twisted links. "It is impossible for Fenrir to break through this," they said; and they were loud in their thanks to Thor and praises of his **prowess**; only Father Odin kept a grave, sad silence.

When Fenrir came into the court to receive his food from Tyr, it was agreed that Thor and Tyr were to seize and bind him. They held their weapons in readiness, for they expected a fierce struggle; but, to their surprise, Fenrir quietly allowed the chain to be wound round him, and lay down at his ease, while Thor, with two strokes of Miolnir, rivetted the last link into one of the strongest stones on which the court rested. Then, when the Aesir were about to congratulate each other on their victory, he slowly raised his **ponderous** form, which seemed to **dilate** in the rising. With one bound forward [he] snapped the chain like a silken thread, and walked leisurely to his lair, as if no unusual thing had befallen him.

The Aesir, with downcast faces, stood looking at each other. Once more Thor was the first to speak. "He who breaks through Laeding," he said, "only brings upon himself the still harder bondage of Dromi." And having uttered these words, he again lifted Miolnir from the ground, and, weary as he was, returned to the smithy and resumed his place at the anvil.

Part Three

For three days and nights Thor worked, and, when he once more appeared before Father Odin, he carried in his hand Dromi—the "Strong Binding." This chain exceeded Laeding in strength by one half, and was so heavy that Asa Thor himself staggered under its weight; and yet Fenrir showed no fear of allowing himself to be bound by it, and it cost him very little more effort than on the first evening to free himself from its fetters.

Part Four

After this second failure Odin again called a council of Aesir in Gladsheim, and Thor stood among the others, silent and shamefaced.

It was now Frey who ventured first to offer an opinion. "Thor, Tyr, and other brave sons of the Aesir," he said, "have passed their lives valiantly in fighting against giants and monsters, and, doubtless, much wise lore has come to them through these adventures. I, for the most part, have spent my time peacefully in woods and fields, watching how the seasons follow each other, and how the silent, dewy night ever leads up the brightly-smiling day; and, in this watching, many things have been made plain to me which have not, perhaps, been thought worthy of regard by my brother Lords. One thing that I have learned is, the wondrous strength that lies in little things, and that the labour carried on in darkness and silence ever brings forth the grandest birth. Thor and Miolnir have failed to forge a chain strong enough to bind Fenrir; but, since we cannot be helped by the mighty and renowned, let us turn to the unknown and weak.

"In the caverns and dim places of the earth live a tiny race of people, who are always working with unwearied, noiseless fingers. With Asa Odin's permission, I will send my messenger, Skirnir, and entreat aid of them; and we shall, perhaps, find that what passes the might of Asgard may be accomplished in the secret places of Svartheim."

The face of Asa Odin brightened as Frey spoke, and, rising immediately from his seat, he broke up the council, and entreated Frey to lose no time in returning to Alfheim and despatching Skirnir on his mission.

Narration and Discussion

Odin had hoped that "the wholesome, bright air of Gladsheim…would, perhaps, have power to change the cruel nature [Fenrir] had inherited from his father, and make him worthy of his place as a dweller in the City of Lords." How was that working out?

Why do you think even the strong chains that Thor made could not bind Fenrir?

Do you think Frey's idea might work?

Something to think about (for adults and older students): The Victorians (such as the Kearys) were very interested in the idea of people having royal or noble "blood," as we see in fairytales such as Andersen's "The Real Princess." Many of them also believed that bad traits inherited from parents or grandparents could not be changed. What do you think? Charlotte Mason taught something different, although even she might have had a hard time dealing with Fenrir.

> Children are born *persons*. They are not born either good or bad, but with possibilities for good and for evil. (Educational Principles #1 and #2, as listed in *Philosophy of Education*)

Something else to think about: Odin spoke of "the evil which they had allowed to grow up among them unnoticed." If we have allowed a bad habit to take hold in our lives, how can we change it?

Creative narration: Drama? Visual Art?

(Lesson 33) The Secret of Svartheim

Introduction

Skirnir heads into the realm of the dwarfs, to see if they can make an unbreakable chain for Fenrir. (The problem after that is how they are going to get it on him.)

Vocabulary

sagacity: wisdom

his wondrous sword: that is, the sword which Frey had given him

Will-o'-the-wisp: a ghostly light seen over swampy areas

tidings: news

Reading

Part One

In spite of the cloud that hung over Asgard all was fair and peaceful in Alfheim.

Gerda, the radiant Alf Queen, made there perpetual sunshine with her bright face. The little elves loved her, and fluttered round her, keeping up a continual merry chatter, which sounded through the land like the sharp ripple of a brook over stony places; and Gerda answered them in low, sweet tones, as the answering wind sounds among the trees.

These must have been pleasant sounds to hear after the ringing of Miolnir and the howling of Fenrir; but Frey hardly gave himself time to greet Gerd and his elves before he summoned Skirnir into his presence, and acquainted him with the danger that hung over Asgard, and the important mission which the Aesir had determined to trust to his **sagacity**. Skirnir listened, playing with the knot of **his wondrous sword**, as he was wont to do, in order to make known to every one that he possessed it; for, to confess the truth, it was somewhat too heavy for him to wield.

"This is a far different mission," he said, "from that on which you once sent me, to woo fairest Gerd; but, as the welfare of Asgard requires it, I will depart at once, though I have little liking for the dark caves and cunning people."

Frey thanked him, and, putting a small key into his hand, which was, indeed, the key to the gate of Svartheim, he bade him farewell, and Skirnir set out on his journey.

Part Two

The road from Alfheim to Svartheim is not as long as you would be apt to imagine. Indeed, it is possible for a careless person to wander from one region to another without being at once aware of it. Skirnir, having the key in his hand, took the direct way. The entrance-gate stands at the opening of a dim mountain-cave. Skirnir left his horse without, and entered; the air was heavy, moist, and warm, and it required the keenest glances of Skirnir's keen eyes to see his way. Innumerable narrow, winding paths, all leading downwards, opened themselves before him. As he followed the widest, a faint clinking sound of hammers met his ear, and, looking round, he saw groups of little men at work on every side. Some were wheeling small wheelbarrows full of lumps of shining metal along the ledges of the rock; some, with elfin pickaxes and spades, were digging ore from the mountain-side; some, herded together in little caves, were busy kindling fires, or working with tiny hammers on small anvils. As he continued his downward path the last remnant of daylight faded away; but he was not in total darkness, for now he perceived that each worker carried on his head a lantern, in which burned a pale, dancing light. Skirnir knew that each light was a **Will-o'-the-wisp**, which the dwarf who carried it had caught and imprisoned to light him in his work during the day, and which he must restore to the earth at night.

Part Three

For many miles Skirnir wandered on lower and lower. On every side of him lay countless heaps of treasure—gold, silver, diamonds, rubies, emeralds—which the cunning workers stowed away silently in their dark hiding-places. At length he came to the very middle of the mountain, where the rocky roof rose to an immense height, and where he found himself in a brilliantly-lighted palace. Here, in truth, were hung all the lights in the world, which, on dark, moonless nights, are carried out by dwarfs to deceive the eyes of men. Corpse-lights, Will-o'-the-wisps, the sparks from glow-worms' tails, the light in fireflies' wings—these, carefully hung up in tiers round and round the hall, illuminated the palace with a cold blue light, and revealed to Skirnir's eyes the grotesque and hideous shapes of the tiny beings around him. Hump-backed, cunning-eyed, open-mouthed, they stood round, laughing, and whispering, and pointing with shrivelled fingers. One among them, a little taller than the rest, who sat on a golden seat thickly set with diamonds, appeared to be a kind of chief among them, and to him Skirnir addressed his message.

Cunning and wicked as these dwarfs were, they entertained a wholesome fear of Odin, having never forgotten their one interview with him in Gladsheim; and, therefore, when they heard from whom Skirnir came, with many uncouth gesticulations they bowed low before him, and declared themselves willing to obey All-father's commands. They asked for two days and two nights in which to complete their task, and during that time Skirnir remained their guest in Svartheim.

He wandered about, and saw strange sights. He saw the great earth central fire, and [those] whose task it is ceaselessly to feed it with fuel; he saw the diamond-makers, who change the ashes of the great fire into brilliants; and the dwarfs, whose business it is to fill the cracks in the mountain-sides with pure veins of silver and gold, and lead them up to places where they will one day meet the eyes of men. Nearer the surface he visited the workers in iron and the makers of salt-mines; he drank of their strange-tasting mineral waters, and admired the splendour of their silver-roofed temples and dwellings of solid gold.

Part Four

At the end of two days Skirnir re-entered the audience-hall, and then the chief of the dwarfs put into his hand a slender chain. You can imagine what size it was when I tell you that the dwarf chief held it lightly balanced on his forefinger; and when it rested on Skirnir's hand it felt to him no heavier than a piece of thistle-down.

The Svart King laughed loud when he saw the disappointment on Skirnir's face. "It seems to you a little thing," he said; "and yet I assure you that in making it we have used up all the materials in the whole world fit for the purpose. No such chain can ever be made again, neither will the least atom of the substances of which it is made be found more. It is fashioned out of six things. The noise made by the footfall of cats; the beards of women; the roots of stones; the sinews of bears; the breath of fish; and the spittle of birds. Fear not with this to bind Fenrir; for no stronger chain will ever be made till the end of the world."

Skirnir now looked with wonder at his chain, and, after having thanked the dwarfs, and promised to bring them a reward from Odin, he set forth on his road home, and, by the time of the evening meal, reached Valhalla, and gladdened the hearts of the

Aesir by the **tidings** of his success.

Narration and Discussion

Describe the dwarfs' realm, using any creative means you like.

Why did the dwarfs use "impossible things" to make the strongest chain in the world? (Are all those things impossible? Don't bears have sinews, or fish have breath?)

Creative narration #1: Can you think of any truly "impossible things?"

> "I have got ivory, apes, and peacocks...hummingbirds' tongues, angels' feathers, and unicorns' horns...frankincense, ambergris, and myrrh...a pound of butter, two dozen eggs, and a sack of sugar—sorry, my wife wrote that in there." (James Thurber, *Many Moons*)

Creative narration #2: What is in the *Asgard Daily News* today? New flavors of mead? Pet-keeping advice?

(Lesson 34) Honour

Introduction

The Aesir conspire to get the dwarfs' chain around Fenrir's neck.

Vocabulary

vied: competed

loath: reluctant, unwilling

no deceit is intended: In some versions of the story, Fenrir is promised that, if he cannot break this final chain, he will then be released from it.

annihilation: complete destruction

compass ends: accomplish things

Places

Amsvartnir: the lake containing the island **Lyngvi**; it does not seem to be a real place.

Reading

Part One

Far away to the north of Asgard, surrounded by frowning mountains, the dark lake, **Amsvartnir**, lies, and, above the level of its troubled waters, burns **Lyngvi**, the island of sweet broom, flaming like a jewel on the dark brow of Hela. In this lonely isle, to which no ship but Skidbladnir could sail, the Aesir, with Fenrir in the midst, assembled to try the strength of the dwarfs' chain.

Fenrir prowled round his old master, Tyr, with a look of savage triumph in his cruel eyes, now licking the hand that had so long fed him, and now shaking his great head, and howling defiantly. The Aesir stood at the foot of Gioll, the sounding rock, and passed Gleipnir, the chain, from one to another, talking about it, while Fenrir listened. "It was much stronger than it looked," they said; and Thor and Tyr **vied** with each other in their efforts to break it; while Bragi declared his belief that there was no one among Aesir or giants capable of performing so great a feat, "unless," he added, "it should be you, Fenrir."

This speech roused the pride of Fenrir; and, after looking long at the slender chain and the faces of the Aesir, he answered, "**Loath** am I to be bound by this chain; but, lest you should doubt my courage, I will consent that you should bind me, provided one of you put his hand into my mouth as a pledge that **no deceit is intended**."

There was a moment's silence among the Aesir when they heard this, and they looked at one another. Odin looked at Thor, and Thor looked at Bragi, and Frey fell behind, and put his hand to his side, where the all-conquering sword, which he alone could wield, no longer rested.

At length Tyr stepped forward valiantly, and put his strong right hand, with which he had so often fed him, into the wolf's cruel jaws. At this signal the other Aesir threw the chain round the monster's neck, bound him securely with one end, and fastened the other to the great rock Gioll. When he was bound Fenrir rose, and shook himself, as he had done before; but in vain he raised himself up, and bounded forward—the more he struggled the more firmly the slender chain bound him.

At this sight the Aesir set up a loud shout of joy; for they saw their enemy conquered, and the danger that threatened Asgard averted. Only Tyr was silent, for in the struggle he had lost his hand.

Part Two

Then Thor thrust his sword into the mouth of Fenrir, and a foaming dark flood burst forth, roared down the rock and under the lake, and began its course through the country a turbid river. So it will roll on till Ragnarok be come.

The sails of Skidbladnir now spread themselves out to the wind; and the Aesir, seated in the magic ship, floated over the lake silently in the silent moonlight; while, from the top of Bifrost, over the Urda fount and the dwelling of the Norns, a song floated down. "Who," asked one voice, "of all the Aesir has won the highest honour?" and, singing, another voice made answer, "Tyr has won the highest honour; for, of all the Aesir, he has the most worthily employed his gift."

"Frey gave his sword for fairest Gerd."

"Odin bought for himself wisdom at the price of his right eye."

"Tyr, not for himself, but for others, has sacrificed his strong right hand."

Explaining Things, and Looking Ahead

The wolf Fenrir is **annihilation**; he was destined to swallow the chief of the gods at Ragnarok. We see him here as destruction chained until his time for mischief should come again—the destructive side of nature morally and physically is personified in him. Why the dwarfs should be able to make a chain strong enough to bind him, which the gods had failed to do, is a puzzle. May it mean that subtlety can **compass ends** which force has to relinquish; or possibly a better thing than subtlety, gentleness?

Har says of [Tyr], "he is the most daring and intrepid of the gods, hence a man who surpasses all others in valour is called Tyr-strong." His having only one hand refers partly to his character of war god, and means that the victory can only be awarded to one side. "Thou never couldst settle a strife betwixt two," was said to his shame, and, we may add, to that of all war gods for ever.

Tyr gives his name to Tuesday, as Odin to Wednesday, Thor to Thursday, and Freyja or Frigga to Friday. Some suggest that Loki is the patron of Saturday. He—Loki—forms the subject of the next chapter.

Narration and Discussion

How did the Aesir trick Fenrir into being bound with the chain?

Why were they rather quiet as they returned home?

For further thought: What do you think of the idea that subtlety or gentleness may do what force cannot? Can you give any examples?

Creative narration: Interview one or more of the Aesir about these events.

(Lesson 35) Chapter Eight: The Punishment of Loki

Introduction

Loki has lost all favour with the Aesir and runs away. But he can't hide forever.

Vocabulary

vigilance: watchfulness

Names

Kvasir: "But isn't Kvasir dead and his blood turned into mead?" This story and the earlier one about Kvasir come from two different "books," and they were told at various times without worrying about which part of the story happened first.

Har: an ancient sage who sits on a high throne (possibly Odin)

Reading

Part One

After the death of Baldur, Loki never again ventured to intrude himself into the presence of the Aesir. He knew well enough that he had now done what could never be forgiven him, and that, for the future, he must bend all his cunning and **vigilance** to the task of hiding himself for ever from the eyes of those whom he had so injured, and escaping the just punishment he had brought upon himself.

"The world is large, and I am very cunning," said Loki to himself, as he turned his back upon Asgard, and wandered out into Manheim. "There is no end to the thick woods, and no measure for the deep waters; neither is there any possibility of counting the various forms under which I shall disguise myself. All-father will never be able to find me; I have no cause to fear." But, though Loki repeated this over and over again to himself, he *was* afraid.

He wandered far into the thick woods, and covered himself with the deep waters; he climbed to the tops of misty hills, and crouched in the dark of hollow caves; but above the wood, and through the water, and down into the darkness, a single ray of calm, clear light seemed always to follow him, and he knew that it came from the eye of All-father, who was watching him from Air Throne.

Then he tried to escape the judging eye by disguising himself under various shapes. Sometimes he was an eagle on a lonely mountain-crag; sometimes he hid himself as one among a troop of timid reindeer; sometimes he lay in the nest of a wood-pigeon; sometimes he swam, a bright-spotted fish, in the sea; but, wherever he was, among living creatures, or alone with dead nature, everything seemed to know him, and to find some voice in which to say to him, "You are Loki, and you have killed Baldur." Air, earth, or water, there was no rest for him anywhere.

Part Two

Tired at last of seeking what he could nowhere find, Loki built himself a house by the side of a narrow, glittering river which, at a lower point, flashed down from a high rock into the sea below. He took care that his house should have four doors in it, that he might look out on every side, and catch the first glimpse of the Aesir when they came, as he knew they would come, to take him away. Here his wife, Siguna, and his two sons, Ali and Nari, came to live with him.

Siguna was a kind woman, far too good and kind for Loki. She felt sorry for him now that she saw he was in great fear, and that every living thing had turned against him, and she would have hidden him from the just anger of the Aesir if she could; but the two sons cared little about their father's dread and danger; they spent all their time in quarrelling with each other; and their loud, angry voices, sounding above the waterfall, would speedily have betrayed the hiding-place, even if All-father's piercing eye had not already discovered it. "If only the children would be quiet," Siguna used to say anxiously every day. But Loki said nothing; he was beginning to know by experience that there was [something] about his children that could never be kept quiet or hidden away.

At last, one day when he was sitting in the middle of his house looking alternately out of all the four doors, and amusing himself as well as he could by making a fishing net, he spied in the distance the whole company of the Aesir approaching his house. The sight of them coming all together—beautiful, and noble, and free—pierced Loki with a pang that was worse than death. He rose without daring to look again, threw his net on a fire that burned on the floor, and, rushing to the side of the little river, he turned himself into a salmon, swam down to the deepest, stillest pool at the bottom, and hid himself between two stones.

Part Three

The Aesir entered the house, and looked all round in vain for Loki, till **Kvasir**, one of Odin's sons, famous for his keen sight, spied out the remains of the fishing-net in the fire; then Odin knew at once that there was a river near, and that it was there where Loki had hidden himself. He ordered his sons to make a fresh net, and to cast it into the water, and drag out whatever living thing they could find there.

It was done as he desired. Thor held one end of the net, and all the rest of the Aesir drew the other through the water. When they pulled it up the first time, however, it was empty, and they would have gone away disappointed, had not Kvasir, looking earnestly at the meshes of the net, discovered that something living had certainly touched them. They then added a weight to the net, and threw it with such force that it reached the bottom of the river, and dragged up the stones in the pool.

Loki now saw the danger he was in of being caught in the net, and, as there was no other way of escape, he rose to the surface, swam down the river as quickly as he could, and leaped over the net into the waterfall. He swam and leaped quickly as a flash of lightning, but not so quickly but that the Aesir saw him, knew him through his disguise, and resolved that he should no longer escape them.

They divided into two bands. Thor waded down the river to the waterfall; the other

Aesir stood in a group below. Loki swam backwards and forwards between them. Now he thought he would dart out into the sea, and now that he would spring over the net back again into the river. This last seemed the readiest way of escape, and, with the greatest speed, he attempted it. Thor, however, was watching for him, and, as soon as Loki leaped out of the water, he stretched out his hand, and caught him while he was yet turning in the air. Loki wriggled his slippery, slimy length through Thor's fingers; but the Thunderer grasped him tightly by the tail, and, holding him in this manner in his hand, waded to the shore. There Father Odin and the other Aesir met him; and, at Odin's first searching look, Loki was obliged to drop his disguise, and, cowering and frightened, to stand in his proper shape before the assembled Lords. One by one they turned their faces from him; for, in looking at him, they seemed to see over again the death of Baldur the Beloved.

Part Four

I told you that there were high rocks looking over the sea not far from Loki's house. One of these, higher than the rest, had midway four projecting stones, and to these the Aesir resolved to bind Loki in such a manner that he should never again be able to torment the inhabitants of Manheim or Asgard by his evil-doings. Thor proposed to return to Asgard, to bring a chain with which to bind the prisoner; but Odin assured him that he had no need to take such a journey. "Loki," he said, "has already forged for himself a chain stronger than any you can make. While we have been occupied in catching him, his two sons, Ali and Nari, transformed into wolves by their evil passions, have fought with, and destroyed, each other. With their sinews we must make a chain to bind their father, and from that he can never escape."

It was done as Asa Odin said. A rope was made of the dead wolves' sinews, and, as soon as it touched Loki's body, it turned into bands of iron, and bound him immovably to the rock. Secured in this manner the Aesir left him. But his punishment did not end here. A snake, whose fangs dropped venom, glided to the top of the rock, and leaned his head over to peer at Loki. The eyes of the two met and fixed each other. The serpent could never move away afterwards; but every moment a burning drop from his tongue fell down on Loki's shuddering face.

In all the world there was only one who pitied him. His kind wife ever afterwards stood beside him, and held a cup over his head to catch the poison. When the cup was full, she was obliged to turn away to empty it, and drops of poison fell again on Loki's face. He shuddered and shrank from it, and the whole earth trembled. So will he lie bound till Ragnarok be come.

[*Note: the rest of this chapter has been shortened from the original text.*]

Explaining Things, and Looking Ahead

[The German scholar Karl Joseph Simrock] says that Loki…represents the guilty conscience of the gods…a personification of the consciousness of sin. His attempts at concealment, the four doors of his house placed every way that he might be alert in descrying danger, his making the net by which he was caught…his being bound with the [sinews] of his own children—results of evil deeds—all carry out this idea. He is (says Simrock) the Bad itself as well as the consciousness of it. He is sin chained, as Fenrir is destruction chained. The gods are moral power; they are his chains, for it is said that when he shudders they tremble. And yet, how real he has become in this myth, so much a person that we can scarcely help wishing him to escape by means of his ingenious disguises, and are certainly glad that at last some one is left to pity him—the faithful wife, standing by, who wards off from him so much of his punishment.

We now come to Ragnarok; and "first," as **Har** said, "there will come a winter." But that is not exactly how we tell the story.

Narration and Discussion

Do you think Loki's punishment was too cruel?

A tough question: If Baldur could die, and Loki's sons could kill each other, why didn't the Aesir kill Loki outright?

Creative narration: What is in the *Asgard Daily News* today? Is there room for anything besides the capture of Loki?

(Lesson 36) Chapter Nine: Ragnarok, or, The Twilight of the Gods

Introduction

Odin, one evening, is drawn by dreams into Baldur's empty palace. He sees a vision of Ragnarok, the end-of-Aesir-time, in all its gory details; and we are left wondering whether it did happen as he foresaw. That is not simply because the Kearys wanted a child-friendly version of the story; even adult readers of the original *Eddas* are not sure about the ending.

> "Had Ragnarok happened yet? Was it still to happen? I did not know then. I am not certain now." (Neil Gaiman, *Norse Mythology*)

(Chronology aside, this is not a "gentle" story—be prepared.)

Vocabulary

luminous: light-filled, glowing

Year Four: Heroes of Asgard

cleft in twain: cut in two

summit: top

Naglfar: a boat made from the nail clippings of the dead

sated: filled up

rent the wolf in twain: tore him in half

golden tablets: In Neil Gaiman's *Norse Mythology*, these are golden chess pieces.

Names

Hrym: a giant who was prophesied to sail the ship **Naglfar** during **Ragnarok**

Beli: a giant

Places

Jarnvid: the Iron Wood

Reading

Part One

Since the day that Baldur died no one had walked in the bright halls of Broadblink—no one had even stepped through the expanded gates. Instead of undimmed brightness, a soft, **luminous** mist now hung over the palace of the dead Asa, and the Asyniur whispered to one another that it was haunted by wild dreams.

"I have seen them," Freyja used to say; "I have seen them float in at sunset through the palace windows and the open doors; every evening I can trace their slight forms through the rosy mist; and I know that those dreams are wild and strange from the shuddering that I feel when I look at them, or if ever they glance at me."

So the Asyniur never went into Broadblink, and though the Aesir did not think much about the dreams, they never went there either.

But one day it happened that Odin stood in the opening of the palace gates at sunset. The evening was clear and calm, and he stood watching the western sky until its crimson faded into soft blue grey; then the colours of the flowers began to mix one with another—only the tall white and yellow blossoms stood out alone—the distance became more dim. It was twilight, and there was silence over the earth whilst the night and the evening drew near to one another. Then a young dream came floating through the gates into Broadblink. Her sisters were already there; but she had only just been born, and, as she passed Odin, she touched him with a light hand, and drew him along with her into the palace.

She led him into the same hall in which Baldur had dreamed, and there Odin saw the night sky above him, and the broad branches of Yggdrasil swaying in the breeze. The Norns stood under the great ash; the golden threads had dropped from their fingers; and Urd and Verdandi stood one on each side of Skuld, who was still veiled. For a long time the three stood motionless, but at length Urd and Verdandi raised each a cold hand, and lifted the veil slowly from Skuld's face. Odin looked breathlessly within the veil, and the eyes of Skuld dilated as he looked, grew larger and larger, melted into one another, and, at last, expanded into boundless space. In the midst of [that] space lay the world, with its long shores, and vast oceans, ice mountains, and green plains; Aesirland in the midst, with Manheim all round it; then the wide sea, and, far off, the frost-bound shores of Jotunheim. Sometimes there was night and sometimes day; summer and winter gave place to one another; and Odin watched the seasons as they changed, rejoiced in the sunshine, and looked calmly over the night.

But at last, during one sunrise, a wolf came out of **Jarnvid**, and began to howl at the sun. The sun did not seem to heed him, but walked majestically up the sky to her mid-day point; then the wolf began to run after her, and chased her down the sky again to the low west. There the sun opened her bright eye wide, and turned round at bay; but the wolf came close up to her, and opened his mouth, and swallowed her up. The earth shuddered, and the moon rose. Another wolf was waiting for the moon with wide jaws open, and, while yet pale and young, he, too, was devoured. The earth shuddered again; it was covered with cold and darkness, while frost and snow came driving from the four corners of heaven. Winter and night, winter and night, there was now nothing but winter.

Part Two

A dauntless eagle sat upon the height of the Giantess' Rock, and began to strike his harp. Then a light red [rooster] crowed over the Bird Wood. A gold-combed [rooster] crowed over Asgard, and over Helheim a [rooster] of sooty red. From a long way underground, Garm began to howl, and at last Fenrir broke loose from his rock-prison, and ran forth over the whole earth. Then brother contended with brother, and war had no bounds. A hard age was that.

> "An axe age,
>
> A sword age,
>
> Shields oft **cleft in twain**;
>
> A storm age,
>
> A wolf age,
>
> Ere the earth met its doom."

Confusion rioted in the darkness. At length Heimdall ran up Bifrost, and blew his Giallar horn, whose sound went out into all worlds, and Yggdrasil, the mighty ash, was shaken from its root to its **summit**.

After this Odin saw himself ride forth from Asgard to consult Mimir at the Well of Wisdom. Whilst he was there Jormungand turned mightily in his place, and began to plough the ocean, which caused it to swell over every shore, so that the world was covered with water to the base of its high hills.

Then the ship **Naglfar** was seen coming over the sea with its prow from the east, and the giant **Hrym** was the steersman. All Jotunheim resounded, and the dwarfs stood moaning before their stony doors.

Then heaven was cleft in twain, and a flood of light streamed down upon the dark earth. The sons of Muspell, the sons of fire, rode through the breach, and at the head of them rode [*omission*] Surtr, their leader, before and behind whom fire raged, and whose sword outshone the sun. He led his flaming bands from heaven to earth over Bifrost, and the tremulous bridge broke in pieces beneath their tread.

Then the earth shuddered again; even giantesses stumbled; and men trod the way to Helheim in such crowds that Garm was **sated** with their blood, broke loose, and came up to earth to look upon the living.

Confusion rioted, and Odin saw himself, at the head of all the Aesir, ride over the tops of the mountains to Vigrid, the high, wide battlefield, where the giants were already assembled, headed by Fenrir, Garm, Jormungand, and Loki. Surtr was there, too, commanding the sons of fire, whom he had drawn up in several shining bands on a distant part of the plain.

Part Three

Then the great battle began in earnest. First, Odin went forth against Fenrir, who came on, opening his enormous mouth; the lower jaw reached to the earth, the upper one to heaven, and would have reached further had there been space to admit of it. Odin and Fenrir fought for a little while only, and then Fenrir swallowed the Aesirs' Father; but Vidar stepped forward, and, putting his foot on Fenrir's lower jaw, with his hand he seized the other, and **rent the wolf in twain**.

In the meantime Tyr and Garm had been fighting until they had killed each other. Heimdall slew Loki, and Loki slew Heimdall. Frey, **Beli**'s radiant slayer, met Surtr in battle, and was killed by him. Many terrible blows were exchanged ere Frey fell; but the Fire King's sword outshone the sun, and where was the sword of Frey?

Thor went forth against Jormungand; the strong Thunderer raised his arm—he feared no evil—he flung Miolnir at the monster serpent's head. Jormungand leaped up a great height in the air, and fell down to the earth again without life; but a stream of venom poured forth from his nostrils as he died. Thor fell back nine paces from the strength of his own blow; he bowed his head to the earth, and was choked in the poisonous flood; so the monster serpent was killed by the strong Thunderer's hand; but in death Jormungand slew his slayer.

Then all mankind forsook the earth, and the earth itself sank down slowly into the ocean. Water swelled over the mountains, rivers gurgled through thick trees, deep currents swept down the valleys—nothing was to be seen on the earth but a wide flood. The stars fell from the sky, and flew about hither and thither. At last, smoky clouds drifted upward from the infinite deep, encircling the earth and the water; fire burst forth from the midst of them, red flames wrapped the world, roared through the branches of Yggdrasil, and played against heaven itself. The flood swelled, the fire raged; there was now nothing but flood and fire.

"Then," said Odin, in his dream, "I see the end of all things. The end is like the beginning, and it will now be forever as if nothing had ever been."

Part Four

But, as he spoke, the fire ceased suddenly; the clouds rolled away; a new and brighter sun looked out of heaven; and he saw arise a second time the earth from ocean.

It rose slowly as it had sunk. First, the waters fell back from the tops of new hills that rose up fresh and verdant; raindrops like pearls dripped from the freshly budding trees, and fell into the sea with a sweet sound; waterfalls splashed glittering from the high rocks; eagles flew over the mountain streams; earth arose spring-like; unsown fields bore fruit; there was no evil, and all nature smiled.

Then from Memory's Forest came forth a new race of men, who spread over the whole earth, and who fed on the dew of the dawn. There was also a new city on Asgard's Hill—a city of gems; and Odin saw a new hall standing in it, fairer than the sun, and roofed with gold. Above all, the wide blue expanded, and into that fair city came Modi and Magni, Thor's two sons, holding Miolnir between them. Vali and Vidar came, and the deathless Hoenir; Baldur came up from the deep, leading his blind brother Hodur peacefully by the hand; there was no longer any strife between them. Two brothers' sons inhabited the spacious Wind-Home.

Part Five

Then Odin watched how the Aesir sat on the green plain, and talked of many things. "Garm is dead," said Hod to Baldur, "and so are Loki, and Jormungand, and Fenrir, and the world rejoices; but did our dead brothers rejoice who fell in slaying them?"

"They did, Hod," answered Baldur; "they gave their lives willingly for the life of the world"; and, as he listened, Odin felt that this was true; for, when he looked upon that beautiful and happy age, it gave him no pain to think that he must die before it came—that, though for many, it was not for him.

By and by Hoenir came up to Hod and Baldur with something glittering in his hand—something that he had found in the grass; and as he approached he said, "Behold the **golden tablets**, my brothers, which in the beginning of time were given to the Aesir's Father, and were lost in the Old World." Then they all looked eagerly at the tablets, and, as they bent over them, their faces became even brighter than before.

"There is no longer any evil thing," said Odin; "not an evil sight, nor an evil sound." But as he spoke dusky wings rose out of Niflheim, and the dark-spotted serpent,

Nidhogg, came flying from the abyss, bearing dead carcasses on his wings—cold death, undying.

Then the joy of Odin was drowned in the tears that brimmed his heart, and it was as if the eternal gnawer had entered into his soul. "Is there, then, no victory over sin?" he cried. "Is there no death to Death?" and with the cry he woke. His dream had faded from him.

Part Six

He stood in the palace gates alone with night, and the night was dying. Long since the rosy clasp of evening had dropped from her; she had turned through darkness eastward, and looked earnestly towards dawn. It was twilight again, for the night and the morning drew near to one another. A star stood in the east—the morning star—and a coming brightness smote the heavens. Out of the light a still voice came advancing, swelling, widening, until it filled all space. "Look forth," it said, "upon the groaning earth, with all its cold, and pain, and cruelty, and death. Heroes and giants fight and kill each other; now giants fall, and heroes triumph; now heroes fall, and giants rise; they can but combat, and the earth is full of pain. Look forth, and fear not; but when the worn-out faiths of nations shall totter like old men, turn eastward, and behold the light that lighteth every man; for there is nothing dark it doth not lighten; there is nothing hard it cannot melt; there is nothing lost it will not save."

Explaining Things

Of course the *Eddas* do not say anything about Odin seeing Ragnarok in a dream, or about his having any idea of a light that was to come; but, divested of this slender veil, the story as it here stands is almost an exact likeness of the northern myth. In one *Edda* it is given as the prophecy of a Vala, and the last line is "Now she will descend," meaning that she had finished her prophesying, and would come down from her high seat.

[*omission*]

The only allusions that can be relied on as genuine which the Eddas contain to a higher god than Odin is one very obscure [part] which says, speaking of Ragnarok,—

"Then comes the Mighty One,

To the great judgment,

The powerful from above

Who rules over all

He shall doom pronounce

And strifes allay,

Holy peace establish

Which shall ever be."

Narration and Discussion

Neil Gaiman writes, "It was the fact that the world and the story ends, and the way that it ends and is reborn, that made the gods and the frost giants and the rest of them tragic heroes, tragic villains. Ragnarok made the Norse world linger for me, seem strangely present and current…" Do you agree, or does this battle-heavy ending just seem too violent and sad?

Something to think about: *"Is there, then, no victory over sin?"* he cried. *"Is there no death to Death?"* How might you respond?

Creative narration: Could you make a final version of the *Asgard Daily News*?

Poetic Epilogue: Tegnér's Drapa, by Henry Wadsworth Longfellow

I heard a voice, that cried,
"Balder the Beautiful
Is dead, is dead!"
And through the misty air
Passed like the mournful cry
Of sunward sailing cranes.

I saw the pallid corpse
Of the dead sun
Borne through the Northern sky.
Blasts from Niffelheim
Lifted the sheeted mists
Around him as he passed.

And the voice forever cried,
"Balder the Beautiful
Is dead, is dead!"
And died away
Through the dreary night,
In accents of despair.

Balder the Beautiful,
God of the summer sun,
Fairest of all the Gods!
Light from his forehead beamed,
Runes were upon his tongue,
As on the warrior's sword.

All things in earth and air
Bound were by magic spell
Never to do him harm;
Even the plants and stones;
All save the mistletoe,
The sacred mistletoe!

Hoeder, the blind old God,
Whose feet are shod with silence,
Pierced through that gentle breast
With his sharp spear, by fraud
Made of the mistletoe,
The accursed mistletoe!

They laid him in his ship,
With horse and harness,
As on a funeral pyre.
Odin placed
A ring upon his finger,

And whispered in his ear.

They launched the burning ship!
It floated far away
Over the misty sea,
Till like the sun it seemed,
Sinking beneath the waves.
Balder returned no more!

So perish the old Gods!
But out of the sea of Time
Rises a new land of song,
Fairer than the old.
Over its meadows green
Walk the young bards and sing.

Build it again,
O ye bards,
Fairer than before!
Ye fathers of the new race,
Feed upon morning dew,
Sing the new Song of Love!

The law of force is dead!
The law of love prevails!
Thor, the thunderer,
Shall rule the earth no more,
No more, with threats,
Challenge the meek Christ.

Sing no more,
O ye bards of the North,
Of Vikings and of Jarls!
Of the days of Eld
Preserve the freedom only,
Not the deeds of blood!

Year Five: *The Age of Fable*, by Thomas Bulfinch

AO Book of Mythology

Preface/Introduction

Any edition of *Bulfinch's Mythology* (all three books) or *The Age of Fable* (just the first volume) will contain various prefaces and introductions. The preface to the 1910 Dent's edition states that:

> "The Age of Fable" has come to be ranked with older books like "Pilgrim's Progress," "Gulliver's Travels," "The Arabian Nights," "Robinson Crusoe," and five or six other productions of world-wide renown as a work with which every one must claim some acquaintance before his education can be called really complete. Many readers of the present edition will probably recall coming in contact with the work as children, and, it may be added, will no doubt discover from a fresh perusal the source of numerous bits of knowledge that have remained stored in their minds since those early years.

One of the most interesting introductions is that which begins the (1991) Harper Collins *Bulfinch's Mythology*, edited by Richard P. Martin. Martin tells the story of how, during the 1849 Gold Rush, Thomas Bulfinch (a Harvard College graduate who was then working as a Boston bank clerk) heard a great deal of street chatter, and read newspaper stories as well, which referred to ancient myths and adventures. For instance, men sailing off on ships to look for gold were referred to as "Argonauts." Bulfinch wondered if the people using those terms actually knew what they meant. So, much like someone posting on today's social media, he wrote an article about Jason and the Argonauts for "a showy pictorial newspaper." The article was so popular that the newspaper asked him for more, and Bulfinch got a book deal out of it (in 1855).

In his own "Author's Preface," he pondered the need for such a book.

> But how is mythology to be taught to one who does not learn it through the medium of the languages of Greece and Rome? To devote study to a species of learning which relates wholly to false marvels and obsolete faiths is not to be expected of the general reader in a practical age like this. The time even of the young is claimed by so many sciences of facts and things that little can be spared for set treatises on a science of mere fancy.

And this is his attempt at an answer:

> If no other knowledge deserves to be called useful but that which helps to enlarge our possessions or to raise our station in society, then Mythology has no claim to the appellation. But if that which tends to make us happier and better can be called useful, then we claim that epithet for our subject. For Mythology is the handmaid of literature; and literature is one of the best allies of virtue and promoters of happiness.

> Without a knowledge of mythology much of the elegant literature of our own language cannot be understood and appreciated. When Byron calls Rome "the Niobe of nations," or says of Venice, "She looks a Sea-Cybele fresh from ocean," he calls up to the mind of one

familiar with our subject, illustrations more vivid and striking than the pencil could furnish, but which are lost to the reader ignorant of mythology.

Bulfinch also defended his storytelling format (as Eustace Bright might have done in *Tanglewood Tales*) by criticizing dull reference books.

> Shall we be told that answers to such queries may be found in notes, or by a reference to the Classical Dictionary? We reply, the interruption of one's reading by either process is so annoying that most readers prefer to let an allusion pass unapprehended rather than submit to it. Moreover, such sources give us only the dry facts without any of the charm of the original narrative; and what is a poetical myth when stripped of its poetry? The story of Ceyx and Halcyone, which fills a chapter in our book, occupies but eight lines in the best (Smith's) Classical Dictionary; and so of others...Our work is an attempt to solve this problem, by telling the stories of mythology in such a manner as to make them a source of amusement. We have endeavored to tell them correctly, according to the ancient authorities, so that when the reader finds them referred to he may not be at a loss to recognize the reference. **Thus we hope to teach mythology not as a study, but as a relaxation from study; to give our work the charm of a story-book, yet by means of it to impart a knowledge of an important branch of education.**

By including bits of poetry by English and American writers, Bulfinch tried to show how the stories stretched from their first hearers, to Milton and Tennyson and Longfellow, to Forty-Niners looking for gold, and to readers (including children) making their first acquaintance.

> Our work is not for the learned, nor for the theologian, nor for the philosopher, but for the reader of English literature, of either sex, who wishes to comprehend the allusions so frequently made by public speakers, lecturers, essayists, and poets, and those which occur in polite conversation.

The Dent's edition adds one thoughtful point:

> His book has the singular merit of provoking further inquiry and leaving the reader tantalized and quite unsatisfied . His Ulysses and Aeneas send the new-come traveller in these realms of gold clamouring to Homer, and his notes on the Dryads and Water Deities open the road at the end of which waves the Golden Bough of the new classical mythologists. It was, in fact, a service or pioneer book that he wished to offer... to the new beginner and the young scholar.

In other words, this book is a starting place, but not an end. As Charlotte Mason wrote,

> No one knoweth the things of a man but the spirit of a man which is in him; therefore, there is no education but self-education, and as soon as a young child begins his education he does so as a student.

Our business is to give him mind-stuff, and both quality and quantity are essential. Naturally, each of us possesses this mind-stuff only in limited measure, but we know where to procure it; for the best thought the world possesses is stored in books; we must open books to children, the best books... (*Philosophy of Education*, p. 26)

And that is, really, all you need to know before beginning.

Term Examinations on *The Age of Fable*

The original examination questions provided for *The Age of Fable* were a bit different from typical "Tell what you know of this event" questions. In the original PNEU exams, they are found under the topic of "Composition," and the students were asked to write a story in either prose or verse, about one given character (depending on what was covered during the term): for instance, Arion, Cadmus, Ceyx, Phaeton, Daphne, or Orion. As this seems a simple and useful pattern to follow, we will not suggest more detailed questions.

However, for older students or those who want a little more, the following may be an interesting alternative: provide two stanzas from one of the poems that Bulfinch includes, or (even better) one that students have not yet seen. Ask them to a) continue the poem, in the style of the author, or b) write the opening stanzas of a similar poem but about another character.

Year Five: The Age of Fable

Chapter One

(Lesson 1) Introductory Chapter (First Part)

Introduction

The first three Lesson s, making up the first chapter of *The Age of Fable*, tell about the ancient Greek view of the world, and then they give a rather whirlwind tour of the major gods and goddesses. There are a lot of names, and not much explanation. It's like sitting beside someone as they flip through family photos, and if you haven't encountered these people before, the names probably won't mean much. It's certainly not going to be easy to narrate such a passage!

To make things more difficult, in the nineteenth century, it was common to use the Roman names of gods instead of Greek names (when there were close equivalents), likely because the study of Latin was more common than that of Greek. Apparently this convention was so widespread that even professors of Greek were known to use Roman names in their personal correspondence.

A second additional difficulty is that, when we do write the Greek names, there are often variations in spelling (Heracles or Herakles). A third is that, throughout the Greek/Roman world, there were minor and local deities who were often variations on the major ones; those are the kinds of things that still keep scholars busy.

However, there are a couple of ways to get around these problems. The first option is to start making your own chart of the Greek gods as you come across them, with a parallel list of their Roman names. (Bulfinch attempts to help here by giving the Greek names in parentheses.) You could do this in a notebook, or use file cards.

Another idea is to find a readymade chart, in a reference book or online; print it out or copy it if you can; and then use your printout as a sort of Bingo card, marking off names as you learn about them. An online search for "chart of Greek and Roman god names" should bring up several options. Some websites and books will also have "family trees" of the gods, which can be helpful. Not all charts will contain every minor deity that Bulfinch mentions, but a good one should cover at least the major names.

A third option is simply to listen for the names you already know, and don't worry too much about those you don't. Most of them will be repeated in the more detailed stories in the rest of the book. Enjoy the "family photos," but don't stress too much yet about who's who.

But we will begin first with a view of the world.

Vocabulary

> **the finest productions of poetry and art:** Bulfinch includes a number of myth-related excerpts from English, American, and German poetry. His examples of sculpture and painting are fewer, but still important; perhaps that will encourage students to explore classically-inspired art in more detail.

pass into oblivion: be forgotten

fancy: imagination

exempt from: free of, not subject to [that thing]

happy: blessed, fortunate

Names

Hyperboreans: Those who were believed to live beyond the North Wind, in a realm of perpetual sunshine.

Moore: Irish poet Thomas Moore (1779-1852)

Aethiopia: To the ancient Greeks, this could refer to the country of Libya; but it was also used to mean (as stated here) a more general, happy place somewhere far away to the south.

Places

Mediterranean: the large sea surrounding Greece (and other countries)

Euxine: the Black Sea

Elysian Plain: also called the Elysian Fields or Elysium, or the Isles of the Blessed; a place of happy afterlife

Reading

Prologue

The religions of ancient Greece and Rome are extinct. The so-called divinities of Olympus have not a single worshipper among living men. They belong now not to the department of theology, but to those of literature and taste. There they still hold their place, and will continue to hold it, for they are too closely connected with **the finest productions of poetry and art**, both ancient and modern, to **pass into oblivion**.

We propose to tell the stories relating to them which have come down to us from the ancients, and which are alluded to by modern poets, essayists, and orators. Our readers may thus at the same time be entertained by the most charming fictions which **fancy** has ever created, and put in possession of information indispensable to everyone who would read with intelligence the elegant literature of his own day.

In order to understand these stories, it will be necessary to acquaint ourselves with the ideas of the structure of the universe which prevailed among the Greeks—the people from whom the Romans, and other nations through them, received their science and religion.

Part One

The Greeks believed the earth to be flat and circular, their own country occupying the middle of it, the central point being either Mount Olympus, the abode of the gods, or Delphi, so famous for its oracle. The circular disk of the earth was crossed from west to east and divided into two equal parts by the *Sea*, as they called the **Mediterranean**, and its continuation the **Euxine**, the only seas with which they were acquainted.

Around the earth flowed the *River Ocean*, its course being from south to north on the western side of the earth, and in a contrary direction on the eastern side. It flowed in a steady, equable current, unvexed by storm or tempest. The sea, and all the rivers on earth, received their waters from it.

The northern portion of the earth was supposed to be inhabited by a happy race named the **Hyperboreans**, dwelling in everlasting bliss and spring beyond the lofty mountains whose caverns were supposed to send forth the piercing blasts of the north wind, which chilled the people of Hellas (Greece). Their country was inaccessible by land or sea. They lived **exempt from** disease or old age, from toils and warfare. **Moore** has given us the "Song of a Hyperborean," beginning

"I come from a land in the sun-bright deep,

Where golden gardens glow,

Where the winds of the north, becalmed in sleep,

Their conch shells never blow."

On the south side of the earth, close to the stream of Ocean, dwelt a people **happy** and virtuous as the Hyperboreans. They were named the **Aethiopians**. The gods favored them so highly that they were wont to leave at times their Olympian abodes and go to share their sacrifices and banquets.

On the western margin of the earth, by the stream of Ocean, lay a happy place named the **Elysian Plain**, whither mortals favored by the gods were transported without tasting of death, to enjoy an immortality of bliss. This happy region was also called the "Fortunate Fields," and the "Isles of the Blessed."

We thus see that the Greeks of the early ages knew little of any real people except those to the east and south of their own country, or near the coast of the Mediterranean. Their imagination meantime peopled the western portion of this sea with giants, monsters, and enchantresses; while they placed around the disk of the earth, which they probably regarded as of no great width, nations enjoying the peculiar favor of the gods, and blessed with happiness and longevity.

Narration and Discussion

Bulfinch writes "The religions of ancient Greece and Rome are extinct." Many people look at the ancient stories as mainly religious, and so do not want to read them. What are some reasons Bulfinch gives to read mythology? Do you agree? Can you think of any others?

Creative narration: Imagine a conversation between someone from the ancient world, and someone from a later time, about what they know or believe to be true about the world around them.(Perhaps they are talking about what they have learned in geography class.) Is there anything they could agree on?

(Lesson 2) Introductory Chapter (Second Part)

Introduction

After a brief look at the Sun, the Moon, and the Ocean, Bulfinch begins to explain about the supposed earliest gods and goddesses (the Titans), and then the later *pantheon* of gods who were believed to live on Mount Olympus. Remember, if you are making or marking off a chart of names, that Bulfinch gives the Roman equivalent first, and then a Greek name in parentheses.

Vocabulary

Wain or Bear: the constellation Ursa Major. If you have not read much yet about astronomy, you may want to find a book showing constellations (*Find the Constellations*, by H. A. Rey, is one classic), or an online star map. According to Greek mythology, there is a reason that the Bear doesn't set like the others (see **Lesson 10**).

Celestials: those of the sky; the gods

repaired: went

quaffed: drank

lyre: a harp with a U-shaped frame

azure: blue

steeds: horses

cosmogony, or account of the creation: story of how the world was made

Chaos: This will be explained more in **Lesson 4**.

vivified: brought to life

espoused: married

administered a draught: gave a drink

disgorge: spit out

vanquished: conquered

Atlas was condemned... Those who have read *Tanglewood Tales* will remember this.

Names

Milton: John Milton (1608-1674), English poet and author of *Paradise Lost*

Jupiter: Sometimes called Jove; the Roman equivalent of the Greek god Zeus. (See notes in **Lesson 1** about dealing with the rest of the names.)

Hebe (hee-bee): the goddess of youth, who served as the gods' cupbearer

Cowper: William Cowper (1731-1800), English poet and hymn writer, also known for his translation of **Homer's** works

Homer: the greatest of the ancient Greek poets and storytellers

Minerva: The Roman equivalent of the Greek goddess Athena

Vulcan: the Roman god of fire and metalworking (Greek: Hephaestus, Hephaestos)

Saturn (Cronos): Cronos was, supposedly, an unemployed Titan who moved to Italy and became known as Saturn.

Titans: the generation of Greek gods who ruled before those on Olympus

Places

Mount Olympus: a mountain located in Thessaly, believed to be the home of the twelve major Greek gods

Tartarus: the place where the wicked go after death; also, the prison for the **Titans**. "Tartarus" was personified as one of the earliest beings.

Reading

Part One

The Dawn, the Sun, and the Moon were supposed to rise out of the Ocean, on the eastern side, and to drive through the air, giving light to gods and men. The stars, also, except those forming the **Wain or Bear**, and others near them, rose out of and sank into the stream of Ocean. There the sun-god embarked in a winged boat, which conveyed him round by the northern part of the earth, back to his place of rising in the east. **Milton** alludes to this in his "Comus":

"Now the gilded car of day

His golden axle doth allay

In the steep Atlantic stream,

And the slope Sun his upward beam

Shoots against the dusky pole,

Pacing towards the other goal

Of his chamber in the east."

Part Two

The abode of the gods was on the summit of **Mount Olympus**, in Thessaly. A gate of clouds, kept by the goddesses named the Seasons, opened to permit the passage of the **Celestials** to earth, and to receive them on their return. The gods had their separate dwellings; but all, when summoned, **repaired** to the palace of **Jupiter,** as did also those deities whose usual abode was the earth, the waters, or the underworld. It was also in the great hall of the palace of the Olympian king that the gods feasted each day on ambrosia and nectar, their food and drink, the latter being handed round by the lovely goddess **Hebe**. Here they conversed of the affairs of heaven and earth; and as they **quaffed** their nectar, Apollo, the god of music, delighted them with the tones of his **lyre**, to which the Muses sang in responsive strains. When the sun was set, the gods retired to sleep in their respective dwellings.

The following lines from the "Odyssey" (in **Cowper's** translation) will show how **Homer** conceived of Olympus:

"So saying, **Minerva**, goddess **azure**-eyed,

Rose to Olympus, the reputed seat

Eternal of the gods, which never storms

Disturb, rains drench, or snow invades, but calm

The expanse and cloudless shines with purest day.

There the inhabitants divine rejoice

For ever."

The robes and other parts of the dress of the goddesses were woven by Minerva and the Graces; and everything of a more solid nature was formed of the various metals. **Vulcan** was architect, smith, armorer, chariot builder, and artist of all work in Olympus. He built of brass the houses of the gods; he made for them the golden shoes with which they trod the air or the water, and moved from place to place with the speed of the wind, or even of thought. He also shod with brass the celestial **steeds**, which whirled the chariots of the gods through the air, or along the surface of the sea.

He was able to bestow on his workmanship self-motion, so that the tripods (chairs and tables) could move of themselves in and out of the celestial hall. He even endowed with intelligence the golden handmaidens whom he made to wait on himself.

Jupiter, or Jove (Zeus), though called the father of gods and men, had himself a beginning. **Saturn (Cronos)** was his father, and Rhea (Ops) his mother. Saturn and Rhea were of the race of **Titans**, who were the children of Earth and Heaven, which sprang from Chaos, of which we shall give a further account in [**Lesson 4**].

There is another **cosmogony, or account of the creation**, according to which Earth, Erebus, and Love were the first of beings. Love (Eros) issued from the egg of Night, which floated on **Chaos**. By his arrows and torch he pierced and **vivified** all things, producing life and joy.

Part Three: The Family Photo Album

Saturn and Rhea were not the only Titans. There were others, whose names were Oceanus, Hyperion, Iapetus, and Ophion (males); and Themis, Mnemosyne, Eurynome (females). They are spoken of as the elder gods, whose dominion was afterwards transferred to others. Saturn yielded to Jupiter, Oceanus to Neptune, Hyperion to Apollo. Hyperion was the father of the Sun, Moon, and Dawn. He is therefore the original sun-god, and is painted with the splendor and beauty which were afterwards bestowed on Apollo [*omission*].

Ophion and Eurynome ruled over Olympus till they were dethroned by Saturn and Rhea. [*omission for length*] The representations given of Saturn are not very consistent; for on the one hand his reign is said to have been the golden age of innocence and purity, and on the other he is described as a monster who devoured his children.

[*omission for length*]

Jupiter, however, escaped this fate, and when grown up **espoused** Metis (Prudence), who **administered a draught** to Saturn which caused him to **disgorge** his children. Jupiter, with his brothers and sisters, now rebelled against their father Saturn and his brothers the Titans; **vanquished** them, and imprisoned some of them in **Tartarus**, inflicting other penalties on others. **Atlas was condemned to bear up the heavens on his shoulders.**

On the dethronement of Saturn, Jupiter with his brothers Neptune (Poseidon) and Pluto [called Dis or Dis Pater by the Romans, especially in earlier times; but Hades by the Greeks] divided his dominions. Jupiter's portion was the heavens, Neptune's the ocean, and Pluto's the realms of the dead. Earth and Olympus were common property.

Narration and Discussion

If you have read *The Heroes of Asgard* or similar books, do any of these stories remind you of Norse mythology? Does Olympus sound a bit like Asgard?

There are no human beings yet in the story. (They will be created in **Lesson 4**.) How do you think they might be viewed by this race of "gods?"

Creative narration #1: Imagine a conversation between Jupiter, Neptune, and Pluto dividing things up. (Why doesn't anybody want Earth?)

Creative narration #2: Write a to-do list or diary entry for Vulcan.

(Lesson 3) Introductory Chapter (Third Part)

Introduction

Here we go through a catalogue of the major Greek/Roman gods, some of the minor ones, and then a few that the Romans could not match up with any Greek gods they knew of. (The numbers in **Part One** are added for clarity.)

Vocabulary

zephyr: gentle breeze

attired: dressed

girdle: belt, sash

commerce: business

caduceus: a wand with two serpents twined around it, now used as a symbol of healing

beneficent: kind

presidence: rule, headship

insolent: rude, arrogant

divinities, deities: divine beings; gods and goddesses

Names

Spenser: Edmund Spenser (1552/53-1599), English poet known for his poem *The Faerie Queene*

Pan: in Greek mythology, the god who is associated with the wild country, with shepherds, and with music played on pipes. Those who have read *The Wind in the*

Year Five: The Age of Fable

Willows will remember Pan.

Faunus: Faunus was the first of a group of goat-footed creatures called Fauns, similar to the Greek satyrs already mentioned. Students who have read *The Lion, The Witch and The Wardrobe* will recognize Fauns. Bulfinch notes that we must not confuse Faunus with the goddess Fauna, as in "Flora and Fauna."

Places

Arcadia: part of the Peloponnese (the southern part of Greece)

Reading

Part One: More of the Family

1. Jupiter was king of gods and men. The thunder was his weapon, and he bore a shield called Aegis, made for him by Vulcan. The eagle was his favorite bird, and bore his thunderbolts.
2. Juno (Hera) was the wife of Jupiter, and queen of the gods. Iris, the goddess of the rainbow, was her attendant and messenger. The peacock was her favorite bird.
3. [Neptune is usually given third place, though Bulfinch does not mention him here.]
4. Vulcan (Hephaestos), the celestial artist, was the son of Jupiter and Juno. He was born lame, and his mother was so displeased at the sight of him that she flung him out of heaven. Other accounts say that Jupiter kicked him out for taking part with his mother in a quarrel which occurred between them. Vulcan's lameness, according to this account, was the consequence of his fall. [*omission for length*]
5. Mars (Ares), the god of war, was the son of Jupiter and Juno.
6. Phoebus Apollo, or simply Apollo, the god of archery, prophecy, and music, was the son of Jupiter and Latona, and brother of Diana (Artemis). (More about him in **Lesson 7**.) He was god of the sun, as …
7. Diana, his sister, was the goddess of the moon.
8. Venus (Aphrodite), the goddess of love and beauty, was the daughter of Jupiter and Dione. Others say that Venus sprang from the foam of the sea. The **zephyr** wafted her along the waves to the Isle of Cyprus, where she was received and **attired** by the Seasons, and then led to the assembly of the gods. All were charmed with her beauty, and each one demanded her for his wife. Jupiter gave her to Vulcan, in gratitude for the service he had rendered in forging thunderbolts. So the most beautiful of the goddesses became the wife of the most ill-favored of gods. Venus possessed an embroidered **girdle** called Cestus, which had the power of inspiring love. Her favorite birds were swans

and doves, and the plants sacred to her were the rose and the myrtle.

Cupid (Eros), the god of love, was the son of Venus [and so is not listed among the Twelve]. He was her constant companion; and, armed with bow and arrows, he shot the darts of desire into the bosoms of both gods and men. [*omission for length*]

9. Minerva (Pallas, Athene), the goddess of wisdom, was the offspring of Jupiter, without a mother; she sprang forth from his head completely armed. Her favorite bird was the owl, and the plant sacred to her, the olive. [*omission for length*]
10. Mercury (Hermes) was the son of Jupiter and Maia. He presided over **commerce**, wrestling and other gymnastic exercises, even over thieving, and everything, in short, which required skill and dexterity. He was the messenger of Jupiter, and wore a winged cap and winged shoes. He bore in his hand a rod entwined with two serpents, called the **caduceus**. Mercury is said to have invented the lyre. He found, one day, a tortoise, of which he took the shell, made holes in the opposite edges of it, and drew cords of linen through them, and the instrument was complete. The cords were nine, in honor of the nine Muses. Mercury gave the lyre to Apollo, and received from him in exchange the caduceus.
11. Ceres (Demeter) was the daughter of Saturn and Rhea. She had a daughter named Proserpine (Persephone), who became the wife of Pluto, and queen of the realms of the dead. Ceres presided over agriculture.
12. Bacchus (Dionysus), the god of wine, was the son of Jupiter and Semele. He represents not only the intoxicating power of wine, but its social and **beneficent** influences likewise, so that he is viewed as the promoter of civilization, and a lawgiver and lover of peace. [An alternative twelfth, mentioned in "Roman Divinities," is Vesta (Hestia), goddess of the hearth.]

Part Two: Other Gods and Interesting Beings

The Muses were the daughters of Jupiter and Mnemosyne (Memory). They presided over song, and prompted the memory. They were nine in number, to each of whom was assigned the **presidence** over some particular department of literature, art, or science. Calliope was the muse of epic poetry, Clio of history, Euterpe of lyric poetry, Melpomene of tragedy, Terpsichore of choral dance and song, Erato of love poetry, Polyhymnia of sacred poetry, Urania of astronomy, Thalia of comedy.

The Graces were goddesses presiding over the banquet, the dance, and all social enjoyments and elegant arts. They were three in number. Their names were Euphrosyne, Aglaia, and Thalia. **Spenser** describes the office of the Graces thus:

"These three on men all gracious gifts bestow

Which deck the body or adorn the mind,

> To make them lovely or well-favored show;
> As comely carriage, entertainment kind,
> Sweet semblance, friendly offices that bind,
> And all the complements of courtesy;
> They teach us how to each degree and kind
> We should ourselves demean, to low, to high,
> To friends, to foes; which skill men call Civility."

The Fates were also three—Clotho, Lachesis, and Atropos. Their office was to spin the thread of human destiny, and they were armed with shears, with which they cut it off when they pleased. They were the daughters of Themis (Law), who sits by Jove on his throne to give him counsel.

The Erinnyes, or Furies, were three goddesses who punished by their secret stings the crimes of those who escaped or defied public justice. The heads of the Furies were wreathed with serpents, and their whole appearance was terrific and appalling. Their names were Alecto, Tisiphone, and Megaera. They were also called Eumenides.

Nemesis was also an avenging goddess. She represents the righteous anger of the gods, particularly towards the proud and **insolent**.

Pan was the god of flocks and shepherds. His favorite residence was in **Arcadia**.

The Satyrs were deities of the woods and fields. They were conceived to be covered with bristly hair, their heads decorated with short, sprouting horns, and their feet like goats' feet.

Momus was the god of laughter, and Plutus [*not to be confused with Pluto*] was the god of wealth.

[*omission for length*]

Part Three: Roman Divinities

Saturn was an ancient Italian deity. It was attempted to identify him with the Grecian god Cronos, and [it was said] that after his dethronement by Jupiter he fled to Italy, where he reigned during what was called the Golden Age. In memory of his beneficent dominion, the feast of Saturnalia was held every year in the winter season. Then all public business was suspended, declarations of war and criminal executions were postponed, friends made presents to one another and the slaves were indulged with great liberties. A feast was given them at which they sat at table, while their masters served them, to show the natural equality of men, and that all things belonged equally to all, in the reign of Saturn.

Faunus, the grandson of Saturn, was worshipped as the god of fields and shepherds, and also as a prophetic god. His name in the plural, Fauns, expressed a class of gamesome deities, like the Satyrs of the Greeks.

Quirinus was a war god, said to be no other than Romulus, the founder of Rome, exalted after his death to a place among the gods.

[At this point Bulfinch moves to the equivalent of a bulleted list]

Bellona, a war goddess.
Terminus, the god of landmarks [*omission*].
Pales, the goddess presiding over cattle and pastures.
Pomona presided over fruit trees. [She is described in **Year Five Lesson 25**.]
Flora, the goddess of flowers.
Lucina, the goddess of childbirth.

Vesta (the Hestia of the Greeks) was a deity presiding over the public and private hearth [and is sometimes called the twelfth god of Olympus, instead of Bacchus]. A sacred fire, tended by six virgin priestesses called Vestals, flamed in her temple. As the safety of the city was held to be connected with its conservation, the neglect of the virgins, if they let it go out, was severely punished, and the fire was rekindled from the rays of the sun.

"Liber" is the [alternative] Latin name of Bacchus; and "Mulciber" of Vulcan.

Janus was the porter of heaven. He opens the year, the first month being named after him. He is the guardian deity of gates, on which account he is commonly represented with two heads, because every door looks two ways. His temples at Rome were numerous. In war time the gates of the principal one were always open. In peace they were closed; but they were shut only once between the reign of Numa and that of Augustus.

The Penates were the gods who were supposed to attend to the welfare and prosperity of the family. Their name is derived from Penus, the pantry, which was sacred to them. Every master of a family was the priest to the Penates of his own house. The Lares, or Lars, were also household gods, but differed from the Penates in being regarded as the deified spirits of mortals. The family Lars were held to be the souls of the ancestors, who watched over and protected their descendants. The words Lemur and Larva more nearly correspond to our word Ghost.

The Romans believed that every man had his Genius, and every woman her Juno: that is, a spirit who had given them being, and was regarded as their protector through life. On their birthdays men made offerings to their Genius, women to their Juno.

Narration and Discussion

If you were a Greek or Roman child growing up, do you think you would find such a great number of gods and goddesses confusing?

Have you seen anything like the "Three Fates" in other stories?

Do you notice any other names that are now used in everyday speech? (Examples: nemesis; fury)

Creative narration: Thomas Babington Macaulay names some of the gods in a poem called "Prophecy of Capus."

"Pomona loves the orchard,
  And Liber loves the vine,
And Pales loves the straw-built shed
  Warm with the breath of kine;
And Venus loves the whisper
  Of plighted youth and maid,
In April's ivory moonlight,
  Beneath the chestnut shade."

Could you write similar lines about the other gods described in this reading?

For further exploration: How many names of planets can you find in the lists of gods?

Chapter Two

(Lesson 4) Earth, Man, and a Gift

Introduction

Bulfinch writes, "The creation of the world is a problem naturally fitted to excite the liveliest interest of man, its inhabitant. The ancient pagans, not having the information on the subject which we derive from the pages of Scripture, had their own way of telling the story, which is as follows."

Vocabulary

wore one aspect: looked like each other

office: task, responsibility

had been so prodigal of his resources: had used everything so freely

Names

Prometheus, Epimetheus: Those who have read *The Water-Babies* may remember

Mother Carey's story of Prometheus and Epimetheus.

Reading

Part One

Before earth and sea and heaven were created, all things **wore one aspect**, to which we give the name of Chaos—a confused and shapeless mass, nothing but dead weight, in which, however, slumbered the seeds of things. Earth, sea, and air were all mixed up together; so the earth was not solid, the sea was not fluid, and the air was not transparent. God and Nature at last interposed, and put an end to this discord, separating earth from sea, and heaven from both. The fiery part, being the lightest, sprang up, and formed the skies; the air was next in weight and place. The earth, being heavier, sank below; and the water took the lowest place, and buoyed up the earth.

Here some god—it is not known which—gave his good offices in arranging and disposing the earth. He appointed rivers and bays their places, raised mountains, scooped out valleys, distributed woods, fountains, fertile fields, and stony plains. The air being cleared, the stars began to appear, fishes took possession of the sea, birds of the air, and four-footed beasts of the land.

But a nobler animal was wanted, and Man was made. It is not known whether the creator made him of divine materials, or whether in the earth, so lately separated from heaven, there lurked still some heavenly seeds. **Prometheus** took some of this earth, and kneading it up with water, made man in the image of the gods. He gave him an upright stature, so that while all other animals turn their faces downward, and look to the earth, he raises his to heaven, and gazes on the stars.

Part Two

Prometheus was one of the Titans, a gigantic race, who inhabited the earth before the creation of man. To him and his brother **Epimetheus** was committed the **office** of making man, and providing him and all other animals with the faculties necessary for their preservation. Epimetheus undertook to do this, and Prometheus was to overlook his work, when it was done.

Epimetheus accordingly proceeded to bestow upon the different animals the various gifts of courage, strength, swiftness, sagacity; wings to one, claws to another, a shelly covering to a third, etc. But when man came to be provided for, who was to be superior to all other animals, Epimetheus **had been so prodigal of his resources** that he had nothing left to bestow upon him. In his perplexity he resorted to his brother Prometheus, who, with the aid of Minerva, went up to heaven, and lighted his torch at the chariot of the sun, and brought down fire to man.

With this gift man was more than a match for all other animals. It enabled him to make weapons wherewith to subdue them; tools with which to cultivate the earth; to warm his dwelling, so as to be comparatively independent of climate; and finally to introduce the arts and to coin money, the means of trade and commerce.

Narration and Discussion

Are there any ideas about this account of creation that you especially like? How do they fit with what is taught elsewhere in the ancient world, or today?

Creative narration #1: Imagine that you are a parent or grandparent in the Greek/Roman world, answering a child's questions about where things came from. What would you tell them? If you were the child, what questions might you still have?

Creative narration #2: Dramatize the conversation between Epimetheus and Prometheus, about how the equipping of the animals has been going, and the problem that there is nothing much left for the humans.

(Lesson 5) Pandora, and the Golden Age

Introduction

Many people are familiar with the story of Pandora's Box, and you may have read about it yourself in *A Wonder Book*. What is less well known is her connection with Epimetheus; and also the idea that Pandora was the first woman, who had been given the gifts of beauty, music, etc.; but also, unfortunately, curiosity.

The second part of this reading explains the passing of the different "ages," starting with a Golden Age in which there was no war or crime, but then moving on through increasingly worse times. (We will read how the gods responded to this terrible state of things in **Lesson 6**.)

Vocabulary

presumption: arrogance, disrespect

noxious articles: nasty things

fitting: equipping

he had had no occasion: he hadn't needed

hapless: unlucky, unfortunate

magistrate: judge

perpetual: everlasting

succeeded: followed

brazen: Bronze

cultivated in common: farmed as one big piece of land, rather than each family working its own property

lay prostrate: collapsed, lay unconscious

Names

the unwiser son of Japhet: Epimetheus

him who had stole Jove's authentic fire: Prometheus

Astraea: Bulfinch gives us this note: "The goddess of innocence and purity. After leaving earth, she was placed among the stars, where she became the constellation Virgo—the Virgin. Themis (Justice) was the mother of Astraea. She is represented as holding aloft a pair of scales, in which she weighs the claims of opposing parties."

Reading

Part One

Woman was not yet made. The story (absurd enough!) is that Jupiter made her, and sent her to Prometheus and his brother, to punish them for their **presumption** in stealing fire from heaven; and man, for accepting the gift.

The first woman was named Pandora. She was made in heaven, every god contributing something to perfect her. Venus gave her beauty, Mercury persuasion, Apollo music, etc. Thus equipped, she was conveyed to earth, and presented to Epimetheus, who gladly accepted her, though cautioned by his brother to beware of Jupiter and his gifts.

Epimetheus had in his house a jar, in which were kept certain **noxious articles**, for which, in **fitting** man for his new abode, **he had had no occasion**. Pandora was seized with an eager curiosity to know what this jar contained; and one day she slipped off the cover and looked in. Forthwith there escaped a multitude of plagues for **hapless** man,—such as gout, rheumatism, and colic for his body, and envy, spite, and revenge for his mind,—and scattered themselves far and wide. Pandora hastened to replace the lid! but, alas! the whole contents of the jar had escaped, one thing only excepted, which lay at the bottom, and that was *hope*. So we see at this day, whatever evils are abroad, hope never entirely leaves us; and while we have *that*, no amount of other ills can make us completely wretched.

Another story is that Pandora was sent in good faith, by Jupiter, to bless man; that she was furnished with a box, containing her marriage presents, into which every god had put some blessing. She opened the box incautiously, and the blessings all escaped, *hope* only excepted. This story seems more probable than the former; for how could *hope*, so precious a jewel as it is, have been kept in a jar full of all manner of evils, as in the former statement?

[The following verse has been moved from the end of the chapter so that it can be discussed here.]

The comparison of Eve to Pandora is too obvious to have escaped Milton, who introduces it in Book IV of "Paradise Lost":

"More lovely than Pandora, whom the gods

Endowed with all their gifts; and O, too like

In sad event, when to **the unwiser son**

Of Japhet brought by Hermes, she insnared

Mankind with her fair looks, to be avenged

On **him who had stole Jove's authentic fire**."

Part Two

The world being thus furnished with inhabitants, the first age was an age of innocence and happiness, called the *Golden Age*. [Bulfinch does not explain how this could be so with all Pandora's plagues set free, but we must take him at his word.] Truth and right prevailed, though not enforced by law, nor was there any **magistrate** to threaten or punish. The forest had not yet been robbed of its trees to furnish timbers for vessels, nor had men built fortifications round their towns. There were no such things as swords, spears, or helmets. The earth brought forth all things necessary for man, without his labor in ploughing or sowing. **Perpetual** spring reigned, flowers sprang up without seed, the rivers flowed with milk and wine, and yellow honey distilled from the oaks.

Then **succeeded** the *Silver Age*, inferior to the golden, but better than that of brass. Jupiter shortened the spring, and divided the year into seasons. Then, first, men had to endure the extremes of heat and cold, and houses became necessary. Caves were the first dwellings, and leafy coverts of the woods, and huts woven of twigs. Crops would no longer grow without planting. The farmer was obliged to sow the seed, and the toiling ox [was forced] to draw the plough.

Next came the **Brazen** *Age*, more savage of temper, and readier to the strife of arms, yet not altogether wicked.

The hardest and worst was the *Iron Age*. Crime burst in like a flood; modesty, truth, and honor fled. In their places came fraud and cunning, violence, and the wicked love of gain. Then seamen spread sails to the wind, and the trees were torn from the mountains to serve for keels to ships, and vex the face of Ocean. The earth, which till now had been **cultivated in common**, began to be divided off into possessions. Men were not satisfied with what the surface produced, but must dig into its [deepest places], and draw forth from thence the ores of metals. Mischievous iron, and more mischievous gold, were produced. War sprang up, using both as weapons; the guest was not safe in his friend's house; and sons-in-law and fathers-in-law, brothers and sisters, husbands and wives, could not trust one another. Sons wished their fathers dead, that they might come to the inheritance; family love **lay prostrate**. The earth was wet with slaughter, and the gods abandoned it, one by one, till **Astraea** alone was left, and finally she also took her departure.

Part Three

It was a favorite idea of the old poets that these goddesses would one day return, and bring back the Golden Age. In the "Messiah" of [Alexander] **Pope** [which he translated from the works of the Roman poet Virgil], this idea occurs:

"All crimes shall cease, and ancient fraud shall fail,

Returning Justice lift aloft her scale,

Peace o'er the world her olive wand extend,

And white-robed Innocence [*Astraea*] from heaven descend."

The English poet John Milton used this image in "On the Morning of Christ's Nativity":

Yes, Truth and Justice then

  Will down return to men,

 The enamelled arras of the rainbow wearing;

  And Mercy set between,

  Throned in celestial sheen,

 With radiant feet the tissued clouds down steering;

  And Heaven, as at some festival,

 Will open wide the gates of her high palace-hall.

[A more familiar reference might be the final verse of "It Came Upon a Midnight Clear":

For lo! the days are hastening on
  By prophet bards foretold,
When, with the ever circling years
  Shall come the age of gold...]

Narration and Discussion

If you have read the story of Pandora's Box before, how does Bulfinch's version differ?

In the story of the different ages, what seemed to go wrong between the different times? Do you think Pandora's "Hope" had disappeared? (A hint for what might lie ahead: Genesis 6:5-7.)

Something to think about: In this story, we read of people becoming greedy and violent because of their desire for gold and other precious metals. Have we changed at all since that time?

Creative narration: Write a journal entry for a) Pandora or b) Astraea.

(Lesson 6) Prometheus and Deucalion

Introduction

The next story may seem surprisingly familiar to many readers.

Vocabulary

conflagration: huge fire

fell a prey to hunger: died of hunger

prostrate: flat out

retrieve their miserable affairs: make things better

revolved the oracle: thought about the message

sagacity: wisdom

hard: hardy, strong

incensed against them: angry with them

preyed on: ate

magnanimous: large-spirited, generous

treated this theme: written about this

Names

Deucalion: Deucalion is viewed as the "Greek Noah." This story is also told in Chapter IV of *The Story of the Greeks*, by H. A. Guerber.

Byron: George Gordon Byron, 6th Baron Byron, referred to as Lord Byron or simply Byron (1788-1824), English Romantic poet

Shelley: Percy Bysshe Shelley (1792-1822), English Romantic poet

Places

Parnassus: a mountain range in central Greece, thought to be the home of the Muses. In Ovid's version of this story (the one Bulfinch is using), Deucalion builds a large chest, and he and his wife use it to survive the flood; they then land on Mount Parnassus.

Reading

Part One: The Flood

Jupiter, seeing this state of things, burned with anger. He summoned the gods to council. They obeyed the call, and took the road to the palace of heaven. The road, which any one may see in a clear night, stretches across the face of the sky, and is called the Milky Way. Along the road stand the palaces of the illustrious gods; the common people of the skies live apart, on either side.

Jupiter addressed the assembly. He set forth the frightful condition of things on the earth, and closed by announcing his intention to destroy the whole of its inhabitants, and provide a new race, unlike the first, who would be more worthy of life, and much better worshippers of the gods. So saying he took a thunderbolt, and was about to launch it at the world, and destroy it by burning; but recollecting the danger that such a **conflagration** might set heaven itself on fire, he changed his plan, and resolved to drown it.

The north wind, which scatters the clouds, was chained up; the south was sent out, and soon covered all the face of heaven with a cloak of pitchy darkness.

[*Bulfinch switches to the present tense, apparently intending the next paragraph to be read with full dramatic effect.*]

The clouds, driven together, resound with a crash; torrents of rain fall; the crops are laid low; the year's labor of the husbandman perishes in an hour. Jupiter, not satisfied with his own waters, calls on his brother Neptune to aid him with his. He lets loose the rivers, and pours them over the land. At the same time, he heaves the land with an earthquake, and brings in the reflux of the ocean over the shores. Flocks, herds, men, and houses are swept away, and temples, with their sacred enclosures, profaned.

If any edifice remained standing, it was overwhelmed, and its turrets lay hid beneath the waves. Now all was sea, sea without shore. Here and there an individual remained on a projecting hilltop, and a few, in boats, pulled the oar where they had lately driven the plough.

[*More present tense.*]
The fishes swim among the tree-tops; the anchor is let down into a garden. Where

the graceful lambs played but now, unwieldy sea calves gambol. The wolf swims among the sheep, the yellow lions and tigers struggle in the water. The strength of the wild boar serves him not, nor his swiftness the stag. The birds fall with weary wing into the water, having found no land for a resting-place.

Part Two

Those living beings whom the water spared **fell a prey to hunger**. **Parnassus** alone, of all the mountains, overtopped the waves; and there **Deucalion**, and his wife Pyrrha, of the race of Prometheus, found refuge—he a just man, and she a faithful worshipper of the gods.

Jupiter, when he saw none left alive but this pair, and remembered their harmless lives and pious demeanor, ordered the north winds to drive away the clouds, and disclose the skies to earth, and earth to the skies. Neptune also directed Triton to blow on his shell, and sound a retreat to the waters. The waters obeyed, and the sea returned to its shores, and the rivers to their channels.

Then Deucalion thus addressed Pyrrha: "O wife, only surviving woman, joined to me first by the ties of kindred and marriage, and now by a common danger, would that we possessed the power of our ancestor Prometheus, and could renew the race as he at first made it! But as we cannot, let us seek yonder temple, and inquire of the gods what remains for us to do."

They entered the temple, deformed as it was with slime, and approached the altar, where no fire burned. There they fell **prostrate** on the earth, and prayed the goddess to inform them how they might **retrieve their miserable affairs**. The oracle answered, "Depart from the temple with head veiled and garments unbound, and cast behind you the bones of your mother."

They heard the words with astonishment. Pyrrha first broke silence: "We cannot obey; we dare not profane the remains of our parents." They sought the thickest shades of the wood, and **revolved the oracle** in their minds. At length Deucalion spoke: "Either my **sagacity** deceives me, or the command is one we may obey without impiety. The earth is the great parent of all; the stones are her bones; these we may cast behind us; and I think this is what the oracle means. At least, it will do no harm to try."

They veiled their faces, unbound their garments, and picked up stones, and cast them behind them. The stones (wonderful to relate) began to grow soft, and assume shape. By degrees, they put on a rude resemblance to the human form, like a block half-finished in the hands of the sculptor. The moisture and slime that were about them became flesh; the stony part became bones; the veins remained veins, retaining their name, only changing their use.

Those thrown by the hand of the man became men, and those by the woman became women. It was a **hard** race, and well adapted to labor, as we find ourselves to be at this day, giving plain indications of our origin.

Part Three: The Fate of Prometheus

Prometheus has been a favorite subject with the poets. He is represented as the friend of mankind, who interposed in their behalf when Jove was **incensed against them**, and who taught them civilization and the arts. But as, in so doing, he transgressed the will of Jupiter, he drew down on himself the anger of the ruler of gods and men. Jupiter had him chained to a rock on Mount Caucasus, where a vulture **preyed on** his liver, which was renewed as fast as [it was] devoured. This state of torment might have been brought to an end at any time by Prometheus, if he had been willing to submit to his oppressor; for he possessed a secret which involved the stability of Jove's throne, and if he would have revealed it, he might have been at once taken into favor. But that he disdained to do. He has therefore become the symbol of **magnanimous** endurance of unmerited suffering, and strength of will resisting oppression.

Byron and **Shelley** have both **treated this theme**. The following are Byron's lines:

"Titan! to whose immortal eyes

The sufferings of mortality,

Seen in their sad reality,

Were not as things that gods despise;

What was thy pity's recompense?

A silent suffering, and intense;

The rock, the vulture, and the chain;

All that the proud can feel of pain;

The agony they do not show;

The suffocating sense of woe.

"Thy godlike crime was to be kind;

To render with thy precepts less

The sum of human wretchedness,

And strengthen man with his own mind.

And, baffled as thou wert from high,

Still, in thy patient energy

In the endurance and repulse

Of thine impenetrable spirit,

Which earth and heaven could not convulse,

A mighty Lesson we inherit."

Byron also employs the same allusion in his "Ode to Napoleon Bonaparte":

"Or, like the thief of fire from heaven,

Wilt thou withstand the shock?

And share with him—the unforgiven—

His vulture and his rock?"

Narration and Discussion

How is the flood story similar to others you have heard? Are there important differences?

The story of Prometheus chained to the rock is a famous one. Do you agree with Byron that "A mighty Lesson we inherit?" How so?

Something to think about: Jupiter intended to form "a new race, unlike the first, who would be more worthy of life, and much better worshippers of the gods." Do you think that happened?

Creative narration: Retell the Greek flood story in any way you like.

Chapter Three
(Lesson 7) Apollo and Daphne

Introduction

The next several readings have one theme in common: romantic love, in all its flavors. Some characters (divine, human, or something in between) want what they cannot have; others have it, but then lose it by malice or accident. Someone has said that Norse myths are mostly fighting and lies, while Greek myths are about love and lies: see if you agree (about the love, the lies, or both).

Many of these myths are also "why" stories, explaining the origins of plants, animals, or constellations.

Vocabulary

produced an excessive fertility: made things grow wildly

Pythian Games: games (sports, music competitions, etc.) held at Delphi every four years, in honour of Apollo

malice: hatred, ill-will

elated: in a great mood

the former: the first one

the latter: the one named last

nymph: a female nature deity

forthwith: immediately

abhorred: hated, detested

spoils of the chase: the meat brought home from hunting

clown: a rough country person

balm: ointment

amatory verses: love poems

filled his arms with bays: caught only an armful of laurel leaves

Names

Python: a mighty serpent, sometimes appearing more like a dragon

Apollo: Apollo is the only god in the Greek/Roman pantheon (list of gods) to share the same name in both. It is thought that the Romans recognized this Greek god as so mighty and unique that they didn't want to risk angering him by changing his name.

Daphne: In Greek, "daphne" is the word for "laurel."

Cupid: in Greek, Eros

Waller: Edmund Waller (1606-1687), English politician and poet

Phoebus (FEE-buhs): another name for **Apollo**, the Greek god of light, music, and poetry, among other things. Phoebus means "bright."

Reading

Part One: Apollo

The slime with which the earth was covered by the waters of the flood **produced an excessive fertility**, which called forth every variety of production, both bad and good. Among the rest, **Python**, an enormous serpent, crept forth, the terror of the people, and lurked in the caves of Mount Parnassus. **Apollo** slew him with his arrows—weapons which he had not before used against any but feeble animals, hares, wild goats, and such game. In commemoration of this illustrious conquest, he instituted the **Pythian Games**, in which the victor in feats of strength, swiftness of foot, or in the chariot race was crowned with a wreath of beech leaves; for the laurel was not yet adopted by Apollo as his own tree.

The famous statue of Apollo called the Belvedere [*more in* **Year Five Lesson 36**] represents the god after this victory over the serpent Python. To this Byron alludes in his [poem] "Childe Harold," iv., 161:

"... The lord of the unerring bow,

The god of life, and poetry, and light,

The Sun, in human limbs arrayed, and brow

All radiant from his triumph in the fight

The shaft has just been shot; the arrow bright

With an immortal's vengeance; in his eye

And nostril, beautiful disdain, and might

And majesty flash their full lightnings by,

Developing in that one glance the Deity."

Part Two: Daphne

Daphne was Apollo's first love. It was not brought about by accident, but by the **malice** of **Cupid**. Apollo saw [Cupid] playing with his bow and arrows; and being himself **elated** with his recent victory over Python, he said to him, "What have you to do with warlike weapons, saucy boy? Leave them for hands worthy of them. Behold the conquest I have won by means of them over the vast serpent who stretched his poisonous body over acres of the plain! Be content with your torch, child, and kindle up your flames, as you call them, where you will, but presume not to meddle with my weapons."

Venus's boy heard these words, and rejoined, "Your arrows may strike all things else, Apollo, but mine shall strike *you*." So saying, he took his stand on a rock of Parnassus, and drew from his quiver two arrows of different workmanship, one to excite love, the other to repel it. **The former** was of gold and sharp pointed, **the latter** blunt and tipped with lead. With the leaden shaft he struck the **nymph** Daphne, the daughter of the river god Peneus, and with the golden one Apollo, through the heart.

Forthwith the god was seized with love for the maiden, and she **abhorred** the thought of loving. Her delight was in woodland sports and in the **spoils of the chase**. Many lovers sought her, but she spurned them all, ranging the woods, and taking no thought of [marriage]. Her father often said to her, "Daughter, you owe me a son-in-law; you owe me grandchildren." She, hating the thought of marriage as a crime, with her beautiful face tinged all over with blushes, threw arms around her father's neck, and said, "Dearest father, grant me this favor, that I may always remain unmarried, like Diana." He consented, but at the same time said, "Your own face will forbid it."

Apollo loved her, and longed to obtain her; and he who gives oracles to all the world was not wise enough to look into his own fortunes. He saw her hair flung loose over her shoulders, and said, "If so charming in disorder, what would it be if arranged?" He saw her eyes bright as stars; he saw her lips, and was not satisfied with only seeing them. He admired her hands and arms, naked to the shoulder, and whatever was hidden from view he imagined more beautiful still. He followed her; she fled, swifter than the wind, and delayed not a moment at his entreaties.

"Stay," said he, "daughter of Peneus; I am not a foe. Do not fly me as a lamb flies the wolf, or a dove the hawk. It is for love I pursue you. You make me miserable, for fear you should fall and hurt yourself on these stones, and I should be the cause. Pray run slower, and I will follow slower. I am no **clown**, no rude peasant. Jupiter is my father, and I am lord of Delphos and Tenedos, and know all things, present and future. I am the god of song and the lyre. My arrows fly true to the mark; but, alas! an arrow more fatal than mine has pierced my heart! I am the god of medicine, and know the virtues of all healing plants. Alas! I suffer a malady that no **balm** can cure!"

The nymph continued her flight, and left his plea half uttered. And even as she fled she charmed him. The wind blew her garments, and her unbound hair streamed loose behind her. The god grew impatient to find his wooings thrown away, and, sped by Cupid, gained upon her in the race. It was like a hound pursuing a hare, with open jaws ready to seize, while the feebler animal darts forward, slipping from the very grasp. So flew the god and the virgin—he on the wings of love, and she on those of fear.

The pursuer is the more rapid, however, and gains upon her, and his panting breath blows upon her hair. Her strength begins to fail, and, ready to sink, she calls upon her father, the river god: "Help me, Peneus! open the earth to enclose me, or change my form, which has brought me into this danger!"

Scarcely had she spoken, when a stiffness seized all her limbs; her bosom began to be enclosed in a tender bark; her hair became leaves; her arms became branches; her foot stuck fast in the ground, as a root; her face, became a tree-top, retaining nothing of its former self but its beauty. Apollo stood amazed. He touched the stem, and felt the flesh tremble under the new bark. He embraced the branches, and lavished kisses on the wood. The branches shrank from his lips.

"Since you cannot be my wife," said he, "you shall assuredly be my tree. I will wear you for my crown; I will decorate with you my harp and my quiver; and when the great Roman conquerors lead up the triumphal pomp to the Capitol, you shall be woven into wreaths for their brows. And, as eternal youth is mine, you also shall be always green, and your leaf know no decay."

The nymph, now changed into a Laurel tree, bowed its head in grateful acknowledgment.

Part Three

The story of Apollo and Daphne is often alluded to by the poets. **Waller** applies it to the case of one whose **amatory verses**, though they did not soften the heart of his mistress, yet won for the poet wide-spread fame:

> "Yet what he sung in his immortal strain,
>
> Though unsuccessful, was not sung in vain.
>
> All but the nymph that should redress his wrong,
>
> Attend his passion and approve his song.
>
> Like **Phoebus** thus, acquiring unsought praise,
>
> He caught at love and **filled his arms with bays**."

[*omission for length*]

Narration and Discussion

Why was Cupid so angry with Apollo? What does a story like this tell us about the relationships between the gods?

Could Peneus have perhaps thought of some other solution to save Daphne?

Something to think about: Is love something that strikes like an arrow, or something we choose by free will?

Something more to think about: Bulfinch writes "That Apollo should be the god both of music and poetry will not appear strange, but that medicine should also be assigned to his province, may." What might music have to do with medicine? (1 Samuel 16:23; Psalm 57:7; Psalm 135:3; James 5:13)

(Lesson 8) Pyramus and Thisbe

Introduction

This story is supposed to have happened in ancient Babylonia; but it has inspired storytellers in many cultures ever since.

Vocabulary

neighborhood: living so close together

remarked: noticed

descried: saw

slake: quench

rent: ripped, tore

hapless: unlucky

scabbard: long pouch to hold a sword; sheath

ratified: confirmed, carried out

sepulcher: tomb

Davy's Safety Lamp: a wick lamp used in flammable atmospheres (such as in coal mines), invented in 1815 by Sir Humphrey Davy. A version of the lamp has been used more recently in Olympic torch relays.

burlesqued: spoofed, done in a humorous way

Names

Semiramis: or Shammuramat, a legendary queen of Assyria

Aurora (Greek: Eos): the Roman goddess of dawn. (More about her in **Year Six Lesson 12**.)

Reading

Part One

Pyramus was the handsomest youth, and Thisbe the fairest maiden, in all Babylonia, where **Semiramis** reigned. Their parents occupied adjoining houses; and **neighborhood** brought the young people together, and acquaintance ripened into love. They would gladly have married, but their parents forbade. One thing, however, they could not forbid—that love should glow with equal ardor in the [hearts] of both. They conversed by signs and glances, and the fire burned more intensely for being covered up.

In the wall that parted the two houses there was a crack, caused by some fault in the structure. No one had **remarked** it before, but the lovers discovered it. What will not love discover! It afforded a passage to the voice; and tender messages used to pass backward and forward through the gap. As they stood, Pyramus on this side, Thisbe on that, their breaths would mingle. "Cruel wall," they said, "why do you keep two lovers apart? But we will not be ungrateful. We owe you, we confess, the privilege of transmitting loving words to willing ears." Such words they uttered on different sides of the wall; and when night came and they must say farewell, they pressed their lips upon the wall, she on her side, he on his, as they could come no nearer.

Next morning, when **Aurora** had put out the stars, and the sun had melted the frost from the grass, they met at the accustomed spot. Then, after lamenting their hard fate, they agreed, that next night, when all was still, they would slip away from watchful eyes, leave their dwellings and walk out into the fields; and to insure a meeting, [go] to a well-known edifice standing without the city's bounds, called the Tomb of Ninus, and that the one who came first should await the other at the foot of a certain tree. It was a white mulberry tree, and stood near a cool spring. All was agreed on, and they waited impatiently for the sun to go down beneath the waters and night to rise up from them. Then cautiously Thisbe stole forth, unobserved by the family, her head covered with a veil, made her way to the monument and sat down under the tree.

As she sat alone in the dim light of the evening she **descried** a lioness, her jaws reeking with recent slaughter, approaching the fountain to **slake** her thirst. Thisbe fled at the sight, and sought refuge in the hollow of a rock. As she fled she dropped her veil. The lioness, after drinking at the spring, turned to retreat to the woods, and seeing the veil on the ground, tossed and **rent** it with her bloody mouth.

Part Two

Pyramus, having been delayed, now approached the place of meeting. He saw in the sand the footsteps of the lion, and the color fled from his cheeks at the sight. Presently he found the veil all rent and bloody. "O **hapless** girl," said he, "I have been the cause of thy death! Thou, more worthy of life than I, hast fallen the first victim. I will follow. I am the guilty cause, in tempting thee forth to a place of such peril, and not being myself on the spot to guard thee. Come forth, ye lions, from the rocks, and tear this guilty body with your teeth." He took up the veil, carried it with him to the appointed tree, and covered it with kisses and with tears. "*My* blood also shall stain your texture," said he, and drawing his sword plunged it into his heart. The blood spurted from the wound, and tinged the white mulberries of the tree all red; and, sinking into the earth, reached the roots, so that the red color mounted through the trunk to the fruit.

Part Three

By this time Thisbe, still trembling with fear, yet wishing not to disappoint her lover, stepped cautiously forth, looking anxiously for the youth, eager to tell him the danger she had escaped. When she came to the spot and saw the changed color of the mulberries, she doubted whether it was the same place. While she hesitated, she saw the form of one struggling in the agonies of death. She started back; a shudder ran through her frame as a ripple on the face of the still water when a sudden breeze sweeps over it. But as soon as she recognized her lover, she screamed and beat her breast, embracing the lifeless body, pouring tears into its wounds, and imprinting kisses on the cold lips. "O Pyramus," she cried, "what has done this? Answer me, Pyramus; it is your own Thisbe that speaks. Hear me, dearest, and lift that drooping head!"

At the name of Thisbe Pyramus opened his eyes, then closed them again. She saw her veil stained with blood and the **scabbard** empty of its sword. "Thy own hand has slain thee, and for my sake," she said. "I too can be brave for once, and my love is as strong as thine. I will follow thee in death, for I have been the cause; and death which alone could part us shall not prevent my joining thee. And ye, unhappy parents of us both, deny us not our united request. As love and death have joined us, let one tomb contain us. And thou, tree, retain the marks of slaughter. Let thy berries still serve for memorials of our blood." So saying she plunged the sword into her [heart].

Her parents **ratified** her wish, the gods also ratified it. The two bodies were buried in one **sepulchre**, and the tree ever after brought forth purple berries, as it does to this day.

Part Four

Moore, in the "Sylph's Ball," speaking of **Davy's Safety Lamp**, is reminded of the wall that separated Thisbe and her lover:

"O for that Lamp's metallic gauze,

    That curtain of protecting wire,

Which Davy delicately draws

    Around illicit, dangerous fire!

The wall he sets 'twixt Flame and Air,

    (Like that which barred young Thisbe's bliss,)

Through whose small holes this dangerous pair

    May see each other, but not kiss."

[*omission for length*]

If any of our young readers can be so hard-hearted as to enjoy a laugh at the expense of poor Pyramus and Thisbe, they may find an opportunity by turning to Shakespeare's play of the "Midsummer Night's Dream," where it is most amusingly **burlesqued**.

Narration and Discussion

Do you find "Pyramus and Thisbe" sad, or are you more "hard-hearted" as Bulfinch says?

It is interesting that Bulfinch refers here to "A Midsummer Night's Dream." How might the story of "Apollo and Daphne" also relate to that play? Can you think of another Shakespeare play that is like "Pyramus and Thisbe?"

Creative narration: Moore's poem takes a myth (two sweethearts separated by a wall) and applies the idea to something else quite different (a safety lamp). Choose a myth you have heard OR something you have seen in nature, and write or draw about something that it reminds you of.

(Lesson 9) Cephalus and Procris

Introduction

This is a story that starts with Cephalus, whose only crime was being too good-looking; but it also carries a Lesson about jealousy and trust.

Vocabulary

javelin: spear

entreaties: pleadings

ravenous: extremely hungry

credulous: gullible, easy to convince

stanch: stop

Names

Cephalus (SEF-uh-luhs)

Procris (PRO-cris)

Reading

Part One

Cephalus was a beautiful youth and fond of manly sports. He would rise before the dawn to pursue the chase. Aurora saw him when she first looked forth, fell in love with him, and stole him away.

But Cephalus was just married to a charming wife whom he devotedly loved. Her name was Procris. She was a favorite of Diana, the goddess of hunting, who had given her a dog which could outrun every rival, and a **javelin** which would never fail of its mark; and Procris gave these presents to her husband. Cephalus was so happy in his wife that he resisted all the **entreaties** of Aurora, and she finally dismissed him in displeasure, saying, "Go, ungrateful mortal, keep your wife, whom, if I am not much mistaken, you will one day be very sorry you ever saw again."

Cephalus returned, and was as happy as ever in his wife and his woodland sports. Now it happened some angry deity had sent a **ravenous** fox to annoy the country; and the hunters turned out in great strength to capture it. Their efforts were all in vain; no dog could run it down; and at last they came to Cephalus to borrow his famous dog, whose name was Lelaps. No sooner was the dog let loose than he darted off, quicker than their eye could follow him. If they had not seen his footprints in the sand they would have thought he flew. Cephalus and others stood on a hill and saw the race. The fox tried every art; he ran in a circle and turned on his track, the dog close upon him, with open jaws, snapping at his heels, but biting only the air. Cephalus was about to use his javelin, when suddenly he saw both dog and [fox] stop instantly. The heavenly powers who had given both were not willing that either should conquer. In the very attitude of life and action they were turned into stone. So lifelike and natural did they look, you would have thought, as you looked at them, that one was going to bark, the other to leap forward.

Part Two

Cephalus, though he had lost his dog, still continued to take delight in the chase. He would go out at early morning, ranging the woods and hills unaccompanied by anyone, needing no help, for his javelin was a sure weapon in all cases. Fatigued with hunting, when the sun got high he would seek a shady nook where a cool stream flowed, and, stretched on the grass, with his garments thrown aside, would enjoy the breeze.

Sometimes he would say aloud, "Come, sweet breeze, come and fan my breast, come and allay the heat that burns me." Someone passing by one day heard him talking in this way to the air, and, foolishly believing that he was talking to some maiden, went and told the secret to Procris, Cephalus's wife. Love is **credulous**. Procris, at the sudden shock, fainted away. Presently recovering, she said, "It cannot be true; I will not believe it unless I myself am a witness to it." So she waited, with anxious heart, till the next morning, when Cephalus went to hunt as usual. Then she stole out after him, and concealed herself in the place where the informer directed her.

Cephalus came as he was wont when tired with sport, and stretched himself on the green bank, saying, "Come, sweet breeze, come and fan me; you know how I love you! you make the groves and my solitary rambles delightful." He was running on in this way when he heard, or thought he heard, a sound as of a sob in the bushes. Supposing it some wild animal, he threw his javelin at the spot. A cry from his beloved Procris told him that the weapon had too surely met its mark. He rushed to the place, and found her bleeding, and with sinking strength endeavoring to draw forth from the wound the javelin, her own gift. Cephalus raised her from the earth, strove to **stanch** the blood, and called her to revive and not to leave him miserable, to reproach himself with her death.

She opened her feeble eyes, and forced herself to utter these few words: "I implore you, if you have ever loved me, if I have ever deserved kindness at your hands, my husband, grant me this last request; do not marry that odious Breeze!"

This disclosed the whole mystery: but alas! what advantage to disclose it now! She died; but her face wore a calm expression, and she looked pityingly and forgivingly on her husband when he made her understand the truth.

Part Three

Moore, in his "Legendary Ballads," has one on Cephalus and Procris, beginning thus:

> "A hunter once in a grove reclined,
> > To shun the noon's bright eye,
> And oft he wooed the wandering wind
> > To cool his brow with its sigh
> While mute lay even the wild bee's hum,
> > Nor breath could stir the aspen's hair,
> His song was still, 'Sweet Air, O come!'
> > While Echo answered, 'Come, sweet Air!'"

Narration and Discussion

Are there any similarities between this story and "Pyramus and Thisbe?"

How might the story have ended differently?

Creative narration: Could you continue Moore's poem?

Chapter Four

(Lesson 10) Juno and Her Rivals

Introduction

Those who defy a goddess may end up as cows, bears, or the spots on a peacock's tail.

Vocabulary

her husband: Jupiter (Zeus)

heifer: young cow

loath: unwilling

suffered: allowed

vile: nasty

dispatch: get rid of

satiated: filled, satisfied

low: make cow noises, moo

supplication: begging for help or mercy

transfixing: shooting

assented: agreed

Names

Juno: a major goddess, the wife of Jupiter. (Greek: Hera)

Io: an Argive princess, and ancestor of kings and heroes such as Perseus and Cadmus. One of the moons of Jupiter is named for **Io**, and another is named for **Callisto.** (A third is named for **Europa**, a story familiar to those who have read *Tanglewood Tales*.)

Argus: or Argos Panoptes," meaning "All-Seeing Argus" or "All-Eyes"

Leigh Hunt: James Henry Leigh Hunt (1784-1859), English essayist, critic, and poet

Keats: John Keats (1795-1821), English Romantic poet

J. R. Lowell: James Russell Lowell (1819-1891), American Romantic poet

Places

Ionian sea: part of the Mediterranean Sea, between Italy and Greece

Illyria: a region of southeastern Europe, in the Balkan Peninsula

Mount Haemus: part of the Balkan Mountains in southeastern Europe

Thracian strait: later called the **Bosphorus** or **Bosporus**; it connects the Black Sea to the Sea of Marmara.

Scythia, [land of the]Cimmerians: parts of western Asia

Nile: the river that runs through Egypt

Reading

Part One: Io

    Juno one day perceived it suddenly grow dark, and immediately suspected that **her husband** had raised a cloud to hide some of his doings that would not bear the light. She brushed away the cloud, and saw her husband on the banks of a glassy river, with a beautiful **heifer** standing near him. Juno suspected the heifer's form concealed some fair nymph of mortal mould—as was, indeed the case; for it was **Io**, the daughter of the river god Inachus, whom Jupiter had been flirting with, and, when he became aware of the approach of his wife, had changed [her] into that form.
    Juno joined her husband, and, noticing the heifer, praised its beauty, and asked whose it was, and of what herd. Jupiter, to stop [her] questions, replied that it was a fresh creation from the earth. Juno asked to have it as a gift.
    What could Jupiter do? He was **loath** to give his mistress to his wife; yet how refuse so trifling a present as a simple heifer? He could not, without exciting suspicion; so he consented. The goddess was not yet relieved of her suspicions; so she delivered the heifer to **Argus**, to be strictly watched.
    Now Argus had a hundred eyes in his head, and never went to sleep with more than two at a time, so that he kept watch of Io constantly. He **suffered** her to feed through the day, and at night tied her up with a **vile** rope round her neck. She would have stretched out her arms to implore freedom of Argus, but she had no arms to stretch out, and her voice was a bellow that frightened even herself. She saw her father and her sisters, went near them, and suffered them to pat her back, and heard them admire her beauty. Her father reached her a tuft of grass, and she licked the outstretched hand. She longed to make herself known to him, and would have uttered her wish; but, alas! words were wanting.
    At length she bethought herself of writing, and inscribed her name—it was a short one—with her hoof on the sand. Inachus recognized it, and discovering that his daughter, whom he had long sought in vain, was hidden under this disguise, mourned over her, and, embracing her white neck, exclaimed, "Alas! my daughter, it would have been a less grief to have lost you altogether!" While he thus lamented, Argus, observing, came and drove her away, and took his seat on a high bank, from whence he could see all around in every direction.

Part Two: A Story Within the Story

    Jupiter was troubled at beholding the sufferings of his mistress, and calling Mercury, told him to go and **despatch** Argus. Mercury made haste, put his winged slippers on his feet, and cap on his head, took his sleep-producing wand, and leaped down from the heavenly towers to the earth. There he laid aside his wings, and kept only his wand, with which he presented himself as a shepherd driving his flock. As he strolled on he blew upon his pipes. (These were what are called the Syrinx or Pandean pipes.) Argus listened with delight, for he had never seen the instrument before. "Young man," said he, "come and take a seat by me on this stone. There is no better place for your flocks to graze in than hereabouts, and here is a pleasant shade such as shepherds love."

Mercury sat down, talked, and told stories till it grew late, and played upon his pipes his most soothing strains, hoping to lull the watchful eyes to sleep, but all in vain; for Argus still contrived to keep some of his eyes open though he shut the rest.

Among other stories, Mercury told him how the instrument on which he played was invented. "There was a certain nymph, whose name was Syrinx, who was much beloved by the satyrs and spirits of the wood; but she would have none of them, but was a faithful worshipper of Diana, and followed the chase. You would have thought it was Diana herself, had you seen her in her hunting dress, only that her bow was of horn and Diana's of silver. One day, as she was returning from the chase, Pan met her, told her just this, and added more of the same sort. She ran away, without stopping to hear his compliments, and he pursued till she came to the bank of the river, where he overtook her, and she had only time to call for help on her friends the water nymphs. They heard and consented. Pan threw his arms around what he supposed to be the form of the nymph, and found he embraced only a tuft of reeds! As he breathed a sigh, the air sounded through the reeds, and produced a plaintive melody. The god, charmed with the novelty and with the sweetness of the music, said, 'Thus, then, at least, you shall be mine.' And he took some of the reeds, and placing them together, of unequal lengths, side by side, made an instrument which he called Syrinx, in honor of the nymph."

Before Mercury had finished his story he saw Argus's eyes all asleep. As his head nodded forward on his breast, Mercury with one stroke cut his neck through, and tumbled his head down the rocks. O hapless Argus! The light of your hundred eyes is quenched at once! Juno took them and put them as ornaments on the tail of her peacock, where they remain to this day.

Part Three

But the vengeance of Juno was not yet **satiated**. She sent a gadfly to torment Io, who fled over the whole world from its pursuit. She swam through the **Ionian sea**, which derived its name from her, then roamed over the plains of **Illyria**, ascended **Mount Haemus**, and crossed the **Thracian strait**, thence named the **Bosphorus (cow-ford)**, rambled on through **Scythia**, and the country of the **Cimmerians**, and arrived at last on the banks of the **Nile**.

At length Jupiter interceded for her, and upon his promising not to pay her any more attentions, Juno consented to restore her to her [own] form. It was curious to see her gradually recover her former self. The coarse hairs fell from her body, her horns shrank up, her eyes grew narrower, her mouth shorter; hands and fingers came instead of hoofs to her forefeet; in fine there was nothing left of the heifer, except her beauty. At first she was afraid to speak, for fear she should **low**, but gradually she recovered her confidence and was restored to her father and sisters.

In a poem dedicated to **Leigh Hunt,** by **Keats**, the following allusion to the story of Pan and Syrinx occurs:

"So did he feel who pulled the bough aside,

That we might look into a forest wide,

. . . . . .

Telling us how fair trembling Syrinx fled

Arcadian Pan, with such a fearful dread.

Poor nymph—poor Pan—how he did weep to find

Nought but a lovely sighing of the wind

Along the reedy stream; a half-heard strain.

Full of sweet desolation, balmy pain."

Part Four: Callisto

Callisto was another maiden who excited the jealousy of Juno, and the goddess changed her into a bear. "I will take away," said she, "that beauty with which you have captivated my husband." Down fell Callisto on her hands and knees; she tried to stretch out her arms in **supplication**—they were already beginning to be covered with black hair. Her hands grew rounded, became armed with crooked claws, and served for feet; her mouth, which Jove used to praise for its beauty, became a horrid pair of jaws; her voice, which if unchanged would have moved the heart to pity, became a growl, more fit to inspire terror. Yet her former disposition remained, and with continual groaning, she bemoaned her fate, and stood upright as well as she could, lifting up her paws to beg for mercy, and felt that Jove was unkind, though she could not tell him so. Ah, how often, afraid to stay in the woods all night alone, she wandered about the neighborhood of her former haunts; how often, frightened by the dogs, did she, so lately a huntress, fly in terror from the hunters! Often she fled from the wild beasts, forgetting that she was now a wild beast herself; and, bear as she was, was afraid of the bears.

One day a youth espied her as he was hunting. She saw him and recognized him as her own son, now grown a young man. She stopped and felt inclined to embrace him. As she was about to approach, he, alarmed, raised his hunting spear, and was on the point of **transfixing** her, when Jupiter, beholding, arrested the crime, and snatching away both of them, placed them in the heavens as the Great and Little Bear.

Part Five

Juno was in a rage to see her rival so set in honor, and hastened to ancient Tethys and Oceanus, the powers of Ocean, and in answer to their inquiries thus told the cause of her coming: "Do you ask why I, the queen of the gods, have left the heavenly plains and sought your depths? Learn that I am supplanted in heaven—my place is given to another. You will hardly believe me; but look when night darkens the world, and you shall see the two of whom I have so much reason to complain exalted to the heavens, in that part where the circle is the smallest, in the neighborhood of the pole. Why should anyone hereafter tremble at the thought of offending Juno, when such rewards are the consequence of my displeasure? See what I have been able to effect! I forbade her to wear the human form—she is placed among the stars! So do my punishments result—such is the extent of my power! Better that she should have resumed her former shape, as I permitted Io to do. Perhaps he means to marry her, and put me away! But you, my foster-parents, if you feel for me, and see with displeasure this unworthy treatment of me, show it, I beseech you, by forbidding this guilty couple from coming into your waters."

The powers of the ocean **assented**, and consequently the two constellations of the Great and Little Bear move round and round in heaven, but never sink, as the other stars do, beneath the ocean.

> Milton alludes to the fact that the constellation of the Bear never sets, when he says:
> "Let my lamp at midnight hour
> Be seen in some high lonely tower,
> Where I may oft outwatch the Bear," etc.
>
> And Prometheus, in **J. R. Lowell's** poem, says:
> "One after one the stars have risen and set,
> Sparkling upon the hoar frost of my chain;
> The Bear that prowled all night about the fold
> Of the North-star, hath shrunk into his den,
> Scared by the blithesome footsteps of the Dawn."

[*omission for length*]

Narration and Discussion

Is Juno an all-round villain, or does she also have her good side?

Creative narration #1: Which of the three bits of poetry do you like best? Could you illustrate one of them?

Creative narration #2: Imagine a conversation between Io and Callisto; or between Jupiter and Mercury.

(Lesson 11) Diana and Actaeon

Introduction

Another young man loses his human form (and eventually his life) by being in the wrong place at the wrong time. Life in the ancient world could indeed be dangerous.

Vocabulary

stag: male deer

while Phoebus parches the earth: while the sun is so hot and bright

counterfeited: imitated

capacious: large

Names

Actaeon: a famous Theban hero

King Cadmus: founder of the city of Thebes (see **Year Five Lesson 28**)

one frail form: Bulfinch notes that "The allusion is probably to Shelley himself."

Reading

Part One

Thus in two instances we have seen Juno's severity to her rivals; now let us learn how a virgin goddess punished an invader of her privacy.

It was midday, and the sun stood equally distant from either goal, when young **Actaeon**, son of **King Cadmus**, thus addressed the youths who with him were hunting the **stag** in the mountains: "Friends, our nets and our weapons are wet with the blood of our victims; we have had sport enough for one day, and tomorrow we can renew our labors. Now, **while Phoebus parches the earth**, let us put by our implements and indulge ourselves with rest."

There was a valley thick enclosed with cypresses and pines, sacred to the huntress queen, Diana. In the extremity of the valley was a cave, not adorned with art, but nature had **counterfeited** art in its construction, for she had turned the arch of its roof with stones as delicately fitted as if by the hand of man. A fountain burst out from one side, whose open basin was bounded by a grassy rim. Here the goddess of the woods used to come when weary with hunting and [bathe] in the sparkling water.

One day, having repaired thither with her nymphs, she handed her javelin, her quiver, and her bow to one, her robe to another, while a third unbound the sandals from her feet. Then Crocale, the most skilful of them, arranged her hair, and Nephele, Hyale, and the rest drew water in **capacious** urns. While the goddess was thus employed in [her grooming], behold: Actaeon, having quitted his companions, and rambling without any especial object, came to the place, led thither by his destiny.

As he presented himself at the entrance of the cave, the nymphs, seeing a man, screamed and rushed towards the goddess to hide her with their bodies. But she was taller than the rest and overtopped them all by a head. Such a color as tinges the clouds at sunset or at dawn came over the countenance of Diana thus taken by surprise. Surrounded as she was by her nymphs, she yet turned half away, and sought with a sudden impulse for her arrows. As they were not at hand, she dashed the water into the face of the intruder, adding these words: "Now go and tell, if you can, that you have seen Diana unapparelled."

Part Two

Immediately a pair of branching stag's horns grew out of his head, his neck gained in length, his ears grew sharp-pointed, his hands became feet, his arms long legs, his body was covered with a hairy spotted hide. Fear took the place of his former boldness, and the hero fled. He could not but admire his own speed; but when he saw his horns in the water, "Ah, wretched me!" he would have said, but no sound followed the effort. He groaned, and tears flowed down the face which had taken the place of his own. Yet his consciousness remained. What shall he do?—go home to seek the palace, or lie hid in the woods? The latter he was afraid, the former he was ashamed, to do.

While he hesitated, the dogs saw him. First Melampus, a Spartan dog, gave the signal with his bark, then Pamphagus, Dorceus, Lelaps, Theron, Nape, Tigris, and all the rest, rushed after him swifter than the wind. Over rocks and cliffs, through mountain gorges that seemed impracticable, he fled and they followed. Where he had often chased the stag and cheered on his pack, his pack now chased him, cheered on by his huntsmen. He longed to cry out, "I am Actaeon; recognize your master!" but the words came not at his will. The air resounded with the bark of the dogs.

Presently one fastened on his back, another seized his shoulder. While they held their master, the rest of the pack came up and buried their teeth in his flesh. He groaned,—not in a human voice, yet certainly not in a stag's,—and falling on his knees, raised his eyes, and would have raised his arms in supplication, if he had had them. His friends and fellow-huntsmen cheered on the dogs, and looked everywhere for

Actaeon, calling on him to join the sport. At the sound of his name he turned his head, and heard them regret that he should be away. He earnestly wished he was. He would have been well pleased to see the exploits of his dogs, but to feel them was too much. They were all around him, rending and tearing; and it was not till they had torn his life out that the anger of Diana was satisfied.

Part Three

In Shelley's poem "Adonais" is the following allusion to the story of Actaeon:

" 'Midst others of less note came **one frail form**,

A phantom among men: companionless

As the last cloud of an expiring storm,

Whose thunder is its knell; he, as I guess,

Had gazed on Nature's naked loveliness,

Actaeon-like, and now he fled astray

With feeble steps o'er the world's wilderness;

And his own Thoughts, along that rugged way,

Pursued like raging hounds their father and their prey." (Stanza 31)

Narration and Discussion

Why was Diana so angry with Actaeon? Couldn't she have said "Oops, that was awkward," and accepted his apology?

Do you think Diana might have regretted her impulsive action, when she heard about what happened to Actaeon?

Creative narration: Write an alternative ending for the story.

Something to think about (for older students or adults): Once we have swallowed the tragic scene of Actaeon's death, it is also interesting (and less violent) to explore Shelley's poem. Is it necessary to be "pursued" in order to create art?

(Lesson 12) Latona and the Rustics

Introduction

The last reading for this term is a short one, and is partly a response to the questions raised by the previous story of Diana. Like mother, like daughter?

Vocabulary

not with impunity: but they didn't get away with it

willows and osiers: twigs for weaving baskets

rustics, clowns: country people, peasants

base: This is not a typo; Bulfinch uses the word "base" rather than "bass," though both could be considered correct.

railing: complaining

detraction: criticism

hinds: farm workers

held…in fee: To hold something "in fee" means to possess it, have full rights to it.

adamantine: strong, unyielding

Names

Latona (Greek name: Leto): The mother of **Apollo** and **Diana**. **Lesson 33** tells the story of her rivalry with **Niobe**.

Places

Lycia: a region of Anatolia (part of present-day Turkey)

Aegean (Sea): the part of the Mediterranean between Greece and Asia

Delos: a small island near Mykonos; the legendary birthplace of Apollo and Diana.

Reading

Part One

Some thought the goddess [Diana] in this instance more severe than was just, while others praised her conduct as strictly consistent with her virgin dignity. As usual, the recent event brought older ones to mind, and one of the bystanders told this story.

"Some countrymen of **Lycia** once insulted the goddess **Latona** [who was, coincidentally, the mother of Diana]; but **not with impunity**. When I was young, my father, who had grown too old for active labors, sent me to Lycia to drive thence some choice oxen, and there I saw the very pond and marsh where the wonder happened.

"Nearby stood an ancient altar, black with the smoke of sacrifice and almost buried among the reeds. I inquired whose altar it might be, whether of Faunus or the Naiads, or some god of the neighboring mountain, and one of the country people replied, 'No mountain or river god possesses this altar, but she whom royal Juno in her jealousy drove from land to land, denying her any spot of earth whereon to rear her twins.

"Bearing in her arms the infant deities, Latona reached this land, weary with her burden and parched with thirst. By chance she espied on the bottom of the valley this pond of clear water, where the country people were at work gathering **willows and osiers**. The goddess approached, and, kneeling on the bank, would have slaked her thirst in the cool stream, but the **rustics** forbade her.

"'Why do you refuse me water?' said she; 'water is free to all. Nature allows no one to claim as property the sunshine, the air, or the water. I come to take my share of the common blessing. Yet I ask it of you as a favor. I have no intention of washing my limbs in it, weary though they be, but only to quench my thirst. My mouth is so dry that I can hardly speak. A draught of water would be nectar to me; it would revive me, and I would own myself indebted to you for life itself. Let these infants move your pity, who stretch out their little arms as if to plead for me;' and the children, as it happened, were stretching out their arms.

"Who would not have been moved with these gentle words of the goddess? But these **clowns** persisted in their rudeness; they even added jeers and threats of violence if she did not leave the place. Nor was this all. They waded into the pond and stirred up the mud with their feet, so as to make the water unfit to drink. Latona was so angry that she ceased to mind her thirst, [and] lifting her hands to heaven exclaimed, 'May they never quit that pool, but pass their lives there!'

"And it came to pass accordingly. They now live in the water, sometimes totally submerged, then raising their heads above the surface or swimming upon it. Sometimes they come out upon the bank, but soon leap back again into the water. They still use their **base** voices in **railing**, and though they have the water all to themselves, are not ashamed to croak in the midst of it. Their voices are harsh, their throats bloated, their mouths have become stretched by constant railing, their necks have shrunk up and disappeared, and their heads are joined to their bodies. Their backs are green, their disproportioned bellies white, and in short they are now frogs, and dwell in the slimy pool."

Part Two (A Sidebar)

This story explains [some puzzling lines] in one of Milton's sonnets, "On the **detraction** which followed upon his writing certain treatises."

> "I did but prompt the age to quit their clogs
>
> By the known laws of ancient liberty,
>
> When straight a barbarous noise environs me
>
> Of owls and cuckoos, asses, apes and dogs.
>
> As when those **hinds** that were transformed to frogs

Railed at Latona's twin-born progeny,
Which after **held** the sun and moon **in fee**."

Part Three

The persecution which Latona experienced from Juno is alluded to in the story. The tradition was that the future mother of Apollo and Diana, flying from the wrath of Juno, besought all the islands of the **Aegean** to afford her a place of rest, but all feared too much the potent queen of heaven to assist her rival. **Delos** alone consented to become the birthplace of the future deities. Delos was then a floating island; but when Latona arrived there, Jupiter fastened it with **adamantine** chains to the bottom of the sea, that it might be a secure resting-place for his beloved.

[*omission for length*]

Narration and Discussion

Should the islands who feared Juno have helped Latona anyway?

Creative narration #1: Act or write out a) a conversation between the islands, or b) an interview with one of the frogs.

Creative narration #2: The scene with Latona could be fun to act out.

Something to think about (for older students and adults): The lines from Milton's sonnet are a reaction to criticism over a treatise (essay) he wrote called "Tetrachordon." Milton wrote poems (such as the above) in response, poking fun at people who didn't like big words or who made "barbarous noise" about his work. Do you think creative forms of writing (including songs) are a good way to respond to "detraction," or to things that make us mad? Can you think of any examples?

Chapter Five

(Lesson 13) Phaeton (First Part)

Introduction

The next few Lesson s take a different theme: that of ambition and greed. First we will read about young Phaeton, who asked to drive the Sun's chariot for a day; then we will get to the story of King Midas, who also had a wish that got too big for him. And, finally, we will hear another story familiar to those who have read *A Wonder Book*, about two people who were contented with what they had.

Vocabulary

own: confess, confirm

sinuous: curving, twisting

imbibed: absorbed, or drunken

august abodes: the beautiful palace (its former home)

vesture: robe

that dreadful lake: the river Styx, in the underworld

rashly: too quickly and without thinking

admonition: warning

Names

Phaeton (or Phaethon): can be pronounced "FYE-ton" or "FAY-ton"

Clymene: pronounced CLEE-men-ee or CLIM-en-ee

Walter Savage Landor: English writer and political activist (1775-1864). He wrote *Gebir* (the long poem from which these lines are taken) when he was twenty years old.

Tethys: goddess of fresh water, married to Oceanus. Also mentioned in **Year Five Lesson 20** and **Year Six Lesson 2**.

Reading

Part One

Phaeton was the son of Apollo and the nymph **Clymene**. One day a schoolfellow laughed at the idea of his being the son of the god, and Phaeton went in rage and shame and reported it to his mother. "If," said he, "I am indeed of heavenly birth, give me, mother, some proof of it, and establish my claim to the honor." Clymene stretched forth her hands towards the skies, and said, "I call to witness the Sun which looks down upon us, that I have told you the truth. If I speak falsely, let this be the last time I behold his light. But it needs not much labor to go and inquire for yourself; the land whence the Sun rises lies next to ours. Go and demand of him whether he will **own** you as a son."

Phaeton heard [this] with delight. He travelled to India, which lies directly in the regions of sunrise; and, full of hope and pride, approached the goal whence his parent begins his course.

The palace of the Sun stood reared aloft on columns, glittering with gold and precious stones, while polished ivory formed the ceilings, and silver the doors. The workmanship surpassed the material; for upon the walls Vulcan had represented earth, sea, and skies, with their inhabitants. In the sea were the nymphs, some sporting in the waves, some riding on the backs of fishes, while others sat upon the rocks and dried their sea-green hair. Their faces were not all alike, nor yet unlike,—but such as sisters' [faces] ought to be.

The earth had its towns and forests and rivers and rustic divinities. Over all was carved the likeness of the glorious heaven; and on the silver doors the twelve signs of the zodiac, six on each side.

[The following verses have been moved here from the end of the chapter.]

In the beautiful lines of **Walter Savage Landor**, descriptive of the Sea-shell, there is an allusion to the Sun's palace and chariot. The water-nymph says:

"...I have **sinuous** shells of pearly hue

Within, and things that lustre have **imbibed**

In the sun's palace porch, where when unyoked

His chariot wheel stands midway on the wave.

Shake one and it awakens; then apply

Its polished lip to your attentive ear,

And it remembers its **august abodes**,

And murmurs as the ocean murmurs there." (Gebir, Book I.)

Part Two

Clymene's son advanced up the steep ascent, and entered the halls of his disputed father. He approached the paternal presence, but stopped at a distance, for the light was more than he could bear. Phoebus, arrayed in a purple **vesture**, sat on a throne, which glittered as with diamonds. On his right hand and his left stood the Day, the Month, and the Year, and, at regular intervals, the Hours. Spring stood with her head crowned with flowers, and Summer, with garment cast aside, and a garland formed of spears of ripened grain, and Autumn, with his feet stained with grape-juice, and icy Winter, with his hair stiffened with hoarfrost. Surrounded by these attendants, the Sun, with the eye that sees everything, beheld the youth dazzled with the novelty and splendor of the scene, and inquired the purpose of his errand. The youth replied, "O light of the boundless world, Phoebus, my father,—if you permit me to use that name,—give me some proof, I beseech you, by which I may be known as yours." He ceased; and his father, laying aside the beams that shone all around his head, bade him approach, and embracing him, said, "My son, you deserve not to be disowned, and I confirm what your mother has told you. To put an end to your doubts, ask what you will, the gift shall be yours. I call to witness **that dreadful lake**, which I never saw, but which we gods swear by in our most solemn engagements."

Phaeton immediately asked to be permitted for one day to drive the chariot of the sun. The father repented of his promise; thrice and four times he shook his radiant head in warning.

"I have spoken **rashly**," said he; "this only request I would fain deny. I beg you to withdraw it. It is not a safe boon, nor one, my Phaeton, suited to your youth and strength. Your lot is mortal, and you ask what is beyond a mortal's power. In your ignorance you aspire to do that which not even the gods themselves may do. None but myself may drive the flaming car of day. Not even Jupiter, whose terrible right arm hurls the thunderbolts. The first part of the way is steep, and such as the horses when fresh in the morning can hardly climb; the middle is high up in the heavens, whence I myself can scarcely, without alarm, look down and behold the earth and sea stretched beneath me. The last part of the road descends rapidly, and requires most careful driving. **Tethys**, who is waiting to receive me, often trembles for me lest I should fall headlong. Add to all this, the heaven is all the time turning round and carrying the stars with it. I have to be perpetually on my guard lest that movement, which sweeps everything else along, should hurry me also away.

"Suppose I should lend you the chariot, what would you do? Could you keep your course while the sphere was revolving under you? Perhaps you think that there are forests and cities, the abodes of gods, and palaces and temples on the way. On the contrary, the road is through the midst of frightful monsters. You pass by the horns of the Bull, in front of the Archer, and near the Lion's jaws, and where the Scorpion stretches its arms in one direction and the Crab in another. Nor will you find it easy to guide those horses, with their breasts full of fire that they breathe forth from their mouths and nostrils. I can scarcely govern them myself, when they are unruly and resist the reins.

"Beware, my son, lest I be the donor of a fatal gift; recall your request while yet you may. Do you ask me for a proof that you are sprung from my blood? I give you a proof in my fears for you. Look at my face—I would that you could look into my breast, you would there see all a father's anxiety. Finally," he continued, "look round the world and choose whatever you will of what earth or sea contains most precious—ask it and fear no refusal. This only I pray you not to urge. It is not honor, but destruction you seek. Why do you hang round my neck and still entreat me? You shall have it if you persist,—the oath is sworn and must be kept,—but I beg you to choose more wisely."

He ended; but the youth rejected all **admonition** and held to his demand.

Narration and Discussion

The Greek concept of the "palace of the sun" (not to mention the chariot) has little to do with our current understanding of where the sun is or how it works. However, if we can set those limits aside for now, we enter a magical and beautifully described "Sun kingdom," somewhere in India (because that seemed to be very far east). Would you like to go there?

Why was Phaeton discontented with his everyday life?

What were the reasons Apollo gave for not granting Phaeton's request? Do you think they were good ones?

Creative narration: You are Phaeton's friend, and he calls you to complain that his father won't let him drive the sun chariot. What would you say?

Something to think about: "Do you ask me for a proof that you are sprung from my blood? I give you a proof in my fears for you." What does Apollo mean by this?

(Lesson 14) Phaeton (Second Part)
Introduction

In this second reading, Phaeton takes off, with numerous cautions and warnings. "If, my son, you will in this at least heed my advice, spare the whip and hold tight the reins." He realizes, too late, that driving the sun's chariot is no joyride.

Vocabulary

ambrosia: the food of the gods (and their horses), brought to Olympus by doves

unguent: ointment

agile: able to move quickly; light-footed

cleave: break apart

ballast: something to weigh it down

prevailed: succeeded

Names

Boötes: The Herdsman, one of the constellations

Reading

Part One

So, having resisted as long as he could, Phoebus at last led the way to where stood the lofty chariot. It was of gold, the gift of Vulcan; the axle was of gold, the pole and wheels of gold, the spokes of silver. Along the seat were rows of chrysolites and diamonds which reflected all around the brightness of the sun. While the daring youth gazed in admiration, the early Dawn threw open the purple doors of the east, and showed the pathway strewn with roses. The stars withdrew, marshalled by the Daystar, which last of all retired also. The father, when he saw the earth beginning to glow, and the Moon preparing to retire, ordered the Hours to harness up the horses. They obeyed, and led forth from the lofty stalls the steeds full fed with **ambrosia**, and attached the reins.

Then the father bathed the face of his son with a powerful **unguent**, and made him capable of enduring the brightness of the flame. He set the rays on his head, and, with a foreboding sigh, said, "If, my son, you will in this at least heed my advice, spare the whip and hold tight the reins. They go fast enough of their own accord; the labor is to hold them in. You are not to take the straight road directly between the five circles, but turn off to the left. Keep within the limit of the middle zone, and avoid the northern and the southern alike. You will see the marks of the wheels, and they will serve to guide you. And, that the skies and the earth may each receive their due share of heat, go not too high, or you will burn the heavenly dwellings, nor too low, or you will set the earth on fire; the middle course is safest and best. And now I leave you to your chance, which I hope will plan better for you than you have done for yourself. Night is passing out of the western gates and we can delay no longer. Take the reins; but if at last your heart fails you, and you will benefit by my advice, stay where you are in safety, and suffer me to light and warm the earth."

The **agile** youth sprang into the chariot [*omission*], and grasped the reins with delight, pouring out thanks to his reluctant parent.

Part Two

Meanwhile the horses fill the air with their snortings and fiery breath, and stamp the ground impatient. Now the bars are let down, and the boundless plain of the universe lies open before them. They dart forward and **cleave** the opposing clouds, and outrun the morning breezes which started from the same eastern goal. The steeds soon perceived that the load they drew was lighter than usual; and as a ship without **ballast** is tossed hither and thither on the sea, so the chariot, without its accustomed weight, was dashed about as if empty. They rush headlong and leave the travelled road. He is alarmed, and knows not how to guide them; nor, if he knew, has he the power.

Then, for the first time, the Great and Little Bear were scorched with heat, and would fain, if it were possible, have plunged into the water; and the Serpent which lies coiled up round the north pole, torpid and harmless, grew warm, and with warmth felt its rage revive. **Boötes**, they say, fled away, though encumbered with his plough, and all unused to rapid motion.

When hapless Phaeton looked down upon the earth, now spreading in vast extent beneath him, he grew pale and his knees shook with terror. In spite of the glare all around him, the sight of his eyes grew dim. He wished he had never touched his father's horses, never learned his parentage, never **prevailed** in his request.

[Phaeton] is borne along like a vessel that flies before a tempest, when the pilot can do no more and betakes himself to his prayers. What shall he do? Much of the heavenly road is left behind, but more remains before. He turns his eyes from one direction to the other; now to the goal whence he began his course, now to the realms of sunset which he is not destined to reach. He loses his self-command, and knows not what to do,—whether to draw tight the reins or throw them loose; he forgets the names of the horses. He sees with terror the monstrous forms scattered over the surface of heaven.

Here the Scorpion extended his two great arms, with his tail and crooked claws stretching over two signs of the zodiac. When the boy beheld him, reeking with poison and menacing with his fangs, his courage failed, and the reins fell from his hands. The horses, when they felt them loose on their backs, dashed headlong, and unrestrained went off into unknown regions of the sky, in among the stars, hurling the chariot over pathless places, now up in high heaven, now down almost to the earth. The moon saw with astonishment her brother's chariot running beneath her own.

Narration and Discussion

What happens as Phaeton drives through the stars? What might happen next?

Have you ever been in a situation that got so out of hand that, like Phaeton, you forgot the names of the horses? What did you do?

Creative narration: Use a star map, or chart of the constellations, as background for an action-figure narration, perhaps with a small toy vehicle for the chariot.

(Lesson 15) Phaeton (Third Part)

Introduction

Phaeton, careening across the sky, causes terrible damage to the earth and even cracks

Year Five: The Age of Fable

open the underworld. Jupiter finally has to step in.

Please note that, though we seldom have to mention having to edit out unacceptable content, there is some in this passage. Those using standard editions of Bulfinch will want to check for that.

Vocabulary

there it still remains concealed: The source of the Nile did indeed remain a mystery for centuries.

essayed: tried

omnipotent: all-powerful

amber: Fossilized resin. The Greek word for amber is *elektron*, which is related to a word meaning "beaming sun." This is where our words like "electric" and "electronics" came from.

Names

Nereus (NEARY-yoos): an underwater deity, something like "The Old Man of the Sea"

Heliades: daughters of Clymene, though not of Apollo. A different version of the story says that they were turned into trees because they harnessed the chariot for Phaeton, without Apollo's permission.

Places

NOTE: Rather than trying to provide geographical information here for the places mentioned, we encourage you to just read the passage, but also to look up any places that pique your interest.

Athos: Richard Halliburton has a story about Mount Athos in *The Complete Book of Marvels*, Chapter 28 "Mount Athos, Country of Men."

(Mount) Helicon: a mountain in Boeotia, supposed to be the home of the Muses

Caucasus: the mountains between the Black Sea and the Caspian Sea

Tartarus: the underworld

Eridanus: a river in central Europe; it is also a constellation of the southern hemisphere

Reading

Part One

The clouds begin to smoke, and the mountain tops take fire; the fields are parched with heat, the plants wither, the trees with their leafy branches burn, the harvest is ablaze! But these are small things. Great cities perished, with their walls and towers; whole nations with their people were consumed to ashes!

The forest-clad mountains burned, **Athos** and Taurus and Tmolus and Oete; Ida, once celebrated for fountains, but now all dry; the Muses' mountain **Helicon**, and Haemus; Aetna, with fires within and without, and Parnassus, with his two peaks, and Rhodope, forced at last to part with his snowy crown. Her cold climate was no protection to Scythia, **Caucasus** burned, and Ossa and Pindus, and, greater than both, Olympus; the Alps high in air, and the Apennines crowned with clouds.

Then Phaeton beheld the world on fire, and felt the heat intolerable. The air he breathed was like the air of a furnace and full of burning ashes, and the smoke was of a pitchy darkness. He dashed forward he knew not whither.

[*omission for content*]

The Libyan desert was dried up to the condition in which it remains to this day. The Nymphs of the fountains, with dishevelled hair, mourned their waters, nor were the rivers safe beneath their banks: Tanais smoked, and Caicus, Xanthus, and Meander; Babylonian Euphrates and Ganges, Tagus with golden sands, and Cayster where the swans resort. Nile fled away and hid his head in the desert, and **there it still remains concealed**. Where he used to discharge his waters through seven mouths into the sea, there seven dry channels alone remained.

The earth cracked open, and through the chinks light broke into **Tartarus**, and frightened the king of shadows and his queen. The sea shrank up. Where before was water, it became a dry plain; and the mountains that lie beneath the waves lifted up their heads and became islands. The fishes sought the lowest depths, and the dolphins no longer ventured as usual to sport on the surface. Even **Nereus**, and his wife Doris, with the Nereids, their daughters, sought the deepest caves for refuge.

Part Two

Thrice Neptune **essayed** to raise his head above the surface, and thrice was driven back by the heat. Earth, surrounded as she was by waters, yet with head and shoulders bare, screening her face with her hand, looked up to heaven, and with a husky voice called on Jupiter:

> "O ruler of the gods, if I have deserved this treatment, and it is your
> will that I perish with fire, why withhold your thunderbolts? Let me
> at least fall by your hand. Is this the reward of my fertility, of my

obedient service? Is it for this that I have supplied herbage for cattle, and fruits for men, and frankincense for your altars? But if I am unworthy of regard, what has my brother Ocean done to deserve such a fate? If neither of us can excite your pity, think, I pray you, of your own heaven, and behold how both the poles are smoking which sustain your palace, which must fall if they be destroyed. Atlas faints, and scarce holds up his burden. If sea, earth, and heaven perish, we fall into ancient Chaos. Save what yet remains to us from the devouring flame. O, take thought for our deliverance in this awful moment!"

Thus spoke Earth, and overcome with heat and thirst, could say no more. Then Jupiter **omnipotent**, calling to witness all the gods, including him who had lent the chariot, and showing them that all was lost unless speedy remedy were applied, mounted the lofty tower from whence he diffuses clouds over the earth, and hurls the forked lightnings. But at that time not a cloud was to be found to interpose for a screen to earth, nor was a shower remaining unexhausted. He thundered, and brandishing a lightning bolt in his right hand launched it against the charioteer, and struck him at the same moment from his seat and from existence!

Phaeton, with his hair on fire, fell headlong, like a shooting star which marks the heavens with its brightness as it falls, and **Eridanus**, the great river, received him and cooled his burning frame.

Part Three

The Italian Naiads reared a tomb for him, and inscribed these words upon the stone:

"Driver of Phoebus' chariot, Phaeton,

Struck by Jove's thunder, rests beneath this stone.

He could not rule his father's car of fire,

Yet was it much so nobly to aspire."

His sisters, the **Heliades**, as they lamented his fate, were turned into poplar trees, on the banks of the river, and their tears, which continued to flow, became **amber** as they dropped into the stream.

[*omission for length*]

Part Four: The Phaeton (Non-Bulfinch Notes)

The word "phaeton" was used in the eighteenth and nineteenth centuries to mean an open, rather "sporty" horse-drawn carriage. In the twentieth century, the same word was adopted to mean an open touring car.

"Jill and Molly drove away in the little phaeton every fair morning over the sunny hills and through the changing woods, filling their hands with asters and golden-rod, their lungs with the pure, invigorating air..." (Louisa May Alcott, *Jack and Jill*)

Narration and Discussion

The Naiads' epitaph for Phaeton said, "He could not rule his father's car of fire, / Yet was it much so nobly to aspire." Do you agree?

Creative narration: In Charlotte Mason's *Philosophy of Education*, we are given a poem about Phaeton, written by a teenage student, which begins like this:

> Phaëton was a wilful youth who always got his way.
> He asked to drive his father's charge upon a certain day.
> But Phoebus knowing well what danger lurketh in the sky;
> Implored of him to wish again and not that task to try...

Can you write some more lines for it?

Chapter Six

(Lesson 16) Midas

Introduction

Many students will know the story of King Midas and the Golden Touch, especially if they have read *A Wonder Book*; but the other stories may be less familiar (along with the inclusion of Bacchus and Silenus).

Vocabulary

sod: clump of grass and dirt

the garden of the Hesperides: The reference is to the "Three Golden Apples of the Hesperides," which will be familiar to students who have read *A Wonder Book*.

repast: meal

consternation: dismay

he strove to divest himself of his power: he tried to get rid of it

temerity: boldness, nerve

acquiesced: agreed

discretion: the ability to keep a secret

oracle: prophecy

subjecting all Asia to his sway: conquering Asia

Names

Bacchus (Greek: Dionysus): The god of wine and also of theater; often included as one of the twelve major gods on Olympus.

Silenus: the tutor and companion of Dionysus. He was a satyr, sometimes pictured as having some of the features of a goat, but other times with the ears or tail of a horse. Silenus is known for wisdom, but also for his appetite for drink.

Then Bacchus and Silenus and the Maenads began a dance, far wilder than the dance of the trees; not merely a dance for fun and beauty (though it was that too) but a magic dance of plenty, and where their hands touched, and where their feet fell, the feast came into existence... (C. S. Lewis, *Prince Caspian*)

Places

River Pactolus: a river near the Aegean coast of modern-day Turkey

Phrygia: a kingdom which is now part of Turkey

Reading

Part One: Midas and the Golden Touch

Bacchus, on a certain occasion, found his old schoolmaster and foster-father, **Silenus**, missing. The old man had been drinking, and in that state wandered away, and was found by some peasants, who carried him to their king, Midas. Midas recognized him, and treated him hospitably, entertaining him for ten days and nights with an unceasing round of jollity. On the eleventh day he brought Silenus back, and restored him in safety to his pupil. Whereupon Bacchus offered Midas his choice of a reward, whatever he might wish. He asked that whatever he might touch should be changed into gold. Bacchus consented, though sorry that he had not made a better choice.

Midas went his way, rejoicing in his new-acquired power, which he hastened to put to the test. He could scarce believe his eyes when he found a twig of an oak, which he plucked from the branch, become gold in his hand. He took up a stone; it changed to gold. He touched a **sod**; it did the same. He took an apple from the tree; you would have thought he had robbed **the garden of the Hesperides**. His joy knew no bounds, and as soon as he got home, he ordered the servants to set a splendid **repast** on the table. Then he found to his dismay that whether he touched bread, it hardened in his hand; or put a morsel to his lips, it defied his teeth. He took a glass of wine, but it flowed down his throat like melted gold.

In **consternation** at the unprecedented affliction, **he strove to divest himself of his power**; he hated the gift he had lately coveted. But all in vain; starvation seemed to await him. He raised his arms, all shining with gold, in prayer to Bacchus, begging to be delivered from his glittering destruction. Bacchus, merciful deity, heard and consented. "Go," said he, "to the **River Pactolus**, trace the stream to its fountain-head, there plunge your head and body in, and wash away your fault and its punishment." He did so, and scarce had he touched the waters before the gold-creating power passed into them, and the river-sands became changed into gold, as they remain to this day.

Part Two: Midas and the Hairy Ears

Thenceforth Midas, hating wealth and splendor, dwelt in the country, and became a worshipper of Pan, the god of the fields. On a certain occasion Pan had the **temerity** to compare his music with that of Apollo, and to challenge the god of the lyre to a trial of skill. The challenge was accepted, and Tmolus, the mountain god, was chosen umpire. The senior took his seat, and cleared away the trees from his ears to listen. At a given signal Pan blew on his pipes, and with his rustic melody gave great satisfaction to himself and his faithful follower Midas, who happened to be present.

Then Tmolus turned his head toward the Sun-god, and all his trees turned with him. Apollo rose, his brow wreathed with Parnassian laurel, while his robe of Tyrian purple swept the ground. In his left hand he held the lyre, and with his right hand struck the strings. Ravished with the harmony, Tmolus at once awarded the victory to the god of the lyre, and all but Midas **acquiesced** in the judgment. He dissented, and questioned the justice of the award. Apollo would not suffer such a depraved pair of ears any longer to wear the human form, but caused them to increase in length, grow hairy, within and without, and movable on their roots; in short, to be on the perfect pattern of those of [a donkey].

Mortified enough was King Midas at this mishap; but he consoled himself with the thought that it was possible to hide his misfortune, which he attempted to do by means of an ample turban or head-dress. But his hairdresser of course knew the secret. He was charged not to mention it, and threatened with dire punishment if he presumed to disobey. But he found it too much for his **discretion** to keep such a secret; so he went out into the meadow, dug a hole in the ground, and stooping down, whispered the story, and covered it up. Before long a thick bed of reeds sprang up in the meadow, and as soon as it had gained its growth, began whispering the story, and has continued to do so, from that day to this, every time a breeze passes over the place.

[*omission for length*]

Part Three: The Father of Midas

Midas was king of **Phrygia**. He was the son of Gordius, a poor countryman, who was taken by the people and made king, in obedience to the command of the **oracle**, which had said that their future king should come in a wagon. While the people were deliberating, Gordius with his wife and son came driving his wagon into the public square. Gordius, being made king, dedicated his wagon to the deity of the oracle, and tied it up in its place with a fast knot. This was the celebrated "Gordian Knot," which, in after-times it was said, whoever should untie should become lord of all Asia.

Many tried to untie it, but none succeeded, till Alexander the Great, in his career of conquest, came to Phrygia [in 333 B.C.]. He tried his skill with as ill success as others, till growing impatient he drew his sword and cut the knot. When he afterwards succeeded in **subjecting all Asia to his sway**, people began to think that he had complied with the terms of the oracle according to its true meaning.

[Editor's note: "Cutting a Gordian Knot" has come to mean attacking a problem head-on, rather than worrying about untangling all the small details first. Sometimes that actually works!

>Turn him to any cause of policy,
>The Gordian Knot of it he will unloose,
>Familiar as his garter... (Shakespeare, *Henry V*)]

Narration and Discussion

In this version of "The Golden Touch," based on the classic Roman version by Ovid, Midas's frustration is caused mainly by his inability to eat anything without it turning to gold. In later retellings, such as Hawthorne's, his daughter is accidentally turned to gold as well, which adds an extra bit of drama. Which version do you prefer?

Would you rather listen to Pan play his pipes, or Apollo play the lyre? What would you do if you were forced to choose between them? (Does that seem like another kind of Gordian knot?)

Creative narration: Imagine an interview with a) Midas's hairdresser, or b) one of the palace servants when Midas had the "Golden Touch."

(Lesson 17) Baucis and Philemon

Introduction

This story will be familiar as "The Miraculous Pitcher" to readers of *A Wonder Book*. Bulfinch tells it with less detail than Hawthorne, and also changes the menu a bit; but it still manages to convey the love and faith that embodied Baucis and Philemon.

Vocabulary

linden tree: a tree with heart-shaped leaves and yellow blossoms

fen-birds: birds living in a wetland (marsh) area

cormorants: diving birds living near water

caduceus: a wand with two serpents twined around it (also mentioned in **Lesson 3**)

pot-herbs: leafy greens (like spinach) or herbs

beguiled: passed

cornel berries: a red fruit, also called the Cornelian cherry

not of the oldest: wine is better when it is aged

eluded their pursuit: got away from them

chastisement: punishment

benignant accents: kindly tones

Names

Baucis (BAH-sis)

Philemon (Fi-LEE-mohn)

The Tyanean shepherd: refers to the local people

Reading

Part One

On a certain hill in Phrygia stands a **linden tree** and an oak, enclosed by a low wall. Not far from the spot is a marsh, formerly good habitable land, but now indented with pools, the resort of **fen-birds** and **cormorants**. Once on a time Jupiter, in, human shape, visited this country, and with him his son Mercury (he of the **caduceus**), without his wings. They presented themselves, as weary travellers, at many a door, seeking rest and shelter, but found all closed, for it was late, and the inhospitable inhabitants would not rouse themselves to open for their reception. At last a humble mansion received them, a small thatched cottage, where **Baucis**, a pious old dame, and her husband **Philemon**, united when young, had grown old together. Not ashamed of their poverty, they made it endurable by moderate desires and kind dispositions. One need not look there for master or for servant; they two were the whole household, master and servant alike.

When the two heavenly guests crossed the humble threshold, and bowed their heads to pass under the low door, the old man placed a seat, on which Baucis, bustling and attentive, spread a cloth, and begged them to sit down. Then she raked out the coals from the ashes, and kindled up a fire, fed it with leaves and dry bark, and with her scanty breath blew it into a flame. She brought out of a corner split sticks and dry branches, broke them up, and placed them under the small kettle. Her husband collected some **pot-herbs** in the garden, and she shred[ded] them from the stalks, and prepared them for the pot. He reached down with a forked stick a flitch of bacon hanging in the chimney, cut a small piece, and put it in the pot to boil with the herbs, setting away the rest for another time. A [beechwood] bowl was filled with warm water, that their guests might wash. While all was doing, they **beguiled** the time with conversation.

On the bench designed for the guests was laid a cushion stuffed with seaweed; and a cloth, only produced on great occasions, but ancient and coarse enough, was spread over that. The old lady, with her apron on, with trembling hand set the table. One leg was shorter than the rest, but a piece of slate put under restored the level. When fixed, she rubbed the table down with some sweet-smelling herbs. Upon it she set some of chaste Minerva's olives, some **cornel berries** preserved in vinegar, and added radishes and cheese, with eggs lightly cooked in the ashes. All were served in earthen dishes, and an earthenware pitcher, with wooden cups, stood beside them. When all was ready, the stew, smoking hot, was set on the table. Some wine, **not of the oldest**, was added; and for dessert, apples and wild honey; and over and above all, friendly faces, and simple but hearty welcome.

Part Two

Now while the repast proceeded, the old folks were astonished to see that the wine, as fast as it was poured out, renewed itself in the pitcher, of its own accord. Struck with terror, Baucis and Philemon recognized their heavenly guests, fell on their knees, and with clasped hands implored forgiveness for their poor entertainment. There was an old goose, which they kept as the guardian of their humble cottage; and they bethought them to make this a sacrifice in honor of their guests. But the goose, too nimble, with the aid of feet and wings, for the old folks, **eluded their pursuit**, and at last took shelter between the gods themselves. They forbade it to be slain; and spoke in these words: "We are gods. This inhospitable village shall pay the penalty of its impiety; you alone shall go free from the **chastisement**. Quit your house, and come with us to the top of yonder hill." They hastened to obey, and, staff in hand, labored up the steep ascent. They had reached to within an arrow's flight of the top, when turning their eyes below, they beheld all the country sunk in a lake, only their own house left standing.

Part Three

While they gazed with wonder at the sight, and lamented the fate of their neighbors, that old house of theirs was changed into a temple. Columns took the place of the corner posts, the thatch grew yellow and appeared a gilded roof, the floors became marble, the doors were enriched with carving and ornaments of gold. Then spoke Jupiter in **benignant accents**: "Excellent old man, and woman worthy of such a husband, speak, tell us your wishes; what favor have you to ask of us?"

Philemon took counsel with Baucis a few moments; then declared to the gods their united wish. "We ask to be priests and guardians of this your temple; and since here we have passed our lives in love and concord, we wish that one and the same hour may take us both from life, that I may not live to see her grave, nor be laid in my own by her."

Their prayer was granted. They were the keepers of the temple as long as they lived. When grown very old, as they stood one day before the steps of the sacred edifice, and were telling the story of the place, Baucis saw Philemon begin to put forth leaves, and old Philemon saw Baucis changing in like manner. And now a leafy crown had grown over their heads, while exchanging parting words, as long as they could speak. "Farewell, dear spouse," they said, together, and at the same moment the bark closed over their mouths.

The Tyanean shepherd still shows [or *long showed*] the two trees, standing side by side, made out of the two good old people.

[*omission for length*]

Narration and Discussion

How did Baucus and Philemon show hospitality to their guests?

Does the village being destroyed remind you of any stories that we have already read?

Something to think about: Would you want to be a tree forever with someone that you love? Does the Bible say anything to help us not fear that separation from loved ones? (John 14:1-6)

Creative narration: Dramatize this story. (Don't forget to include the goose.)

> Ev'n yet, an ancient Tyanaean shows
> A spreading oak, that near a linden grows:
> The neighbourhood confirm the prodigie,
> Grave men, not vain of tongue, or like to lie.
> I saw myself the garlands on their boughs,

And tablets hung for gifts of granted vows;

And off'ring fresher up, with pious pray'r,

The good, said I, are God's peculiar care,

And such as honour heav'n, shall heav'nly honour share.

(*from John Dryden's translation of Ovid*)

Chapter Seven

(Lesson 18) Proserpine (First Part)

Introduction

Those who have read *Tanglewood Tales* will recognize the story "The Pomegranate Seeds." In Hawthorne's version, "Proserpina" was said to be a little girl, stolen by Pluto in order that "he might have something to love." In this more adult version, she is taken to be Pluto's bride.

Vocabulary

his kingdom: the underworld

apprehension: concern, anxiety

embowered in: surrounded by

fervid: intense, burning

trident: three-pronged spear

honey in the comb: honey straight from the beehive

poppy juice: a sleeping drug

Names

Typhon: a monstrous, serpent-like giant, and father of many other monsters

Briareus: also called Aegaeon, "the sea goat"; he had fifty heads and a hundred arms

Enceladus: another giant who is said to be buried beneath Mount Aetna, sometimes alone but possibly with the others named above. One story says that the island of Sicily was thrown on top of him by Athena, during a battle.

that daughter of Ceres: Proserpine (Pro-SER-pee-na), sometimes spelled Proserpina, the daughter of **Jupiter** and **Ceres** (Zeus and Demeter). She is the goddess of springtime, and also queen of the underworld (because of her relationship with **Pluto**). In Greek, her name is **Persephone**.

Celeus (SEE-lee-us or KEE-lee-us): Bulfinch just calls him an old man, but in other versions he is the king of **Eleusis**.

Places

Mount Aetna (or Etna): a volcano on the east coast of Sicily

vale of Enna: located on the island of Sicily, across from the toe of Italy's "boot."

Cyane (SIGH-an-ee, sometimes spelled Kyane): Cyane was a naiad and a friend of Proserpine. Naiads are the spirits of some body of fresh water, like a well or a stream; Cyane's was a river in southeastern Sicily. In Bulfinch's version, it sounds like the river resisted Pluto's kidnapping of Proserpine; but in other versions, it is Cyane in female form who speaks out to him.

Eleusis (Ih-LEW-siss): part of the region of **Attica**, in Greece

Reading

Part One

When Jupiter and his brothers had defeated the Titans and banished them to Tartarus, a new enemy rose up against the gods. They were the giants **Typhon**, **Briareus**, **Enceladus**, and others. Some of them had a hundred arms, others breathed out fire. They were finally subdued and buried alive under **Mount Aetna**, where they still sometimes struggle to get loose, and shake the whole island with earthquakes. Their breath comes up through the mountain, and is what men call the eruption of the volcano.

The fall of these monsters shook the earth, so that Pluto was alarmed, and feared that **his kingdom** would be laid open to the light of day. Under this **apprehension**, he mounted his chariot, drawn by black horses, and took a circuit of inspection to satisfy himself of the extent of the damage. While he was thus engaged, Venus, who was sitting on Mount Eryx playing with her boy Cupid, espied him, and said [to Cupid], "My son, take your darts with which you conquer all, even Jove himself, and send one into the breast of yonder dark monarch, who rules the realm of Tartarus. Why should he alone escape? Seize the opportunity to extend your empire and mine. Do you not see that even in heaven some despise our power? Minerva the wise, and Diana the huntress, defy us; and there is **that daughter of Ceres**, who threatens to follow their example. Now do you, if you have any regard for your own interest or mine, join these two in one."

The boy unbound his quiver, and selected his sharpest and truest arrow; then straining the bow against his knee, he attached the string, and, having made ready, shot the arrow with its barbed point right into the heart of Pluto.

Part Two

In the **vale of Enna** there is a lake **embowered in** woods, which screen it from the **fervid** rays of the sun, while the moist ground is covered with flowers, and Spring reigns perpetual. Here Proserpine was playing with her companions, gathering lilies and violets, and filling her basket and her apron with them, when Pluto saw her, loved her, and carried her off. She screamed for help to her mother and companions; and when in her fright she dropped the corners of her apron and let the flowers fall, childlike she felt the loss of them as an addition to her grief.

The [kidnapper] urged on his steeds, calling them each by name, and throwing loose[ly] over their heads and necks his iron-colored reins. When he reached the River **Cyane**, and it opposed his passage, he struck the river-bank with his **trident**, and the earth opened and gave him a passage to Tartarus.

Part Three

Ceres sought her daughter all the world over. Bright-haired Aurora, when she came forth in the morning, and Hesperus when he led out the stars in the evening, found her still busy in the search. But it was all unavailing. At length, weary and sad, she sat down upon a stone, and continued sitting nine days and nights, in the open air, under the sunlight and moonlight and falling showers. It was where now stands the city of **Eleusis**, then the home of an old man named **Celeus**. He was out in the field, gathering acorns and blackberries, and sticks for his fire. His little girl was driving home their two goats, and as she passed the goddess, who appeared in the guise of an old woman, she said to her, "Mother,"—and the name was sweet to the ears of Ceres,— "why do you sit here alone upon the rocks?" The old man also stopped, though his load was heavy, and begged her to come into his cottage, such as it was. She declined, and he urged her. "Go in peace," she replied, "and be happy in your daughter; I have lost mine." As she spoke, tears—or something like tears, for the gods never weep—fell down her cheeks upon her bosom. The compassionate old man and his child wept with her. Then said he, "Come with us, and despise not our humble roof; so may your daughter be restored to you in safety." "Lead on," said she, "I cannot resist that appeal!" So she rose from the stone and went with them.

As they walked he told her that his only son, a little boy, lay very sick, feverish, and sleepless. She stooped and gathered some poppies. As they entered the cottage, they found all in great distress, for the boy seemed past hope of recovery. Metanira, his mother, received her kindly, and the goddess stooped and kissed the lips of the sick child. Instantly the paleness left his face, and healthy vigor returned to his body. The whole family were delighted—that is, the father, mother, and little girl, for they were all; they had no servants. They spread the table, and put upon it curds and cream, apples, and **honey in the comb**. While they ate, Ceres mingled **poppy juice** in the milk of the boy.

When night came and all was still, she arose, and taking the sleeping boy, moulded his limbs with her hands, and uttered over him three times a solemn charm, then went and laid him in the ashes. His mother, who had been watching what her guest was doing, sprang forward with a cry and snatched the child from the fire. Then Ceres assumed her own form, and a divine splendor shone all around. While they were overcome with astonishment, she said, "Mother, you have been cruel in your fondness to your son. I would have made him immortal, but you have frustrated my attempt. Nevertheless, he shall be great and useful. He shall teach men the use of the plough, and the rewards which labor can win from the cultivated soil." So saying, she wrapped a cloud about her, and, mounting her chariot, rode away.

Narration and Discussion

You may have heard this story before, but not the part about Venus and Cupid setting off these events. Do you think that takes some of the blame away from Pluto?

If you have not heard this story before, what do you think Ceres should do next? What about Proserpine? Is there any way she could escape from Pluto and the underworld?

Something to think about: Celeus and his family welcomed Ceres into their home, much as Baucis and Philemon did. What are the differences between the stories?

Creative narration: Act out a newscast with a "Missing Persons" report on Proserpine. You might also want to interview Celeus and his family.

(Lesson 19) Proserpine (Second Part)

Introduction

The gods and nature creatures are all frantic to get the Proserpine situation fixed, as Ceres' grief has caused everything on earth to dry up and stop producing. But even after Pluto agrees to send her home, one small problem remains.

Vocabulary

girdle: belt

waft it: let it be carried gently through the air

votary: faithful worshiper

cleft: split open

to procure the restitution of her daughter: to get her daughter back

pomegranate: a fruit containing sweet red flesh and edible seeds

Eleusinian mysteries: secret religious rites

allegory: a story in which one character or object stands for something else. What **is the difference between an allegory and a parable?** An allegory is longer and more complex, like *Pilgrim's Progress*; the characters represent abstract ideas such as "Faithful" and "Mercy." A parable is shorter and has one clear message, such as "love your neighbour."

Names

Arethusa: another naiad (and her fountain or spring) of Sicily

Alpheus: a river god, and the river of the same name (see Part Five)

"Spring": probably **Iris**, the goddess of the rainbow

Triptolemus: In other accounts, the name of the baby was Demophon, and Triptolemus was his brother. However, in this version they are the same person.

Dis: another name for Pluto

Places

Elis: a region of Greece

Erebus: Erebus is the original god of darkness (see **Lesson 2**), but the name also refers to the underworld ruled by Pluto

Reading

Part One

Ceres continued her search for her daughter, passing from land to land, and across seas and rivers, till at length she returned to Sicily, whence she at first set out, and stood by the banks of the River Cyane, where Pluto made himself a passage with his prize to his own dominions. The river nymph would have told the goddess all she had witnessed, but dared not, for fear of Pluto; so she only ventured to take up the **girdle** which Proserpine had dropped in her flight, and **waft it** to the feet of the mother. Ceres, seeing this, was no longer in doubt of her loss, but she did not yet know the cause, and laid the blame on the innocent land. "Ungrateful soil," said she, "which I have endowed with fertility and clothed with herbage and nourishing grain, no more shall you enjoy my favors." Then the cattle died, the plough broke in the furrow, the seed failed to come up; there was too much sun, there was too much rain; the birds stole the seeds—thistles and brambles were the only growth.

Part Two: Arethusa's Story

Seeing this, the fountain **Arethusa** interceded for the land.

"Goddess," said she, "blame not the land; it opened unwillingly to yield a passage to your daughter. I can tell you of her fate, for I have seen her. This is not my native country; I came hither from **Elis**. I was a woodland nymph, and delighted in the chase. They praised my beauty, but I cared nothing for it, and rather boasted of my hunting exploits. One day I was returning from the wood, heated with exercise, when I came to a stream silently flowing, so clear that you might count the pebbles on the bottom. The willows shaded it, and the grassy bank sloped down to the water's edge. I approached, I touched the water with my foot. I stepped in knee-deep, and not content with that, I laid my garments on the willows and went in. While I sported in the water, I heard an indistinct murmur coming up as out of the depths of the stream: and made haste to escape to the nearest bank. The voice said, 'Why do you fly, Arethusa? I am **Alpheus**, the god of this stream.' I ran, he pursued; he was not more swift than I, but he was stronger, and gained upon me, as my strength failed.

"At last, exhausted, I cried for help to Diana. 'Help me, goddess! help your **votary**!' The goddess heard, and wrapped me suddenly in a thick cloud. The river god looked now this way and now that, and twice came close to me, but could not find me. 'Arethusa! Arethusa!' he cried. Oh, how I trembled,—like a lamb that hears the wolf growling outside the fold. A cold sweat came over me, my hair flowed down in streams; where my foot stood there was a pool. In short, in less time than it takes to tell it I became a fountain. But in this form Alpheus knew me and attempted to mingle his stream with mine. Diana **cleft** the ground, and I, endeavoring to escape him, plunged into the cavern, and through the [deepest parts] of the earth, came out here in Sicily. While I passed through the lower parts of the earth, I saw your Proserpine. She was sad, but no longer showing alarm in her countenance. Her look was such as became a queen—the queen of **Erebus**; the powerful bride of the monarch of the realms of the dead."

Part Three

When Ceres heard this, she stood for a while like one stupefied; then turned her chariot towards heaven, and hastened to present herself before the throne of Jove. She told the story of her bereavement, and implored Jupiter to interfere **to procure the restitution of her daughter**. Jupiter consented on one condition, namely, that Proserpine should not during her stay in the lower world have taken any food; otherwise, the Fates forbade her release. Accordingly, Mercury was sent, accompanied by **"Spring,"** to demand Proserpine of Pluto.

The wily monarch consented; but, alas! the maiden had taken a **pomegranate** which Pluto offered her, and had sucked the sweet pulp from a few of the seeds. This was enough to prevent her complete release; but a compromise was made, by which she was to pass half the time with her mother, and the rest with her husband Pluto.

Ceres allowed herself to be pacified with this arrangement, and restored the earth to her favor. Now she remembered Celeus and his family, and her promise to his infant son **Triptolemus**. When the boy grew up, she taught him the use of the plough, and how to sow the seed. She took him in her chariot, drawn by winged dragons, through all the countries of the earth, imparting to mankind valuable grains, and the knowledge of agriculture. After his return, Triptolemus built a magnificent temple to Ceres in Eleusis, and established the worship of the goddess, under the name of the **Eleusinian mysteries**, which, in the splendor and solemnity of their observance, surpassed all other religious celebrations among the Greeks.

Part Four

There can be little doubt of this story of Ceres and Proserpine being an **allegory**. Proserpine signifies the seed-corn which when cast into the ground lies there concealed—that is, she is carried off by the god of the underworld. It reappears—that is, Proserpine is restored to her mother, [and] Spring leads her back to the light of day.

Milton [mentions] the story of Proserpine in "Paradise Lost," Book IV, [where he says that the Garden of Eden was even more beautiful than the one where Proserpine gathered flowers]:

"The birds their quire apply; airs, vernal airs,

Breathing the smell of field and grove, attune

The trembling leaves...Not that fair field

Of Enna where Proserpine gathering flowers,

 Herself a fairer flower, by gloomy **Dis**

 Was gathered, which cost Ceres all that pain

 To seek her through the world; nor that sweet grove

Of Daphne by Orontes, and the inspired

Castalian spring, might with this paradise

Of Eden strive."

[*omission for length*]

Narration and Discussion

In *Heroes of Asgard* (**Year Four Lesson 26**), Loki was sent to rescue Iduna, who had been kidnapped. Are there any other similarities in the two stories?

Something to think about: Bulfinch's explanation of what the allegory means is a little different from that of others who simply say that Proserpine represents the returning spring (rather than the seed itself). Does one or the other make more sense to you?

Creative narration #1: Dramatize the scene between the gods, when Ceres arrives to demand the release of Proserpine.

Creative narration #2: If you did a newscast for the last Lesson, you could do a sequel, interviewing Proserpine and anyone else involved.

(Lesson 20) Glaucus and Scylla

Introduction

The next two stories are about falling in love with something, or someone, very different from yourself. Sometimes that works out well; other times, not so much.

In this first one, a fisherman named Glaucus eats a strange plant that makes him crave seawater, and so he jumps in and undergoes a transformation into a "sea-green deity." He falls in love with a nymph named Scylla, but that does not end well at all.

Vocabulary

palate: upper part of the mouth

laving: bathing

metamorphosis: transformation

in this strain: like this

as we shall see…: Those who have read *Tanglewood Tales* will already know the story of the sailors who landed on Circe's island (from the *Odyssey*). As this volume does not include those stories, we refer you to **Further Reading** at the end of the book.

Be not diffident: Don't be so modest

gambolling beasts, the victims of her art: Circe was known to turn people into animals, and these were some of her experiments.

Thus she destroyed six of the companions of Ulysses: Also in the *Odyssey*.

Names

Glaucus: pronounced GLOCK-us

Oceanus and Tethys…: See **Year Six Lesson 2**.

Scylla [#1]: pronounced SEE-lah. Bulfinch calls her a "beautiful maiden," but in other versions of the story she is a naiad, or nymph.

Circe (Sur-see): an enchantress (see note above)

Aeneas: He would grow up to be one of the heroes of the Trojan war.

Reading

Part One

Glaucus was a fisherman. One day he had drawn his nets to land, and had taken a great many fishes of various kinds. So he emptied his net, and proceeded to sort the fishes on the grass. The place where he stood was a beautiful island in the river, a solitary spot, uninhabited, and not used for pasturage of cattle, nor ever visited by any but himself. On a sudden, the fishes, which had been laid on the grass, began to revive and move their fins as if they were in the water; and while he looked on astonished, they one and all moved off to the water, plunged in, and swam away.

He did not know what to make of this, whether some god had done it or some secret power in the herbage. "What herb has such a power?" he exclaimed; and gathering some of it, he tasted it. Scarce had the juices of the plant reached his **palate** when he found himself agitated with a longing desire for the water. He could no longer restrain himself, but bidding farewell to earth, he plunged into the stream.

The gods of the water received him graciously, and admitted him to the honor of their society. They obtained the consent of **Oceanus and Tethys, the sovereigns of the sea**, that all that was mortal in him should be washed away. A hundred rivers poured their waters over him. Then he lost all sense of his former nature and all consciousness. When he recovered, he found himself changed in form and mind. His hair was sea-green, and trailed behind him on the water; his shoulders grew broad, and what had been thighs and legs assumed the form of a fish's tail. The sea-gods complimented him on the change of his appearance, and he fancied himself rather a good-looking personage.

Part Two

One day Glaucus saw the beautiful maiden **Scylla [#1]**, the favorite of the water-nymphs, rambling on the shore, and when she had found a sheltered nook, **laving** her limbs in the clear water. He fell in love with her, and showing himself on the surface, spoke to her, saying such things as he thought most likely to win her to stay; for she turned to run immediately on the sight of him, and ran till she had gained a cliff overlooking the sea. Here she stopped and turned round to see whether it was a god or a sea animal, and observed with wonder his shape and color.

Glaucus, partly emerging from the water, and supporting himself against a rock, said, "Maiden, I am no monster, nor a sea animal, but a god; and neither Proteus nor Triton ranks higher than I. Once I was a mortal, and followed the sea for a living; but now I belong wholly to it." Then he told the story of his **metamorphosis**, and how he had been promoted to his present dignity, and added, "But what avails all this if it fails to move your heart?" He was going on **in this strain**, but Scylla turned and hastened away.

Glaucus was in despair, but it occurred to him to consult the enchantress **Circe**. Accordingly he repaired to her island—the same where afterwards Ulysses landed, **as we shall see in one of our later stories**. After mutual salutations, he said, "Goddess, I entreat your pity; you alone can relieve the pain I suffer. The power of herbs I know as well as any one, for it is to them I owe my change of form. I love Scylla. I am ashamed to tell you how I have sued and promised to her, and how scornfully she has treated me. I beseech you to use your incantations, or potent herbs, if they are more prevailing, not to cure me of my love,—for that I do not wish,—but to make her share it and yield me a like return." To which Circe replied, for she was not insensible to the attractions of the sea-green deity, "You had better pursue a willing object; you are worthy to be sought, instead of having to seek in vain. **Be not diffident**, know your own worth. I protest to you that even I, goddess though I be, and learned in the virtues of plants and spells, should not know how to refuse you. If she scorns you, scorn her; meet one who is ready to meet you half way, and thus make a due return to both at once." To these words Glaucus replied, "Sooner shall trees grow at the bottom of the ocean, and sea-weed on the top of the mountains, than I will cease to love Scylla, and her alone."

Part Three

The goddess was indignant, but she could not punish him, neither did she wish to do so, for she liked him too well; so she turned all her wrath against her rival, poor Scylla. She took plants of poisonous powers and mixed them together, with incantations and charms. Then she passed through the crowd of **gambolling beasts, the victims of her art**, and proceeded to the coast of Sicily, where Scylla lived.

There was a little bay on the shore to which Scylla used to resort, in the heat of the day, to breathe the air of the sea, and to bathe in its waters. Here the goddess poured her poisonous mixture, and muttered over it incantations of mighty power. Scylla came as usual and plunged into the water up to her waist. What was her horror to perceive a brood of serpents and barking monsters surrounding her! At first she could not imagine they were a part of herself, and tried to run from them, and to drive them away; but as she ran she carried them with her, and when she tried to touch her limbs, she found her hands touch only the yawning jaws of monsters. Scylla remained rooted to the spot. Her temper grew as ugly as her form, and she took pleasure in devouring hapless mariners who came within her grasp. **Thus she destroyed six of the companions of Ulysses**, and tried to wreck the ships of **Aeneas**, till at last she was turned into a rock, and as such still continues to be a terror to mariners.

[*omission for length and content*]

Narration and Discussion

What should you probably not do if you see fish jumping back into the water?

Why do you think Scylla ran from Glaucus?

Did anyone in this story end up getting what they wanted?

Creative narration: Write some diary entries for a) Scylla or b) Glaucus.

Further exploration: Various artists in the modern world have painted this story, including Rubens (warning: nudity), Turner, and Waterhouse (look for his painting *Circe Invidiosa*). Imagine that you have been hired to show a scene from the story on a clay vase, or as a sculpture. What scene would you choose? What might it look like?

Chapter Eight

(Lesson 21) Pygmalion

Introduction

On the subject of finding love with someone outside of your own group or species, there isn't anything much stranger than a story of falling in love with a statue. However, the ending is a happy one.

Vocabulary

a statue of ivory: later sources call her **Galatea (#1)**

raiment: clothing

became her: looked beautiful on her

cloths of Tyrian dye: Purple cloth is mentioned in the Bible (Acts 16:14).

festival of Venus: Warning: this is not a family-friendly holiday.

votary: worshiper

nuptials: wedding, marriage

Names

Pygmalion: an artist who thought there could never be a perfect woman

Paphos: In Ovid's version of the story, Paphos was the daughter of Pygmalion and Galatea; others say he was their son but that they also had another daughter. At any rate, the city of **Paphos** is on the southwest coast of the island of Cyprus.

Places

Cyprus: a large island in the Mediterranean Sea

Reading

Part One: Pygmalion

Pygmalion saw so much to blame in women that he came at last to abhor [them all], and resolved to live unmarried. He was a sculptor, and had made with wonderful skill **a statue of ivory**, so beautiful that no living woman came anywhere near it. It was indeed the perfect semblance of a maiden that seemed to be alive, and only prevented from moving by modesty. His art was so perfect that it concealed itself and its product looked like the workmanship of nature.

Pygmalion admired his own work, and at last fell in love with the counterfeit creation. Oftentimes he laid his hand upon it as if to assure himself whether it were living or not, and could not even then believe that it was only ivory. He caressed it, and gave it presents such as young girls love,—bright shells and polished stones, little birds and flowers of various hues, beads and amber. He put **raiment** on its limbs, and jewels on its fingers, and a necklace about its neck. To the ears he hung earrings and strings of pearls upon the breast. Her dress **became her**, and she looked not less charming than when unattired. He laid her on a couch spread with **cloths of Tyrian dye**, and called her his wife, and put her head upon a pillow of the softest feathers, as if she could enjoy their softness.

The **festival of Venus** was at hand—a festival celebrated with great pomp at

Cyprus. [Sacrifices] were offered, the altars smoked, and the odor of incense filled the air. When Pygmalion had performed his part in the solemnities, he stood before the altar and timidly said, "Ye gods, who can do all things, give me, I pray you, for my wife"—he dared not say "my ivory virgin," but said instead— "one like my ivory virgin."

Venus, who was present at the festival, heard him and knew the thought he would have uttered; and as an omen of her favor, caused the flame on the altar to shoot up thrice in a fiery point into the air.

Part Two

When he returned home, he went to see his statue, and leaning over the couch, gave a kiss to the mouth. It seemed to be warm. He pressed its lips again, he laid his hand upon the limbs; the ivory felt soft to his touch and yielded to his fingers [*omission*].

While he stands astonished and glad, though doubting, and fears he may be mistaken, again and again with a lover's ardor he touches the object of his hopes.

It was indeed alive! The veins when pressed yielded to the finger and again resumed their roundness. Then at last the **votary** of Venus found words to thank the goddess, and pressed his lips upon lips as real as his own. The virgin felt the kisses and blushed, and opening her timid eyes to the light, fixed them at the same moment on her lover. Venus blessed the **nuptials** she had formed, and from this union **Paphos** was born, from whom the city, sacred to Venus, received its name.

[*omission for length and content*]

Part Three: Poetic and Dramatic Versions After Bulfinch

The story of "Pygmalion," brief as it is, has inspired operas, ballets, and paintings. Most famously, George Bernard Shaw's play *Pygmalion* tells the story not of an artist and his statue, but of a wealthy, educated man and a poor woman he intends to "re-shape" into something more to his liking. This was the story that became the musical play and film "My Fair Lady."

The English poet Robert Graves (1895-1985) wrote two poems on the subject of "Pygmalion," one of which, "Pygmalion to Galatea," is quite beautiful. Here are the last two stanzas:

> As you are various, so be woman:
> Graceful in going as well armed in doing.
> Be witty, kind, enduring, unsubjected:
> Without you I keep heavy house.
> So be woman!
>
> As you are woman, so be lovely:
> As you are lovely, so be various,

Merciful as constant, constant as various.
So be mine, as I yours for ever.

Narration and Discussion

Was Pygmalion foolish to treat his statue as if it were alive?

After Galatea came to life, do you think they were happy together?

Creative narration: Imagine a busy-morning breakfast conversation in Pygmalion's house.

Something to think about: People in myths seemed to do a great deal of chasing after each other (sometimes under the influence of magic arrows and potions). Have you read about any truly happy couples so far? What do you think their secret was? (If you can dramatize an interview, or imagine a conversation or a letter from one character to another, that could also be a **Creative narration**.)

(Lesson 22) Venus and Adonis

Introduction

Even Venus can get caught in her own traps.

[*Note: The story of Dryope is contained in the original text, but it has been omitted here for both length and suitability.*]

Vocabulary

> **prodigious:** great
>
> **shall be annually renewed:** The Adonia festival was celebrated every year, in midsummer. To remember this event, women would sow fast-growing plants (such as lettuce and fennel) in baskets or shards of pottery, and leave them in the hot sun where they would sprout quickly, but then wither and die. The women would then grieve the "death of Adonis."
>
> **bloody hue:** deep red

Names

> **Adonis:** The Greek name "Adonis" comes from the Canaanite word for "lord," which is closely related to the Hebrew word "Adonai," used in the Bible and also translated

"lord." An "Adonis" now refers to an extremely handsome youth.

the Fates: three goddesses who shape human destiny

Places

Paphos: see "Pygmalion"

Cnidos: or Knidos; a city in what is now Turkey

Amathos: or Amathus, a city in Cyprus

Reading

Part One: Venus and Adonis

Venus, playing one day with her boy Cupid, wounded [herself] with one of his arrows. She pushed him away, but the wound was deeper than she thought. Before it healed she beheld **Adonis**, and was captivated with him. She no longer took any interest in her favorite resorts—**Paphos**, and **Cnidos**, and **Amathos**, rich in metals. She absented herself even from heaven, for Adonis was dearer to her than heaven. Him she followed and bore him company.

She who used to love to recline in the shade, with no care but to cultivate her charms, now rambles through the woods and over the hills, dressed like the huntress Diana; and calls her dogs, and chases hares and stags, or other game that it is safe to hunt, but keeps clear of the wolves and bears, reeking with the slaughter of the herd.

She charged Adonis, too, to beware of such dangerous animals. "Be brave towards the timid," said she; "courage against the courageous is not safe. Beware how you expose yourself to danger and put my happiness to risk. Attack not the beasts that Nature has armed with weapons. I do not value your glory so high as to consent to purchase it by such exposure. Your youth, and the beauty that charms Venus, will not touch the hearts of lions and bristly boars. Think of their terrible claws and **prodigious** strength!" [*omission for content*] Having given him this warning, she mounted her chariot drawn by swans, and drove away through the air.

But Adonis was too noble to heed such counsels. The dogs had roused a wild boar from his lair, and the youth threw his spear and wounded the animal with a sidelong stroke. The beast drew out the weapon with his jaws, and rushed after Adonis, who turned and ran; but the boar overtook him, and buried his tusks in his side, and stretched him, dying, upon the plain.

Part Two

Venus, in her swan-drawn chariot, had not yet reached Cyprus, when she heard coming up through mid-air the groans of her beloved, and turned her white-winged coursers back to earth. As she drew near and saw from on high his lifeless body bathed in blood, she alighted and, bending over it, beat her breast and tore her hair.

Reproaching **the Fates**, she said, "Yet theirs shall be but a partial triumph; memorials of my grief shall endure, and the spectacle of your death, my Adonis, and of my lamentations **shall be annually renewed**. Your blood shall be changed into a flower; that consolation none can envy me." Thus speaking, she sprinkled nectar on the blood; and as they mingled, bubbles rose as in a pool on which raindrops fall, and in an hour's time there sprang up a flower of **bloody hue** like that of the pomegranate.

But it is short-lived. It is said the wind blows the blossoms open, and afterwards blows the petals away; so it is called Anemone, or Wind Flower, from the cause which assists equally in its production and its decay.

Milton alludes to the story of Venus and Adonis in his "Comus":

"Beds of hyacinth and roses
Where young Adonis oft reposes,
Waxing well of his deep wound
In slumber soft, and on the ground
Sadly sits th' Assyrian queen;" etc.

Part Three: Some Things Bulfinch Didn't Mention

Although Bulfinch often quotes the romantic poets, he misses one obvious literary reference: Shelley's poetic tribute to his friend John Keats, titled *Adonais*. Here are a few lines from the poem:

A breaking billow; even whilst we speak

Is it not broken? On the withering flower

The killing sun smiles brightly: on a cheek

The life can burn in blood, even while the heart may break.

In Spenser's epic poem *The Faerie Queene* (AO students will read this in Year Seven), the walls of Castle Joyous are decorated with tapestries showing the story of Adonis.

And, finally, William Shakespeare wrote a poem called "Venus and Adonis" early in his career. (It is not recommended for young readers.) Apparently it was very popular at the time, though critics afterward were not as generous with their praise. C. S. Lewis said that the Venus of Shakespeare's poem reminded him of certain scary female relatives.

Narration and Discussion

Why did Venus begin to dress differently and take up hunting?

Have you ever been so captivated with something that you had time for nothing else, even things you used to enjoy? Or have you been left behind by someone who found a more absorbing friend or interest?

> "Any friendship, even if it be friendship between mother and child, which is over-fond and exclusive, making the one continually necessary to the other, and shutting out other claims of duty and affection, is suspect of the clear Conscience." (Charlotte Mason, *Ourselves Book 2*, p. 21)

Can you think of any other stories about this situation? (One novel about friendship and loyalty is *Sarah and Katie*, by Dori White.)

Creative narration: Imagine a conversation between women planting lettuce as a tribute to Adonis. How might they explain what they are doing?

[*Note: The next story in the book is Apollo and Hyacinthus. It is omitted here for reasons of content.*]

Chapter Nine

(Lesson 23) Ceyx and Halcyone (First Half)

Introduction

King Ceyx, the adored husband of Queen Halcyone, is grieving the death of his brother, and has some big questions for the gods. When he plans to visit a faraway temple, Halcyone does not have a good feeling about it, but there is little she can do.

Vocabulary

direful prodigies: gloomy omens, strange signs

Aeolus being the god of the winds: Bulfinch assumes that Halcyone's father is the god of the winds, but other sources say there is a confusion of names, and that there was more than one Aeolus.

before the moon…: before two months pass

presentiment: feeling about the future, usually bad

Stygian: very dark (refers to the River Styx in the underworld)

surge: great wave

Names

Ceyx: pronounced SAY-ix

Halcyone (or Alcyone): pronounced Al-kee-oh-nee or Al-see-oh-nee

Aeolus: the king of **Aeolia** (see the note under Vocabulary)

Places

Thessaly: another name for **Aeolia**

Carlos in Ionia: Claros (Clarus), located in **Ionia** (on the eastern side of the **Mediterranean Sea**). Claros was the site of a temple to Apollo, and was believed to be a center of prophecy similar to that at **Delphi**. ["Carlos" seems to be a misspelling.]

Reading

Part One

Ceyx was king of **Thessaly**, where he reigned in peace, without violence or wrong. He was son of Hesperus, the Day-star, and the glow of his beauty reminded one of his father.

Halcyone, the daughter of **Aeolus**, was his wife, and devotedly attached to him.

Now Ceyx was in deep affliction for the loss of his brother, and **direful prodigies** following his brother's death made him feel as if the gods were hostile to him. He thought best, therefore, to make a voyage to **Carlos in Ionia**, to consult the oracle of Apollo. But as soon as he disclosed his intention to his wife Halcyone, a shudder ran through her frame, and her face grew deadly pale. "What fault of mine, dearest husband, has turned your affection from me? Where is that love of me that used to be uppermost in your thoughts? Have you learned to feel easy in the absence of Halcyone? Would you rather have me away?" She also endeavored to discourage him, by describing the violence of the winds, which she had known familiarly when she lived at home in her father's house,—**Aeolus being the god of the winds**, and having as much as he could do to restrain them. "They rush together," said she, "with such fury that fire flashes from the conflict. But if you must go," she added, "dear husband, let me go with you, otherwise I shall suffer not only the real evils which you must encounter, but those also which my fears suggest."

These words weighed heavily on the mind of King Ceyx, and it was no less his own wish than hers to take her with him, but he could not bear to expose her to the dangers of the sea. He answered, therefore, consoling her as well as he could, and finished with these words: "I promise, by the rays of my father the Day-star, that if fate permits I will return **before the moon shall have twice rounded her orb**." When he had thus spoken, he ordered the vessel to be drawn out of the ship house, and the oars and sails to be put aboard. When Halcyone saw these preparations she shuddered, as if with a **presentiment** of evil. With tears and sobs she said farewell, and then fell senseless to the ground.

Ceyx would still have lingered, but now the young men grasped their oars and pulled vigorously through the waves, with long and measured strokes. Halcyone raised her streaming eyes, and saw her husband standing on the deck, waving his hand to her. She answered his signal till the vessel had receded so far that she could no longer distinguish his form from the rest. When the vessel itself could no more be seen, she strained her eyes to catch the last glimmer of the sail, till that too disappeared. Then, retiring to her chamber, she threw herself on her solitary couch.

Part Two

Meanwhile they glide out of the harbor, and the breeze plays among the ropes. The seamen draw in their oars, and hoist their sails.

When half or less of their course was passed, as night drew on, the sea began to whiten with swelling waves, and the east wind to blow a gale. The master gave the word to take in sail, but the storm forbade obedience, for such is the roar of the winds and waves his orders are unheard.

The men, of their own accord, busy themselves to secure the oars, to strengthen the ship, to reef the sail. While they thus do what to each one seems best, the storm increases. The shouting of the men, the rattling of the shrouds, and the dashing of the waves, mingle with the roar of the thunder. The swelling sea seems lifted up to the heavens, to scatter its foam among the clouds; then sinking away to the bottom assumes the color of the shoal—a **Stygian** blackness. The vessel shares all these changes. It seems like a wild beast that rushes on the spears of the hunters. Rain falls in torrents, as if the skies were coming down to unite with the sea. When the lightning ceases for a moment, the night seems to add its own darkness to that of the storm; then comes the flash, rending the darkness asunder, and lighting up all with a glare. Skill fails, courage sinks, and death seems to come on every wave.

The men are stupefied with terror. The thought of parents, and kindred, and pledges left at home, comes over their minds. Ceyx thinks of Halcyone. No name but hers is on his lips, and while he yearns for her, he yet rejoices in her absence. Presently the mast is shattered by a stroke of lightning, the rudder broken, and the triumphant **surge** curling over looks down upon, the wreck, then falls, and crushes it to fragments. Some of the seamen, stunned by the stroke, sink, and rise no more; others cling to fragments of the wreck.

Ceyx, with the hand that used to grasp the scepter, holds fast to a plank, calling for help,—alas, in vain,—upon his father and his father-in-law. But oftenest on his lips was the name of Halcyone. To her his thoughts cling. He prays that the waves may bear his body to her sight, and that it may receive burial at her hands. At length the waters overwhelm him, and he sinks.

The Day-star looked dim that night. Since it could not leave the heavens, it shrouded its face with clouds.

Part Three

In the meanwhile Halcyone, ignorant of all these horrors, counted the days till her husband's promised return.

Now she gets ready the garments which he shall put on, and now what she shall wear when he arrives. To all the gods she offers frequent incense, but more than all to Juno. For her husband, who was no more, she prayed incessantly: that he might be safe; that he might come home; that he might not, in his absence, see any one that he would love better than her. But of all these prayers, the last was the only one destined to be granted.

[*It sounds like this story has come to a rather depressing full stop. But there is a second half.*]

Narration and Discussion

Have you ever had a really bad feeling about something, and it turned out afterwards that you were right? Should Ceyx have insisted on going to the temple, even after Halcyone expressed her fears and even fainted before the ship left?

"No name but hers is on his lips, and while he yearns for her, he yet rejoices in her absence." Why?

Something big to think about: Does God always answer our prayers for loved ones' safety? How should we respond when we have prayed but bad things still happen?

> Now, I saw that there stood behind the multitude a chariot and a couple of horses waiting for Faithful, who (so soon as his enemies had slain him) was taken up into it, and straightway was carried up through the clouds with sound of trumpet the nearest way to the Celestial Gate. But as for Christian... he sang, saying,
>
> "Well, Faithful, thou hast faithfully professed
>
> Unto thy Lord, with whom thou shalt be blest,
>
> When faithless ones, with all their vain delights,
>
> Are crying out under their hellish plights.
>
> Sing, Faithful, sing, and let thy name survive;
>
> For though they killed thee, thou art yet alive."
>
> (John Bunyan, *The Pilgrim's Progress*)

For those who like to write: Bulfinch (mostly translating from the Roman writer

Ovid) uses his storytelling skills very well in this passage. What are some words or phrases that help you to see, hear, or even feel what is happening?

(Lesson 24) Ceyx and Halcyone (Second Half)

Introduction

Halcyone will not be consoled after the death of her husband. *"Halcyone is no more,"* she answers, *"she perished with her Ceyx."* (But there is a happy ending.)

Vocabulary

ebony: dark wood

ever and anon: continually

despatch: this word can have different meanings; here it just means "send"

stagnant: lifeless, unmoving (in this case, literally putting people to sleep)

counterfeiting forms: imitating someone else

visage: face

shade: ghost

smote her breast and [tore] her garments: ancient customs that show grief

presaging: warning, predicting

foreboded: warned

epitaph: something written on a tomb

mole: sea wall, embankment to keep the water away from the land

stem its violent ingress: keep the waves from roaring in

seven placid days: This week or two of calm weather is called (for obvious reasons) the Halcyon Days. The phrase is also used now to mean a happy, peaceful time.

Names

Iris: the goddess of the rainbow, who also acted as a messenger for the gods

Somnus: the Roman god of sleep. (In Greek, his name is Hypnos.)

Morpheus: the god of dreams

Icelos (Icelus): a dream spirit

Phantasos: a son of Somnus who appears as objects in dreams

Places

Cimmerian country: a region of west Asia

River Lethe (LEE-thee): a river of the underworld, whose name means "forgetfulness"

Trachine: Trachis, later called **"Heraclea Trachinia"** in honour of Heracles

Reading

Part One

The goddess, at length, could not bear any longer to be pleaded with for one already dead, and to have hands raised to her altars that ought rather to be offering funeral rites. So, calling **Iris**, she said, "Iris, my faithful messenger, go to the drowsy dwelling of **Somnus**, and tell him to send a vision to Halcyone in the form of Ceyx, to make known to her the event."

Iris puts on her robe of many colors, and tingeing the sky with her bow, seeks the palace of the King of Sleep. Near the **Cimmerian country**, a mountain cave is the abode of the dull god Somnus. Here Phoebus dares not come, either rising, at midday, or setting. Clouds and shadows are exhaled from the ground, and the light glimmers faintly. The bird of dawning, with crested head, never there calls aloud to Aurora, nor watchful dog, nor more sagacious goose disturbs the silence. No wild beast, nor cattle, nor branch moved with the wind, nor sound of human conversation, breaks the stillness. Silence reigns there; but from the bottom of the rock the **River Lethe** flows, and by its murmur invites to sleep. Poppies grow abundantly before the door of the cave, and other herbs, from whose juices Night collects slumbers, which she scatters over the darkened earth. There is no gate to the mansion, to creak on its hinges, nor any watchman; but in the midst a couch of black **ebony**, adorned with black plumes and black curtains. There the god reclines, his limbs relaxed with sleep. Around him lie dreams, resembling all various forms, as many as the harvest bears stalks, or the forest leaves, or the seashore sand grains.

As soon as the goddess entered and brushed away the dreams that hovered around her, her brightness lit up all the cave. The god, scarce opening his eyes, and **ever and anon** dropping his beard upon his breast, at last shook himself free from himself, and leaning on his arm, inquired her errand,—for he knew who she was. She answered, "Somnus, gentlest of the gods, tranquillizer of minds and soother of care-worn hearts, Juno sends you her commands that you **despatch** a dream to Halcyone, in the city of

Trachine, representing her lost husband and all the events of the wreck."

Having delivered her message, Iris hasted away, for she could no longer endure the **stagnant** air, and as she felt drowsiness creeping over her, she made her escape, and returned by her bow the way she came. Then Somnus called one of his numerous sons,— **Morpheus**,—the most expert in **counterfeiting forms**, and in imitating the walk, the countenance, and mode of speaking, even the clothes and attitudes most characteristic of each. But he only imitates men, leaving it to another to [im]personate birds, beasts, and serpents. Him they call **Icelos**; and **Phantasos** is a third, who turns himself into rocks, waters, woods, and other things without life. These wait upon kings and great personages in their sleeping hours, while others move among the common people. Somnus chose, from all the brothers, Morpheus, to perform the command of Iris; then laid his head on his pillow and yielded himself to grateful repose.

Part Two

Morpheus flew, making no noise with his wings, and soon came to the [city], where, laying aside his wings, he assumed the form of Ceyx. Under that form, but pale like a dead man, naked, he stood before the couch of the wretched wife. His beard seemed soaked with water, and water trickled from his drowned locks. Leaning over the bed, tears streaming from his eyes, he said, "Do you recognize your Ceyx, unhappy wife, or has death too much changed my **visage**? Behold me, know me, your husband's **shade**, instead of himself. Your prayers, Halcyone, availed me nothing. I am dead. No more deceive yourself with vain hopes of my return. The stormy winds sunk my ship in the Aegean Sea, waves filled my mouth while it called aloud on you. No uncertain messenger tells you this, no vague rumor brings it to your ears. I come in person, a shipwrecked man, to tell you my fate. Arise! give me tears, give me lamentations, let me not go down to Tartarus unwept." To these words Morpheus added the voice, which seemed to be that of her husband; he seemed to pour forth genuine tears; his hands had the gestures of Ceyx.

Halcyone, weeping, groaned, and stretched out her arms in her sleep, striving to embrace his body, but grasping only the air. "Stay!" she cried; "whither do you fly? let us go together." Her own voice awakened her. Starting up, she gazed eagerly around, to see if he was still present, for the servants, alarmed by her cries, had brought a light.

When she found him not, she **smote her breast and [tore] her garments**. She cares not to unbind her hair, but tears it wildly. Her nurse asks what is the cause of her grief. "Halcyone is no more," she answers, "she perished with her Ceyx. Utter not words of comfort, he is shipwrecked and dead. I have seen him, I have recognized him. I stretched out my hands to seize him and detain him. His shade vanished, but it was the true shade of my husband. Not with the accustomed features, not with the beauty that was his, but pale, naked, and with his hair wet with sea-water, he appeared to wretched me. Here, in this very spot, the sad vision stood,"—and she looked to find the mark of his footsteps. "This it was, this that my **presaging** mind **foreboded**, when I implored him not to leave me, to trust himself to the waves. Oh, how I wish, since thou wouldst go, thou hadst taken me with thee! It would have been far better. Then I should have had no remnant of life to spend without thee, nor a separate death to die. If I could bear to live and struggle to endure, I should be more cruel to myself than the sea has been to me. But I will not struggle, I will not be separated from thee, unhappy husband. This time, at least, I will keep thee company. In death, if one tomb may not include us, one **epitaph** shall; if I may not lay my ashes with thine, my name, at least, shall not be separated."

Her grief forbade more words, and these were broken with tears and sobs.

Part Three

It was now morning. She went to the seashore, and sought the spot where she last saw him, on his departure. "While he lingered here, and cast off his tacklings, he gave me his last kiss." While she reviews every object, and strives to recall every incident, looking out over the sea, she descries an indistinct object floating in the water. At first she was in doubt what it was, but by degrees the waves bore it nearer, and it was plainly the body of a man. Though unknowing of whom, yet, as it was of some shipwrecked one, she was deeply moved, and gave it her tears, saying, "Alas! unhappy one, and unhappy, if such there be, thy wife!" Borne by the waves, it came nearer. As she more and more nearly views it, she trembles more and more. Now, now it approaches the shore. Now marks that she recognizes appear. It is her husband! Stretching out her trembling hands towards it, she exclaims, "O dearest husband, is it thus you return to me?"

There was built out from the shore a **mole**, constructed to break the assaults of the sea, and **stem its violent ingress**. She leaped upon this barrier and (it was wonderful she could do so) she flew, and striking the air with wings produced on the instant, skimmed along the surface of the water, an unhappy bird. As she flew, her throat poured forth sounds full of grief, and like the voice of one lamenting. When she touched the mute and bloodless body, she enfolded its beloved limbs with her new-formed wings, and tried to give kisses with her [hard] beak. Whether Ceyx felt it, or whether it was only the action of the waves, those who looked on doubted, but the body seemed to raise its head. But indeed he did feel it, and by the pitying gods both of them were changed into birds.

They mate and have their young ones. For **seven placid days**, in winter time, Halcyone broods over her nest, which floats upon the sea. Then the way is safe to seamen. Aeolus guards the winds and keeps them from disturbing the deep. The sea is given up, for the time, to his grandchildren.

[*omission for length and content*]

Part Four

Milton in his "Hymn on the Nativity," thus alludes to [this story]:

"But peaceful was the night
Wherein the Prince of light
    His reign of peace upon the earth began;
The winds with wonder whist
Smoothly the waters kist
    Whispering new joys to the mild ocean,
Who now hath quite forgot to rave
While birds of calm sit brooding on the charmed wave."

Keats, also, in "Endymion," says:

"O magic sleep! O comfortable bird
That broodest o'er the troubled sea of the mind
Till it is hushed and smooth."

Narration and Discussion

Why do you think the gods went through such a complicated process to send a message to Halcyone? (Do you think these gods understood people very well?)

How did this sad story turn into a "why story" for its first hearers?

Something to think about: The two poetry selections each have interesting thoughts to pick out. In the Milton poem, see if you can figure out the connection between Christ's Nativity and the Halcyon Days. In the second, Keats compares a comforting, peaceful sleep (after a time of worry) to the same thing. How do you find rest when your mind is a "troubled sea?"

Creative narration: Imagine a conversation between an older sailor and a young one, explaining about the "Halcyon Days."

Chapter Ten

(Lesson 25) Vertumnus and Pomona

Introduction

For once we have a cheerful story about a god trying to win the affections of a Hamadryad. Their story is cheerful; but the story he tells her about Iphis is definitely not. Still, whatever it takes…

Vocabulary

curtail: cut back

graft: a shoot or twig inserted into the stem of another plant

free from that which Venus inspires: not interested in romantic love

corn: grain

spurn them: push them away

prudent: wise

favor his suit: tell Anaxarete to favour him

domestics: servants

on her threshold: in her doorway

vernal: springtime

comely: handsome

prevailed: succeeded

owned a mutual flame: admitted that she loved him too

Names

Pomona: the Roman goddess of fruit and nut trees. Her name has come down to us in the word "pome," meaning a fruit with a core such as an apple or pear.

Sylvanus: the Roman god of woodlands, fields, and flocks

Vertumnus: the god of seasons, change, and plant growth

Helen: the legendary Helen of Troy

Penelope: the wife of Ulysses (Odysseus) in the *Odyssey*

Iphis: a shepherd

Anaxarete: can be pronounced "An-AX-a-reet."

Thomson: James Thomson (1700-1748), Scottish poet

Places

Salamis: an ancient city on Cyprus

Reading

The Hamadryads were Wood-nymphs. **Pomona** was of this class, and no one excelled her in love of the garden and the culture of fruit. She cared not for forests and rivers, but loved the cultivated country, and trees that bear delicious apples. Her right hand bore for its weapon not a javelin, but a pruning-knife. Armed with this, she busied herself at one time to repress the too luxuriant growths, and **curtail** the branches that straggled out of place; at another, to split the twig and insert therein a **graft**, making the branch adopt a nursling not its own. She took care, too, that her favorites should not suffer from drought, and led streams of water by them, that the thirsty roots might drink. This occupation was her pursuit, her passion; and she was **free from that which Venus inspires**.

She was not without fear of the country people, and kept her orchard locked, and allowed not men to enter. The Fauns and Satyrs would have given all they possessed to win her, and so would old **Sylvanus**, who looks young for his years, and Pan, who wears a garland of pine leaves around his head. But **Vertumnus** loved her best of all; yet he sped no better than the rest. O how often, in the disguise of a reaper, did he bring her **corn** in a basket, and looked the very image of a reaper! With a hay band tied round him, one would think he had just come from turning over the grass. Sometimes he would have an ox-goad in his hand, and you would have said he had just unyoked his weary oxen. Now he bore a pruning-hook, and personated a vine-dresser; and again, with a ladder on his shoulder, he seemed as if he was going to gather apples. Sometimes he trudged along as a discharged soldier, and again he bore a fishing-rod, as if going to fish. In this way he gained admission to her again and again, and fed his passion with the sight of her.

One day he came in the guise of an old woman, her gray hair surmounted with a cap, and a staff in her hand. She entered the garden and admired the fruit. "It does you credit, my dear," she said, and kissed her, not exactly with an old woman's kiss. She [the woman] sat down on a bank, and looked up at the branches laden with fruit which hung over her. Opposite was an elm entwined with a vine loaded with swelling grapes. She praised the tree and its associated vine, equally. "But," said she, "if the tree stood alone, and had no vine clinging to it, it would have nothing to attract or offer us but its useless leaves. And equally the vine, if it were not twined round the elm, would lie prostrate on the ground. Why will you not take a Lesson from the tree and the vine, and consent to unite yourself with some one? I wish you would. **Helen** herself had not more numerous suitors, nor **Penelope**, the wife of shrewd Ulysses. Even while you **spurn them**, they court you,—rural deities and others of every kind that frequent these mountains. But if you are **prudent** and want to make a good alliance, and will let an old woman advise you,—who loves you better than you have any idea of,—dismiss all the rest and accept Vertumnus, on my recommendation. I know him as well as he knows himself. He is not a wandering deity, but belongs to these mountains. Nor is he like too many of the lovers nowadays, who love any one they happen to see; he loves you, and you only. Add to this, he is young and handsome, and has the art of assuming any shape he pleases, and can make himself just what you command him. Moreover, he loves the same things that you do, delights in gardening, and handles your apples with admiration. But *now* he cares nothing for fruits nor flowers, nor anything else, but only yourself. Take pity on him, and fancy him speaking now with my mouth.

"Remember that the gods punish cruelty, and that Venus hates a hard heart, and will visit such offences sooner or later. To prove this, let me tell you a story, which is well known in Cyprus to be a fact; and I hope it will have the effect to make you more merciful."

Part Two: The "Old Woman" Tells a Story

"**Iphis** was a young man of humble parentage, who saw and loved **Anaxarete**, a noble lady of the ancient family of Teucer. He struggled long with his passion, but when he found he could not subdue it, he came a suppliant to her mansion. First he told his passion to her nurse, and begged her as she loved her foster-child to **favor his suit**. And then he tried to win her **domestics** to his side. Sometimes he committed his vows to written tablets, and often hung at her door garlands which he had moistened with his tears. He stretched himself **on her threshold**, and uttered his complaints to the cruel bolts and bars. She was deafer than the surges which rise in the November gale; harder than steel from the German forges, or a rock that still clings to its native cliff. She mocked and laughed at him, adding cruel words to her ungentle treatment, and gave not the slightest gleam of hope.

"Iphis could not any longer endure the torments of hopeless love, and, standing before her doors, he spake these last words: 'Anaxarete, you have conquered, and shall no longer have to bear my importunities. Enjoy your triumph! Sing songs of joy, and bind your forehead with laurel,—you have conquered! I die; stony heart, rejoice! This at least I can do to gratify you and force you to praise me; and thus shall I prove that the love of you left me but with life. Nor will I leave it to rumor to tell you of my death. I will come myself, and you shall see me die, and feast your eyes on the spectacle."

[*omission for content: Iphis kills himself*]

"The mournful funeral passed through the town, and the pale corpse was borne on a bier to the place of the funeral pile. By chance the home of Anaxarete was on the street where the procession passed, and the lamentations of the mourners met the ears of her whom the avenging deity had already marked for punishment.

"'Let us see this sad procession,' said she, and mounted to a turret, whence through an open window she looked upon the funeral. Scarce had her eyes rested upon the form of Iphis stretched on the bier, when they began to stiffen, and the warm blood in her body to become cold. Endeavoring to step back, she found she could not move her feet; trying to turn away her face, she tried in vain; and by degrees all her limbs became stony like her heart. That you may not doubt the fact, the statue still remains, and stands in the temple of Venus at **Salamis**, in the exact form of the lady. Now think of these things, my dear, and lay aside your scorn and your delays, and accept a lover. So may neither the **vernal** frosts blight your young fruits, nor furious winds scatter your blossoms!"

When Vertumnus had spoken thus, he dropped the disguise of an old woman, and stood before her in his proper person, as a **comely** youth. It appeared to her like the sun bursting through a cloud. He would have renewed his entreaties, but there was no need; his arguments and the sight of his true form **prevailed**, and the Nymph no longer resisted, but **owned a mutual flame**.

Part Three

[*omission for length*]

Pomona was the especial patroness of the Apple orchard, [but she] was also regarded as presiding over other fruits, and as such is invoked by **Thomson** [in his poem "Summer," part of his longer work "The Seasons"]:

"Bear me, Pomona, to thy citron groves,
To where the lemon and the piercing lime,
With the deep orange, glowing through the green,
Their lighter glories blend. Lay me reclined
Beneath the spreading tamarind, that shakes,
Fanned by the breeze, its fever-cooling fruit."

[A few lines later, he also praises the pineapple:

"Witness, thou best Anana, thou the pride
Of vegetable life, beyond whate'er
The poets imaged in the golden age:
Quick let me strip thee of thy tufty coat,
Spread thy ambrosial stores, and feast with Jove!"]

Narration and Discussion

Does Pomona remind you of any of the Norse gods? What are the similarities?

In what creative ways did Vertumnus try to win her love?

If you were Pomona, would the story about Iphis and Anaxarete persuade you to return the love of Vertumnus, or is it a bit over the top?

Creative narration #1: This story would be a good one to act out.

For those who like to write: Write some lines in praise of your favorite fruit or vegetable, in the style of Thomson.

Chapter Eleven
(Lesson 26) Cupid and Psyche (First Half)

Introduction

After that bit of entertainment from Pomona and Vertumnus, we have a story with a little more depth, and one that has inspired other writers including C. S. Lewis. It was not written down by Ovid (the source for many of Bulfinch's stories), but comes from the writings of Apuleius, who lived in the Roman province of Numidia (Algeria) in the second century A.D. (a bit after Plutarch). Edith Hamilton (in her book *Mythology*) says that Apuleius wrote this story more as entertainment than out of religious belief. Others have called it an early example of a fairy tale, as you might guess from an opening like "A certain king and queen had three daughters. The charms of the two elder were more than common, but the beauty of the youngest was so wonderful…".

Vocabulary

poverty: poorness, referring to its limits

homage: worship

chaplets: garlands

ambrosial locks: divine curls

usurp: steal

contumacious: stubborn, disobedient

reap a mortification: earn shame

quiver: bag or container that holds arrows

silken ringlets: soft curls

plebeian: peasant

apartment: room

nuptial pomp: wedding celebration

august: imposing, impressive

down: feathers

admonitions: instructions

nectareous: delicious, sweet

Names

the youngest: As we will find out, her name is **Psyche**. This can be pronounced in various ways, but a common English pronunciation is "SYE-kee." Others prefer to voice the "p." **Psyche** is a Greek word which can be translated as breath, life, or soul.

That royal shepherd: Paris of Troy, called the "shepherd prince"

Zephyr: the god of the west wind; the word also means a gentle breeze

Reading

Part One

A certain king and queen had three daughters. The charms of the two elder were more than common, but the beauty of **the youngest** was so wonderful that the **poverty** of language is unable to express its due praise. The fame of her beauty was so great that strangers from neighboring countries came in crowds to enjoy the sight, and looked on her with amazement, paying her that **homage** which is due only to Venus herself. In fact Venus found her altars deserted, while men turned their devotion to this young virgin. As she passed along, the people sang her praises, and strewed her way with **chaplets** and flowers.

This perversion of homage due only to the immortal powers to the exaltation of a mortal gave great offence to the real Venus. Shaking her **ambrosial locks** with indignation, she exclaimed, "Am I then to be eclipsed in my honors by a mortal girl? In vain then did **that royal shepherd**, whose judgment was approved by Jove himself, give me the palm of beauty over my illustrious rivals, Pallas and Juno. But she shall not so quietly **usurp** my honors. I will give her cause to repent of so unlawful a beauty."

Thereupon she calls her winged son Cupid, mischievous enough in his own nature, and rouses and provokes him yet more by her complaints. She points out Psyche to him and says, "My dear son, punish that **contumacious** beauty; give thy mother a revenge as sweet as her injuries are great; infuse into the bosom of that haughty girl a passion for some low, mean, unworthy being, so that she may **reap a mortification** as great as her present exultation and triumph."

Cupid prepared to obey the commands of his mother. There are two fountains in Venus's garden, one of sweet waters, the other of bitter. Cupid filled two amber vases, one from each fountain, and suspending them from the top of his **quiver**, hastened to the chamber of Psyche, whom he found asleep. He shed a few drops from the bitter fountain over her lips, though the sight of her almost moved him to pity; then touched her side with the point of his arrow. At the touch she awoke, and opened eyes upon Cupid (himself invisible), which so startled him that in his confusion he wounded himself with his own arrow. Heedless of his wound, his whole thought now was to repair the mischief he had done, and he poured the balmy drops of joy over all her **silken ringlets**.

Part Two

Psyche, henceforth frowned upon by Venus, derived no benefit from all her charms. True, all eyes were cast eagerly upon her, and every mouth spoke her praises; but neither king, royal youth, nor **plebeian** presented himself to demand her in marriage. Her two elder sisters of moderate charms had now long been married to two royal princes; but Psyche, in her lonely **apartment**, deplored her solitude, sick of that beauty which, while it procured abundance of flattery, had failed to awaken love.

Her parents, afraid that they had unwittingly incurred the anger of the gods, consulted the oracle of Apollo, and received this answer: "The virgin is destined for the bride of no mortal lover. Her future husband awaits her on the top of the mountain. He is a monster whom neither gods nor men can resist."

This dreadful decree of the oracle filled all the people with dismay, and her parents abandoned themselves to grief. But Psyche said, "Why, my dear parents, do you now lament me? You should rather have grieved when the people showered upon me undeserved honors, and with one voice called me a Venus. I now perceive that I am a victim to that name. I submit. Lead me to that rock to which my unhappy fate has destined me." Accordingly, all things being prepared, the royal maid took her place in the procession, which more resembled a funeral than a **nuptial pomp**, and with her parents, amid the lamentations of the people, ascended the mountain, on the summit of which they left her alone, and with sorrowful hearts returned home.

Part Three

While Psyche stood on the ridge of the mountain, panting with fear and with eyes full of tears, the gentle **Zephyr** raised her from the earth and bore her with an easy motion into a flowery dale. By degrees her mind became composed, and she laid herself down on the grassy bank to sleep. When she awoke refreshed with sleep, she looked round and beheld near by a pleasant grove of tall and stately trees. She entered it, and in the midst discovered a fountain, sending forth clear and crystal waters, and [close] by, a magnificent palace whose **august** front impressed the spectator that it was not the work of mortal hands, but the happy retreat of some god. Drawn by admiration and wonder, she approached the building and ventured to enter. Every object she met filled her with pleasure and amazement. Golden pillars supported the vaulted roof, and the walls were enriched with carvings and paintings representing beasts of the chase and rural scenes, adapted to delight the eye of the beholder. Proceeding onward, she perceived that besides the apartments of state there were others filled with all manner of treasures, and beautiful and precious productions of nature and art.

While her eyes were thus occupied, a voice addressed her, though she saw no one, uttering these words: "Sovereign lady, all that you see is yours. We whose voices you hear are your servants and shall obey all your commands with our utmost care and diligence. Retire, therefore, to your chamber and repose on your bed of **down**, and when you see fit repair to the bath. Supper awaits you in the adjoining alcove when it pleases you to take your seat there."

Part Four

Psyche gave ear to the **admonitions** of her vocal attendants, and after repose and the refreshment of the bath, seated herself in the alcove, where a table immediately presented itself, without any visible aid from waiters or servants, and covered with the greatest delicacies of food and the most **nectareous** wines. Her ears too were feasted with music from invisible performers; of whom one sang, another played on the lute, and all closed in the wonderful harmony of a full chorus.

She had not yet seen her destined husband. He came only in the hours of darkness and fled before the dawn of morning, but his accents were full of love, and inspired a like passion in her. She often begged him to stay and let her behold him, but he would not consent. On the contrary he charged her to make no attempt to see him, for it was his pleasure, for the best of reasons, to keep concealed. "Why should you wish to behold me?" he said; "have you any doubt of my love? have you any wish ungratified? If you saw me, perhaps you would fear me, perhaps adore me, but all I ask of you is to love me. I would rather you would love me as an equal than adore me as a god."

Part Five

This reasoning somewhat quieted Psyche for a time, and while the novelty lasted she felt quite happy. But at length the thought of her parents, left in ignorance of her fate, and of her sisters, precluded from sharing with her the delights of her situation, preyed on her mind and made her begin to feel her palace as but a splendid prison. When her husband came one night, she told him her distress, and at last drew from him an unwilling consent that her sisters should be brought to see her.

So, calling Zephyr, she acquainted him with her husband's commands, and he, promptly obedient, soon brought them across the mountain down to their sister's valley. They embraced her and she returned their caresses. "Come," said Psyche, "enter with me my house and refresh yourselves with whatever your sister has to offer." Then taking their hands she led them into her golden palace, and committed them to the care of her numerous train of attendant voices, to refresh them in her baths and at her table, and to show them all her treasures. The view of these celestial delights caused envy to enter their [hearts], at seeing their young sister possessed of such state and splendor, so much exceeding their own.

They asked her numberless questions, among others what sort of a person her husband was. Psyche replied that he was a beautiful youth, who generally spent the daytime in hunting upon the mountains. The sisters, not satisfied with this reply, soon made her confess that she had never seen him. Then they proceeded to fill her bosom with dark suspicions. "Call to mind," they said, "the Pythian oracle that declared you destined to marry a direful and tremendous monster. The inhabitants of this valley say that your husband is a terrible and monstrous serpent, who nourishes you for a while with dainties [so] that he may by and by devour you. Take our advice. Provide yourself with a lamp and a sharp knife; put them in concealment that your husband may not discover them, and when he is sound asleep, slip out of bed, bring forth your lamp, and see for yourself whether what they say is true or not. If it is, hesitate not to cut off the monster's head, and thereby recover your liberty."

Narration and Discussion

What was Cupid's assignment? Did he carry it out successfully?

Why was Psyche so lonely?

Do you think she should take her sisters' advice?

Something to think about: We have never yet seen Cupid (or Eros) as anything but mischievous, usually causing trouble alongside his mother; he is often portrayed as a child. Here he appears as an adult, showing kindness to Psyche and asking to be "loved as an equal." Do you trust him in this new-and-improved form?

Creative narration: Retell the story so far in a creative way (drama, art, songwriting).

(Lesson 27) Cupid and Psyche (Second Half)

Introduction

Note to self from Psyche: if you're determined to peek at your secret husband, at least try not to drop hot lamp oil on him.

Vocabulary

first sleep: In early times, it was apparently common to go to bed early, to get up for a while, and then to go back to sleep.

repaired thither: went there

sickles and rakes: harvesting tools

sultry: hot

allay: lessen

ruminating on: thinking about

propitiate: regain favour

laid up of: suffering from

the inextricable heap: the hopeless mess

margin: edge

approbation: praise

implacable: impossible to please

infernal shades: spirits of the underworld; the dead

satisfied: convinced, sure

precipitate herself headlong: throw herself off

ambrosia: the drink of the gods

these nuptials shall be perpetual: this marriage will last forever

Names

Proserpine: Because of her marriage to Pluto, Proserpine is referred to as the Queen of the Underworld.

Reading

Part One

Psyche resisted these persuasions as well as she could, but they did not fail to have their effect on her mind, and when her sisters were gone, their words and her own curiosity were too strong for her to resist. So she prepared her lamp and a sharp knife, and hid them out of sight of her husband. When he had fallen into his **first sleep**, she silently rose, and, uncovering her lamp, beheld not a hideous monster, but the most beautiful and charming of the gods, with his golden ringlets wandering over his snowy neck and crimson cheek, with two dewy wings on his shoulders, whiter than snow, and with shining feathers like the tender blossoms of spring. As she leaned the lamp over to have a nearer view of his face a drop of burning oil fell on the shoulder of the god, startled with which he opened his eyes and fixed them full upon her; then, without saying one word, he spread his white wings and flew out of the window.

Psyche, in vain endeavoring to follow him, fell from the window to the ground. Cupid, beholding her as she lay in the dust, stopped his flight for an instant and said, "O foolish Psyche, is it thus you repay my love? After having disobeyed my mother's commands and made you my wife, will you think me a monster and cut off my head? But go; return to your sisters, whose advice you seem to think preferable to mine. I inflict no other punishment on you than to leave you forever. Love cannot dwell with suspicion." So saying, he fled away, leaving poor Psyche prostrate on the ground, filling the place with mournful lamentations.

When she had recovered some degree of composure she looked around her, but the palace and gardens had vanished, and she found herself in the open field not far from the city where her sisters dwelt. She **repaired thither** and told them the whole story of her misfortunes, at which, pretending to grieve, those spiteful creatures inwardly rejoiced. "For now," said they, "he will perhaps choose one of us." With this idea, without saying a word of her intentions, each of them rose early the next morning and ascended the mountains, and having reached the top, called upon Zephyr to receive her and bear her to his lord; then leaping up, and not being sustained by Zephyr, fell down the precipice and was dashed to pieces.

Part Two

Psyche meanwhile wandered day and night, without food or repose, in search of her husband. Casting her eyes on a lofty mountain having on its brow a magnificent temple, she sighed and said to herself, "Perhaps my love, my lord, inhabits there," and directed her steps thither.

She had no sooner entered than she saw heaps of corn, some in loose ears and some in sheaves, with mingled ears of barley. Scattered about lay **sickles and rakes**, and all the instruments of harvest, without order, as if thrown carelessly out of the weary reapers' hands in the **sultry** hours of the day. This unseemly confusion the pious Psyche put an end to, by separating and sorting everything to its proper place and kind, believing that she ought to neglect none of the gods, but endeavor by her piety to engage them all in her behalf.

The holy Ceres, whose temple it was, finding her so religiously employed, thus spoke to her: "O Psyche, truly worthy of our pity, though I cannot shield you from the frowns of Venus, yet I can teach you how best to **allay** her displeasure. Go, then, and voluntarily surrender yourself to your lady and sovereign, and try by modesty and submission to win her forgiveness, and perhaps her favor will restore you the husband you have lost."

Psyche obeyed the commands of Ceres and took her way to the temple of Venus, endeavoring to fortify her mind and **ruminating on** what she should say and how best **propitiate** the angry goddess, feeling that the issue was doubtful and perhaps fatal.

Venus received her with angry countenance. "Most undutiful and faithless of servants," said she, "do you at last remember that you really have a mistress? Or have you rather come to see your sick husband, yet **laid up of** the wound given him by his loving wife? You are so ill-favored and disagreeable that the only way you can merit your lover must be by dint of industry and diligence. I will make trial of your housewifery." Then she ordered Psyche to be led to the storehouse of her temple, where was laid up a great quantity of wheat, barley, millet, vetches, beans, and lentils prepared for food for her pigeons, and said, "Take and separate all these grains, putting all of the same kind in a parcel by themselves, and see that you get it done before evening." Then Venus departed and left her to her task.

Part Three

But Psyche, in a perfect consternation at the enormous work, sat [stupefied] and silent, without moving a finger to **the inextricable heap**. While she sat despairing, Cupid stirred up the little ant, a native of the fields, to take compassion on her. The leader of the ant hill, followed by whole hosts of his six-legged subjects, approached the heap, and with the utmost diligence, taking grain by grain, they separated the pile, sorting each kind to its parcel; and when it was all done, they vanished out of sight in a moment.

Venus at the approach of twilight returned from the banquet of the gods, breathing odors and crowned with roses. Seeing the task done, she exclaimed, "This is no work of yours, wicked one, but his, whom to your own and his misfortune you have enticed." So saying, she threw her a piece of black bread for her supper and went away.

Next morning Venus ordered Psyche to be called and said to her, "Behold yonder grove which stretches along the **margin** of the water. There you will find sheep feeding without a shepherd, with golden-shining fleeces on their backs. Go, fetch me a sample of that precious wool gathered from every one of their fleeces."

Psyche obediently went to the riverside, prepared to do her best to execute the command. But the river god inspired the reeds with harmonious murmurs, which seemed to say, "O maiden, severely tried, tempt not the dangerous flood, nor venture among the formidable rams on the other side, for as long as they are under the influence of the rising sun, they burn with a cruel rage to destroy mortals with their sharp horns or rude teeth. But when the noontide sun has driven the cattle to the shade, and the serene spirit of the flood has lulled them to rest, you may then cross in safety, and you will find the woolly gold sticking to the bushes and the trunks of the trees."

Thus the compassionate river god gave Psyche instructions how to accomplish her task, and by observing his directions she soon returned to Venus with her arms full of the golden fleece; but she received not the **approbation** of her **implacable** mistress, who said, "I know very well it is by none of your own doings that you have succeeded in this task, and I am not satisfied yet that you have any capacity to make yourself useful. But I have another task for you. Here, take this box and go your way to the **infernal shades**, and give this box to **Proserpine** and say, 'My mistress Venus desires you to send her a little of your beauty, for in tending her sick son she has lost some of her own.' Be not too long on your errand, for I must paint myself with it to appear at the circle of the gods and goddesses this evening."

Part Four

Psyche was now **satisfied** that her destruction was at hand, being obliged to go with her own feet directly down to Erebus. Wherefore, to make no delay of what was not to be avoided, she goes to the top of a high tower to **precipitate herself headlong**, thus to descend the shortest way to the shades below. But a voice from the tower said to her, "Why, poor unlucky girl, dost thou design to put an end to thy days in so dreadful a manner? And what cowardice makes thee sink under this last danger who hast been so miraculously supported in all thy former?" Then the voice told her how by a certain cave she might reach the realms of Pluto, and how to avoid all the dangers of the road, to pass by Cerberus the three-headed dog, and prevail on Charon, the ferryman, to take her across the black river and bring her back again. But the voice added, "When Proserpine has given you the box filled with her beauty, of all things this is chiefly to be observed by you, that you never once open or look into the box nor allow your curiosity to pry into the treasure of the beauty of the goddesses."

Psyche, encouraged by this advice, obeyed it in all things, and taking heed to her ways travelled safely to the kingdom of Pluto. She was admitted to the palace of Proserpine, and without accepting the delicate seat or delicious banquet that was offered her, but contented with coarse bread for her food, she delivered her message from Venus. Presently the box was returned to her, shut and filled with the precious commodity. Then she returned the way she came, and glad was she to come out once more into the light of day.

But having got so far successfully through her dangerous task, a longing desire seized her to examine the contents of the box. "What," said she, "shall I, the carrier of this divine beauty, not take the least bit to put on my cheeks to appear to more advantage in the eyes of my beloved husband!" So she carefully opened the box, but found nothing there of any beauty at all, but an infernal and truly Stygian sleep, which being thus set free from its prison, took possession of her, and she fell down in the midst of the road, a sleepy corpse without sense or motion.

Part Five

But Cupid, being now recovered from his wound, and not able longer to bear the absence of his beloved Psyche, slipping through the smallest crack of the window of his chamber which happened to be left open, flew to the spot where Psyche lay, and gathering up the sleep from her body closed it again in the box, and waked Psyche with a light touch of one of his arrows. "Again," said he, "hast thou almost perished by the same curiosity. But now perform exactly the task imposed on you by my mother, and I will take care of the rest."

Then Cupid, as swift as lightning penetrating the heights of heaven, presented himself before Jupiter with his supplication. Jupiter lent a favoring ear, and pleaded the cause of the lovers so earnestly with Venus that he won her consent. On this he sent Mercury to bring Psyche up to the heavenly assembly, and when she arrived, handing her a cup of **ambrosia**, he said, "Drink this, Psyche, and be immortal; nor shall Cupid ever break away from the knot in which he is tied, but **these nuptials shall be perpetual**."

Thus Psyche became at last united to Cupid, and in due time they had a daughter born to them whose name was Pleasure.

Part Six

The fable of Cupid and Psyche is usually considered allegorical. The Greek name for a *butterfly* is Psyche, and the same word means the *soul*. There is no illustration of the immortality of the soul so striking and beautiful as the butterfly, bursting on brilliant wings from the tomb in which it has lain, after a dull, grovelling, caterpillar existence, to flutter in the blaze of day and feed on the most fragrant and delicate productions of the spring. Psyche, then, is the human soul, which is purified by sufferings and misfortunes, and is thus prepared for the enjoyment of true and pure happiness.

In works of art Psyche is represented as a maiden with the wings of a butterfly, along with Cupid, in the different situations described in the allegory.

Milton alludes to the story of Cupid and Psyche in the conclusion of his "Comus":

"Celestial Cupid, her famed son, advanced,

Holds his dear Psyche sweet entranced,

After her wandering labors long,

Till free consent the gods among

Make her his eternal bride;

And from her fair unspotted side

Two blissful twins are to be born,

Youth and Joy; so Jove hath sworn."

[*omission for length*]

Narration and Discussion

Psyche made more than one big mistake in this story, but Cupid did not give up. Can you think of other stories of patient and forgiving love?

Something to think about: C. S. Lewis thought that Apuleius was wrong to make the two sisters merely jealous. He said the story made more sense if the sisters came to visit Psyche but could not see a beautiful palace, only grass and rocks; and that this shows how we can lose out if we refuse to "see." Lewis thought about his version of the story for a long time, and finally turned it into a novel, *Till We Have Faces*. (Those who have read Lewis's final *Narnia* book, *The Last Battle*, will remember that he wrote a similar scene involving dwarves.) Do you agree that his idea is an improvement?

Artwork to look for: Paintings inspired by this story include "The Wedding of Cupid and Psyche" by Raphael; "Psyche's Wedding" by Edward Burne-Jones; "Cupid and Psyche" by Anthony van Dyck; and "Psyche Opening the Golden Box" by John William Waterhouse. (Previewing is recommended.)

Other "Don't Peek" stories: "Whitebear Whittington," an American folktale, "Prince Whitebear," (Danish version), or "East of the Sun and West of the Moon," (Norwegian version, included in the *Blue Fairy Book*). "The Crane Wife" is a Japanese folktale retold by Sumiko Yagawa and translated from Japanese by Katherine Paterson, illustrated by Suekichi Akaba. Another retelling of that story is "The Crane Maiden," by Miyoko Matsutani, translated by Alvin Tresselt, illustrated by Chihiro Iwasaki.

Chapter Twelve

(Lesson 28) Cadmus

Introduction

Those who have read *Tanglewood Tales* will remember "The Dragon's Teeth," which centers on the search for Europa, the lost sister of Prince Cadmus. This version moves through that part quickly, and picks up the story with Cadmus's building of Thebes, and his battle with a dragon.

> "Well," Noël went on, "...We did sow those dragon's teeth in Randall's ten-acre meadow, and what do you think has come up?"
>
> "Toadstools, I should think," was Oswald's contemptible rejoinder.
>
> "They have come up a camp of soldiers," said Noël— "*armed men*. So you see it *was* history. We have sowed army-seed, just like Cadmus, and it has come up. It was a very wet night. I dare say that helped it along."
>
> (*The Wouldbegoods*, by E. Nesbit)

Year Five: The Age of Fable

Cadmus is believed by some to be a real figure in history, but said by others to be entirely made up, somewhat like King Arthur. In any case, this is his story as retold by Bulfinch.

Vocabulary

libation: wine or water that is poured on the ground as an offering

profaned by the axe: damaged by cutting

entrails: innards

odious: hateful

If a serpent's life is so dear to the gods: If the gods (especially Mars) are still so angry that I killed that dragon

serpents: snakes, we assume, rather than dragons

Names

his servants: also called **"the Tyrians,"** since they were from Tyre (in Phoenicia)

Semele, Ino: daughters of Cadmus who came to tragic ends (not recommended as student reading)

Actaeon: see **Year Five Lesson 11**

Pentheus: grandson of Cadmus, whose story is told in a play called *The Bacchae*.

Places

Phoenicia: The **Phoenicians** were a people-group living on the eastern side of the **Mediterranean**; they were famous as ship-builders and sailors. **Agenor**, the father of Cadmus, might have been the king of **Tyre** or **Sidon**.

Thebes: (pronounced Theebs): a city in Boeotia, in central Greece, which holds the distinction of being one of the oldest continually inhabited cities in the world.

Castalian cave: There was a spring in the cave where people washed themselves before seeking advice from the **oracle**.

Cephisus (Seh-FIH-sus or Keh-FIH-sus): a river in northern Boeotia

Enchelians: a tribe in **Illyria**

Reading

Part One: Cadmus vs. the Dragon

Jupiter, under the disguise of a bull, had carried away Europa, the daughter of Agenor, king of **Phoenicia**. Agenor commanded his son Cadmus to go in search of his sister, and not to return without her. Cadmus went and sought long and far for his sister, but could not find her, and not daring to return unsuccessful, consulted the oracle of Apollo to know what country he should settle in. The oracle informed him that he should find a cow in the field, and should follow her wherever she might wander, and where she stopped, should build a city and call it **Thebes**.

Cadmus had hardly left the **Castalian cave**, from which the oracle was delivered, when he saw a young cow slowly walking before him. He followed her close, offering at the same time his prayers to [Apollo]. The cow went on till she passed the shallow channel of **Cephisus** and came out into the plain of Panope. There she stood still, and raising her broad forehead to the sky, filled the air with her lowings. Cadmus gave thanks, and stooping down kissed the foreign soil, then lifting his eyes, greeted the surrounding mountains. Wishing to offer a sacrifice to Jupiter, he sent **his servants** to seek pure water for a **libation**.

Near by there stood an ancient grove which had never been **profaned by the axe**, in the midst of which was a cave, thick covered with the growth of bushes, its roof forming a low arch, from beneath which burst forth a fountain of purest water. In the cave lurked a horrid serpent with a crested head and scales glittering like gold. His eyes shone like fire, his body was swollen with venom, he vibrated a triple tongue, and showed a triple row of teeth. No sooner had the **Tyrians** dipped their pitchers in the fountain, and the in-gushing waters made a sound, than the glittering serpent raised his head out of the cave and uttered a fearful hiss. The vessels fell from their hands, the blood left their cheeks, they trembled in every limb. The serpent, twisting his scaly body in a huge coil, raised his head so as to overtop the tallest trees, and while the Tyrians from terror could neither fight nor fly, slew some with his fangs, others in his folds, and others with his poisonous breath.

Cadmus, having waited for the return of his men till midday, went in search of them. His covering was a lion's hide, and besides his javelin he carried in his hand a lance, and in his breast a bold heart, a surer reliance than either.

When he entered the wood, and saw the lifeless bodies of his men, and the monster with his bloody jaws, he exclaimed, "O faithful friends, I will avenge you, or share your death." So saying, he lifted a huge stone and threw it with all his force at the serpent. Such a block would have shaken the wall of a fortress, but it made no impression on the monster.

Cadmus next threw his javelin, which met with better success, for it penetrated the serpent's scales, and pierced through to his **entrails**. Fierce with pain, the monster turned back his head to view the wound, and attempted to draw out the weapon with his mouth, but broke it off, leaving the iron point rankling in his flesh. His neck swelled with rage, bloody foam covered his jaws, and the breath of his nostrils poisoned the air around. Now he twisted himself into a circle, then stretched himself out on the ground like the trunk of a fallen tree. As he moved onward, Cadmus retreated before him, holding his spear opposite to the monster's opened jaws. The serpent snapped at the weapon and attempted to bite its iron point. At last Cadmus, watching his chance, thrust the spear at a moment when the animal's head thrown back came against the trunk of a tree, and so succeeded in pinning him to its side. His weight bent the tree as he struggled in the agonies of death.

Part Two: The Dragon's Teeth

While Cadmus stood over his conquered foe, contemplating its vast size, a voice was heard (from whence he knew not, but he heard it distinctly) commanding him to take the dragon's teeth and sow them in the earth. He obeyed.

He made a furrow in the ground, and planted the teeth, destined to produce a crop of men. Scarce had he done so when the clods began to move, and the points of spears to appear above the surface. Next helmets with their nodding plumes came up, and next the shoulders and breasts and limbs of men with weapons, and in time a harvest of armed warriors. Cadmus, alarmed, prepared to encounter a new enemy; but one of them said to him, "Meddle not with our civil war." With that, he who had spoken smote one of his earth-born brothers with a sword, and he himself fell pierced with an arrow from another. The latter fell victim to a fourth, and in like manner the whole crowd dealt with each other till all fell, slain with mutual wounds, except five survivors. One of these cast away his weapons and said, "Brothers, let us live in peace!" These five joined with Cadmus in building his city, to which they gave the name of Thebes.

Part Three: "All That Theban Woe"

Cadmus obtained in marriage Harmonia, the daughter of Venus. The gods left Olympus to honor the occasion with their presence, and Vulcan presented the bride with a necklace of surpassing brilliancy, his own workmanship.

But a fatality hung over the family of Cadmus in consequence of his killing the serpent sacred to Mars. **Semele** and **Ino**, his daughters, and **Actaeon** and **Pentheus**, his grandchildren, all perished unhappily, and Cadmus and Harmonia quitted Thebes, now grown **odious** to them, and emigrated to the **country of the Enchelians**, who received them with honor and made Cadmus their king. But the misfortunes of their children still weighed upon their minds; and one day Cadmus exclaimed, "**If a serpent's life is so dear to the gods**, I would I were myself a serpent." No sooner had he uttered the words than he began to change his form. Harmonia beheld it and prayed to the gods to let her share his fate. Both became **serpents**. They live in the woods, but mindful of their origin, they neither avoid the presence of man nor do they ever injure anyone.

[*omission for length*]

Narration and Discussion

Hawthorne's retelling doesn't mention Cadmus turning into a snake; but he does hint at the tragedies of his family: "It seemed as if he were doomed to lose everybody whom he loved, or to see them perish in one way or another." Can you think of anyone in Scripture who lost their friends or family? How did they react?

Creative narration: The English poet Matthew Arnold (1822-1888) wrote a wonderful poem called "Cadmus and Harmonia," which you will now understand when you come across it. Here is the beginning: can you add more lines? Note: there are some rhymes, but not every line has to rhyme.

> Far, far from here,
> The Adriatic breaks in a warm bay
> Among the green Illyrian hills; and there
> The sunshine in the happy glens is fair,
> And by the sea, and in the brakes.
> The grass is cool, the sea-side air
> Buoyant and fresh, the mountain flowers
> More virginal and sweet than ours.
> And there, they say, two bright and aged snakes,
> Who once were Cadmus and Harmonia,
> Bask in the glens or on the warm sea-shore,
> In breathless quiet, after all their ills…

(Lesson 29) The Myrmidons

Introduction

This story is framed as a tale told by Aeacus, the king of Aegina, to a visiting friend who notices that many things have changed since his last visit. Whatever happened to so and so? And who are all these new people who, coincidentally, all seem to be about the same age?

"You're not going to believe it," says Aeacus.

Year Five: The Age of Fable

Vocabulary

Trojan war: the subject of Homer's epic poem the *Iliad*

zealous: enthusiastic, passionate about something; a zealous follower would obey without asking questions

unscrupulous: dishonest, unprincipled

seek assistance: He was looking for soldiers to join his army.

pestilence: disease

credible: believable

Next the disease attacked the country people…: Bulfinch notes: "This description of the plague is copied by Ovid from the account which Thucydides, the Greek historian, gives of the plague of Athens." The Plague of Athens (in 430 B.C.) is also described in Plutarch's *Life of Pericles*.

expedient: helpful; a good idea

charged it on the place of their abode: blamed it on their houses

supplication: prayer

minute: tiny

chide: scold, complain to

tenacious of their gains: keeping a firm hold on what they have

Names

Achilles: the son of **Peleus**, and the grandson of **Aeacus**

Cephalus: Not the same Cephalus as the husband of Procris

Aeacus: the son of **Jupiter (Zeus)** and the nymph **Aegina**, and father of **Peleus**, **Telamon**, and **Phocus**.

Minos (American, **MEE-nohs**; British, **MY-nohs**): the king of Crete

Places

Athens: now the capital city of Greece

Aegina: an island in the Saronic Gulf, 17 miles (27 km) from **Athens**. It is named for **Aegina**, the mother of **Aeacus**.

Crete: a large island near mainland Greece

Reading

Prologue

The Myrmidons were the soldiers of **Achilles**, in the **Trojan war**. From them all **zealous** and **unscrupulous** followers of a political chief are called by that name, down to this day. But the origin of the Myrmidons would not give one the idea of a fierce and bloody race, but rather of a laborious and peaceful one.

Part One: Aeacus's Story

Cephalus, king of **Athens**, arrived in the island of **Aegina** to **seek assistance** of his old friend and ally **Aeacus**, the king, in his war with **Minos**, king of **Crete**. Cephalus was most kindly received, and the desired assistance readily promised. "I have people enough," said **Aeacus**, "to protect myself and spare you such a force as you need."

"I rejoice to see it," replied Cephalus, "and my wonder has been raised, I confess, to find such a host of youths as I see around me, all apparently of about the same age. Yet there are many individuals whom I previously knew, that I look for now in vain. What has become of them?"

Aeacus groaned, and replied with a voice of sadness, "I have been intending to tell you, and will now do so, without more delay, that you may see how from the saddest beginning a happy result sometimes flows.

"Those whom you formerly knew are now dust and ashes! A plague sent by angry Juno devastated the land. She hated it because it bore the name of one of her husband's female favorites. While the disease appeared to spring from natural causes we resisted it, as we best might, by natural remedies; but it soon appeared that the **pestilence** was too powerful for our efforts, and we yielded. At the beginning the sky seemed to settle down upon the earth, and thick clouds shut in the heated air. For four months together a deadly south wind prevailed. The disorder affected the wells and springs; thousands of snakes crept over the land and shed their poison in the fountains.

"The force of the disease was first spent on the lower animals—dogs, cattle, sheep, and birds. The luckless ploughman wondered to see his oxen fall in the midst of their work, and lie helpless in the unfinished furrow. The wool fell from the bleating sheep, and their bodies pined away. The horse, once foremost in the race, contested the palm no more, but groaned at his stall and died an inglorious death. The wild boar forgot his rage, the stag his swiftness, the bears no longer attacked the herds. Everything languished; dead bodies lay in the roads, the fields, and the woods; the air was poisoned by them. I tell you what is hardly **credible**, but neither dogs nor birds would touch them, nor starving wolves. Their decay spread the infection.

"**Next the disease attacked the country people, and then the dwellers in the**

city. At first the cheek was flushed, and the breath drawn with difficulty. The tongue grew rough and swelled, and the dry mouth stood open with its veins enlarged and gasped for the air. Men could not bear the heat of their clothes or their beds, but preferred to lie on the bare ground; and the ground did not cool them, but, on the contrary, they heated the spot where they lay. Nor could the physicians help, for the disease attacked them also, and the contact of the sick gave them infection, so that the most faithful were the first victims. At last all hope of relief vanished, and men learned to look upon death as the only deliverer from disease."

Part Two: The Plague Worsens

"Then they gave way to every inclination, and cared not to ask what was **expedient**, for nothing was expedient. All restraint laid aside, they crowded around the wells and fountains and drank till they died, without quenching thirst. Many had not strength to get away from the water, but died in the midst of the stream, and others would drink of it notwithstanding. Such was their weariness of their sickbeds that some would creep forth, and if not strong enough to stand, would die on the ground. They seemed to hate their friends, and got away from their homes, as if, not knowing the cause of their sickness, they **charged it on the place of their abode**. Some were seen tottering along the road, as long as they could stand, while others sank on the earth, and turned their dying eyes around to take a last look, then closed them in death.

"What heart had I left me, during all this, or what ought I to have had, except to hate life and wish to be with my dead subjects? On all sides lay my people strewn like over-ripened apples beneath the tree, or acorns under the storm-shaken oak. You see yonder a temple on the height. It is sacred to Jupiter. O how many offered prayers there, husbands for wives, fathers for sons, and died in the very act of **supplication**! How often, while the priest made ready for sacrifice, the victim fell, struck down by disease without waiting for the blow!

"At length all reverence for sacred things was lost. Bodies were thrown out unburied, wood was wanting for funeral piles, men fought with one another for the possession of them. Finally there were none left to mourn; sons and husbands, old men and youths, perished alike, unlamented."

Part Three: A New Beginning

"Standing before the altar I raised my eyes to heaven. 'O Jupiter,' I said, 'if thou art indeed my father, and art not ashamed of thy offspring, give me back my people, or take me also away!' At these words a clap of thunder was heard. 'I accept the omen,' I cried; 'O may it be a sign of a favorable disposition towards me!'

"By chance there grew by the place where I stood an oak with wide-spreading branches, sacred to Jupiter. I observed a troop of ants busy with their labor, carrying **minute** grains in their mouths and following one another in a line up the trunk of the tree. Observing their numbers with admiration, I said, 'Give me, O father, citizens as numerous as these, and replenish my empty city.'

"The tree shook and gave a rustling sound with its branches, though no wind agitated them. I trembled in every limb, yet I kissed the earth and the tree. I would not confess to myself that I hoped, yet I did hope.

"Night came on and sleep took possession of my frame oppressed with cares. The tree stood before me in my dreams, with its numerous branches all covered with living, moving creatures. It seemed to shake its limbs and throw down over the ground a multitude of those industrious grain-gathering animals, which appeared to gain in size, and grow larger and larger, and by and by to stand [upright], lay aside their superfluous legs [*omission*], and finally to assume the human form.

"Then I awoke, and my first impulse was to **chide** the gods who had robbed me of a sweet vision and given me no reality in its place. Being still in the temple, my attention was caught by the sound of many voices without; a sound of late unusual to my ears. While I began to think I was yet dreaming, **Telamon**, my son, throwing open the temple gates, exclaimed: 'Father, approach, and behold things surpassing even your hopes!'

"I went forth; I saw a multitude of men, such as I had seen in my dream, and they were passing in procession in the same manner. While I gazed with wonder and delight they approached and kneeling hailed me as their king. I paid my vows to Jove, and proceeded to allot the vacant city to the new-born race, and to parcel out the fields among them I called them "Myrmidons," from the ant (*myrmex*) from which they sprang.

"You have seen these persons; their dispositions resemble those which they had in their former shape. They are a diligent and industrious race, eager to gain, and **tenacious of their gains**. Among them you may recruit your forces. They will follow you to the war, young in years and bold in heart."

Narration and Discussion

The people of Aegina blamed Juno for the plague that swept their island. Might there have been some other reason for the spread of illness?

Do you think Aeacus was a good king? What is your evidence?

Going further: For the people of Aegina, this was the "why-story" of their place. According to the legend, the island began under an angry cloud of revenge, but was then shown mercy and re-populated. Aegina became an important center of trade, and is believed to have been the first city-state in Europe to issue coins. Think about the place you come from (country? state? town?), and see if you can find out its back-story—legendary or factual. Does it help you understand your people a little better?

Year Five: The Age of Fable

Chapter Thirteen

(Lesson 30) Three Stories of Love in Vain

Introduction

We now return to one of the favorite themes of Greek and Roman myth: the search for love, often with the wrong person (such as the enemy who is attacking your father's kingdom). These three stories also repeat a common pattern, that of some unfortunate (or sometimes fortunate) person who is turned into something else.

Vocabulary

lock: bit of hair

repair: go

deportment: manner

hardly mistress of herself: hardly able to keep it together

clement: merciful

dowry: money brought by a bride to her husband

spoil: treasure

animosity: hostility, hate

attended her in the chase: helped her in hunting

shade passed the Stygian river: spirit passed through the underworld

smote their breasts: as a sign of grief

Names

Scylla [#2]: Not the Scylla who was turned into a sea-monster.

Places

Megara (MEG-ah-ra): A town in Greece; in the myths, it is described as more of a kingdom.

Reading

Part One: Nisus and Scylla

Minos, king of Crete, made war upon **Megara**. Nisus was king of Megara, and **Scylla [#2]** was his daughter. The siege had now lasted six months, and the city still held out, for it was decreed by fate that it should not be taken so long as a certain purple **lock**, which glittered among the hair of King Nisus, remained on his head.

There was a tower on the city walls, which overlooked the plain where Minos and his army were encamped. To this tower Scylla used to **repair**, and look abroad over the tents of the hostile army. The siege had lasted so long that she had learned to distinguish the persons of the leaders. Minos, in particular, excited her admiration. Arrayed in his helmet, and bearing his shield, she admired his graceful **deportment**; if he threw his javelin, skill seemed combined with force in the discharge; if he drew his bow, Apollo himself could not have done it more gracefully. But when he laid aside his helmet, and in his purple robes bestrode his white horse with its [bright coverings], and reined in its foaming mouth, the daughter of Nisus was **hardly mistress of herself**; she was almost frantic with admiration. She envied the weapon that he grasped, the reins that he held. She felt as if she could, if it were possible, go to him through the hostile ranks; she felt an impulse to cast herself down from the tower into the midst of his camp, or to open the gates to him, or to do anything else, so only it might gratify Minos.

As she sat in the tower, she talked thus with herself: "I know not whether to rejoice or grieve at this sad war. I grieve that Minos is our enemy; but I rejoice at any cause that brings him to my sight. Perhaps he would be willing to grant us peace, and receive me as a hostage. I would fly down, if I could, and alight in his camp, and tell him that we yield ourselves to his mercy. But then, to betray my father! No! rather would I never see Minos again. And yet no doubt it is sometimes the best thing for a city to be conquered, when the conqueror is **clement** and generous.

"Minos certainly has right on his side. I think we shall be conquered; and if that must be the end of it, why should not love unbar the gates to him, instead of leaving it to be done by war? Better spare delay and slaughter if we can. And O, if any one should wound or kill Minos! No one surely would have the heart to do it; yet ignorantly, not knowing him, one might.

"I will, I will surrender myself to him, with my country as a **dowry**, and so put an end to the war. But how? The gates are guarded, and my father keeps the keys; he only stands in my way. O that it might please the gods to take him away! But why ask the gods to do it? Another woman, loving as I do, would remove with her own hands whatever stood in the way of her love. And can any other woman dare more than I? I would encounter fire and sword to gain my object; but here there is no need of fire and sword. I only need my father's purple lock. More precious than gold to me, that will give me all I wish."

While she thus reasoned, night came on, and soon the whole palace was buried in sleep. She entered her father's bedchamber and cut off the fatal lock; then passed out of the city and entered the enemy's camp. She demanded to be led to the king, and thus addressed him: "I am Scylla, the daughter of Nisus. I surrender to you my country and my father's house. I ask no reward but yourself; for love of you I have done it. See here the purple lock! With this I give you my father and his kingdom." She held out her hand with the fatal **spoil**.

Minos shrunk back and refused to touch it. "The gods destroy thee, infamous woman," he exclaimed; "disgrace of our time! May neither earth nor sea yield thee a resting-place! Surely, my Crete, where Jove himself was cradled, shall not be polluted with such a monster!" Thus he said, and gave orders that equitable terms should be allowed to the conquered city, and that the fleet should immediately sail from the island.

Scylla was frantic. "Ungrateful man," she exclaimed, "is it thus you leave me?—me who have given you victory,—who have sacrificed for you parent and country! I am guilty, I confess, and deserve to die, but not by your hand." As the ships left the shore, she leaped into the water, and seizing the rudder of the one which carried Minos, she was borne along, an unwelcome companion of their course.

A sea-eagle soaring aloft,—it was her father who had been changed into that form,—seeing her, pounced down upon her, and struck her with his beak and claws. In terror she let go the ship and would have fallen into the water, but some pitying deity changed her into a bird. The sea-eagle still cherishes the old **animosity**; and whenever he espies her in his lofty flight you may see him dart down upon her, with beak and claws, to take vengeance for the ancient crime.

Part Two: Echo and Narcissus

Echo was a beautiful nymph, fond of the woods and hills, where she devoted herself to woodland sports. She was a favorite of Diana, and **attended her in the chase.** But Echo had one failing; she was fond of talking, and whether in chat or argument, would have the last word. One day Juno was seeking her husband, who, she had reason to fear, was amusing himself among the nymphs. Echo by her talk contrived to detain the goddess till the nymphs made their escape. When Juno discovered it, she passed sentence upon Echo in these words: "You shall forfeit the use of that tongue with which you have cheated me, except for that one purpose you are so fond of—reply. You shall still have the last word, but no power to speak first."

This nymph saw Narcissus, a beautiful youth, as he pursued the chase upon the mountains. She loved him, and followed his footsteps. O how she longed to address him in the softest accents, and win him to converse! but it was not in her power. She waited with impatience for him to speak first, and had her answer ready.

One day the youth, being separated from his companions, shouted aloud, "Who's here?" Echo replied, "Here." Narcissus looked around, but seeing no one called out, "Come." Echo answered, "Come."

As no one came, Narcissus called again, "Why do you shun me?" Echo asked the same question. "Let us join one another," said the youth. The maid answered with all her heart in the same words, and hastened to the spot, ready to throw her arms about his neck. He started back, exclaiming, "Hands off! I would rather die than you should have me!" "Have me," said she; but it was all in vain. He left her, and she went to hide her blushes in the recesses of the woods.

From that time forth she lived in caves and among mountain cliffs. Her form faded with grief, till at last all her flesh shrank away. Her bones were changed into rocks and there was nothing left of her but her voice. With that she is still ready to reply to any one who calls her, and keeps up her old habit of having the last word.

Part Three: Narcissus and Narcissus

Narcissus's cruelty in this case was not the only instance. He shunned all the rest of the nymphs, as he had done poor Echo. One day a maiden, who had in vain endeavored to attract him, uttered a prayer that he might some time or other feel what it was to love and meet no return of affection. The avenging goddess heard and granted the prayer.

There was a clear fountain, with water like silver, to which the shepherds never drove their flocks, nor the mountain goats resorted, nor any of the beasts of the forest; neither was it defaced with fallen leaves or branches; but the grass grew fresh around it, and the rocks sheltered it from the sun. Hither came one day the youth, fatigued with hunting, heated and thirsty. He stooped down to drink, and saw his own image in the water; he thought it was some beautiful water-spirit living in the fountain. He stood gazing with admiration at those bright eyes, those locks curled like the locks of Bacchus or Apollo, the rounded cheeks, the ivory neck, the parted lips, and the glow of health and exercise over all. He fell in love with himself.

He brought his lips near to take a kiss; he plunged his arms in to embrace the beloved object. It fled at the touch, but returned again after a moment and renewed the fascination. He could not tear himself away; he lost all thought of food or rest, while he hovered over the brink of the fountain gazing upon his own image.

He talked with the supposed spirit: "Why, beautiful being, do you shun me? Surely my face is not one to repel you. The nymphs love me, and you yourself look not indifferent upon me. When I stretch forth my arms you do the same; and you smile upon me and answer my beckonings with the like."

His tears fell into the water and disturbed the image. As he saw it depart, he exclaimed, "Stay, I entreat you! Let me at least gaze upon you, if I may not touch you." With this, and much more of the same kind, he cherished the flame that consumed him, so that by degrees he lost his color, his vigor, and the beauty which formerly had so charmed the nymph Echo. She kept near him, however, and when he exclaimed, "Alas! alas!" she answered him with the same words.

He pined away and died; and when his **shade passed the Stygian river**, it leaned over the boat to catch a look of itself in the waters. The nymphs mourned for him, especially the water-nymphs; and when they **smote their breasts**, Echo smote hers also. They prepared a funeral pile and would have burned the body, but it was nowhere to be found; but in its place a flower, purple within, and surrounded with white leaves, which bears the name and preserves the memory of Narcissus.

[*omission for length*]

Part Four

Milton has imitated the story of Narcissus in the account which he makes Eve give of the first sight of herself reflected in the fountain:

> "That day I oft remember when from sleep
> I first awaked, and found myself reposed
> Under a shade on flowers, much wondering where
> And what I was, whence thither brought, and how.
> Not distant far from thence a murmuring sound
> Of waters issued from a cave, and spread
> Into a liquid plain, then stood unmoved
> Pure as the expanse of heaven; I thither went
> With unexperienced thought, and laid me down
> On the green bank, to look into the clear
> Smooth lake that to me seemed another sky.
> As I bent down to look, just opposite
> A shape within the watery gleam appeared,
> Bending to look on me. I started back;
> It started back; but pleased I soon returned,
> Pleased it returned as soon with answering looks
> Of sympathy and love. There had I fixed
> Mine eyes till now, and pined with vain desire,
> Had not a voice thus warned me: 'What thou seest,
> What there thou seest, fair creature, is thyself;'" etc. (Paradise Lost, Book IV.)

[This poem about Narcissus is a funny one by William Cowper.]

"On An Ugly Fellow"

"Beware, my friend, of crystal brook
Or fountain, lest that hideous hook,
   Thy nose, thou chance to see;
Narcissus' fate would then be thine,
And self-detested thou would'st pine,
   As self-enamoured he."

Narration and Discussion

In "Nisus and Scylla," how did Scylla reason herself into betraying her father? How does our reason sometimes lead us into wrong choices?

> ... [they learn that] reasonable and right are not synonymous terms; that reason is their servant, not their ruler,—one of those servants which help Mansoul in the governance of his kingdom. But no more than appetite, ambition, or the love of ease, is reason to be trusted with the government of a man, much less that of a state; because well-reasoned arguments are brought into play for a wrong course as for a right. (Charlotte Mason, *Philosophy of Education*, p. 142)

In "Echo and Narcissus," what point do you think the storyteller is trying to make? Why is it sometimes better not to have the last word? (Proverbs 21:23; Psalm 141:3; Ecclesiastes 5:2. And more.)

In the second story about Narcissus (the one most famously associated with him), do you think he got what he deserved?

> "Handsome is as handsome does," quoted Marilla. "I've had that said to me before, but I have my doubts about it," remarked skeptical Anne, sniffing at her narcissi. "Oh, aren't these flowers sweet! It was lovely of Mrs. Lynde to give them to me. I have no hard feelings against Mrs. Lynde now. It gives you a lovely, comfortable feeling to apologize and be forgiven, doesn't it?" (L. M. Montgomery, *Anne of Green Gables*)

(Do you think it is coincidental that Marilla and Anne have this discussion while she is holding a bunch of narcissi?)

Creative narration: Choose your favorite of the three stories, and retell it in whatever creative way you like.

(Lesson 31) Two Short Stories About Love

Introduction

The stories in this Lesson are very short, so we have time to explore some of the poetry that Bulfinch thought best amplified them.

Vocabulary

unbound tresses: loose hair

strait: a narrow passage of water, in this case the **Hellespont**. Apparently the distance across is about a mile (1.6 km), but the currents are so strong that they make it feel more like four.

fabulous: made up, not factual

Names

Lord Byron: English poet (see **Lesson 6**)

Reading

Part One: The Short Story of Clytie

Clytie was a water-nymph and in love with Apollo, who made her no return.

So she pined away, sitting all day long upon the cold ground, with her **unbound tresses** streaming over her shoulders.

Nine days she sat and tasted neither food nor drink, her own tears and the chilly dew her only food.

She gazed on the sun when he rose, and as he passed through his daily course to his setting; she saw no other object, her face turned constantly on him.

At last, they say, her limbs rooted in the ground, her face became a [sun]flower, which turns on its stem so as always to face the sun throughout its daily course; for it retains to that extent the feeling of the nymph from whom it sprang.

[*omission for length*]

The sunflower is a favorite emblem of constancy. [The Irish poet Thomas Moore uses it in that way in his famous song "Believe Me, If All Those Endearing Young Charms"]:

"The heart that has truly loved never forgets,

But as truly loves on to the close;

As the sunflower turns on her god when he sets

The same look that she turned when he rose."

[Here is an additional quote from after Bulfinch's time: "Keep your face to the sunshine and you cannot see the shadows. It's what the sunflowers do." (attributed to Helen Keller)]

Part Two: The Even Shorter Story of Hero and Leander

Leander was a youth of Abydos, a town of the Asian side of the **strait** which separates Asia and Europe.

On the opposite shore, in the town of Sestos, lived the maiden Hero, a priestess of Venus.

Leander loved her, and used to swim the strait nightly to enjoy the company of his mistress, guided by a torch which she reared upon the tower for the purpose. But one night a tempest arose and the sea was rough; his strength failed, and he was drowned.

The waves bore his body to the European shore, where Hero became aware of his death, and in her despair cast herself down from the tower into the sea and perished.

[*omission for length*]

The story of Leander's swimming the **Hellespont** was looked upon as **fabulous**, and the feat considered impossible, till **Lord Byron** proved its possibility by performing it himself. In the "Bride of Abydos" he says,

"These limbs that buoyant wave hath borne."

The distance in the narrowest part is almost a mile, and there is a constant current setting out from the Sea of Marmora into the Archipelago. Since Byron's time the feat has been achieved by others; but it yet remains a test of strength and skill in the art of swimming sufficient to give a wide and lasting celebrity to anyone [*omission*] who may dare to make the attempt and succeed in accomplishing it.

In [*omission*] the same poem, Byron thus alludes to this story:

"The winds are high on Helle's wave,

As on that night of stormiest water,

When Love, who sent, forgot to save

The young, the beautiful, the brave,

The lonely hope of Sestos' daughter.

O, when alone along the sky

The turret-torch was blazing high,

Though rising gale and breaking foam,

And shrieking sea-birds warned him home;
And clouds aloft and tides below,
With signs and sounds forbade to go,
He could not see, he would not hear
Or sound or sight foreboding fear.
His eye but saw that light of love,
The only star it hailed above;
His ear but rang with Hero's song,
'Ye waves, divide not lovers long.'
That tale is old, but love anew
May nerve young hearts to prove as true."

Narration and Discussion

On first reading these stories, Clytie, Hero, and Leander may sound more foolish than brave or romantic. (We certainly don't recommend swimming through dangerous currents or throwing oneself off a tower to prove our love.) Does Byron's poem help us to view the story with more sympathy? Are there any lines that you particularly like?

Creative narration: Could you write a very short story about someone who gave everything to show their love?

Chapter Fourteen

(Lesson 32) Minerva and Arachne

Introduction

Minerva (or Athena/Athene), as we know, is the daughter of Jupiter (Zeus), the patron of her namesake city Athens, and the goddess of wisdom (among other things). In these two stories, she shows that she (like the other goddesses) is not to be trifled with.

Vocabulary

aspired to it: wanted to be the chief god of Athens

contended: competed

rude: rough, unfinished

carded: combed and cleaned with a sharp-toothed instrument

spindle: a tool used for spinning

web: In weaving, the **warp** and **weft** (or **woof**) together form the **web**.

adorned it with her needle: embroidered it

homage: great respect

attaches the web to the beam: sets up the loom for weaving

Like the bow, whose long arch…: Bulfinch notes that "This correct description of the rainbow is literally translated from Ovid."

her contest with Neptune: As told in **Part One**

a mighty shield of brass: Minerva's shield is also called her **Aegis**, and this word is now used in English to mean "protection."

failings and errors of the gods: particularly Jupiter (don't forget he is Minerva's father)

could not forbear to admire: could not help admiring

rent: broke

hanged herself: In some versions such as the d'Aulaires' *Book of Greek Myths*, this part is omitted and Arachne is turned immediately into a spider. In a poem by Spenser (not included here), Arachne's jealousy causes her to transform without any extra help.

Names

Leda caressing the swan: Leda was the mother of the brothers Castor and Pollux. Legend says that Jupiter (Zeus) visited her in the form of a swan.

Danae: The mother of Perseus

Europa: See **Year Five, Lesson 30**.

Reading

Part One

Minerva, the goddess of wisdom, was the daughter of Jupiter. She was said to have leaped forth from his brain, mature, and in complete armor. She presided over the useful and ornamental arts, both those of men—such as agriculture and navigation—and those of women,—spinning, weaving, and needlework. She was also a warlike divinity; but it was defensive war only that she patronized, and she had no sympathy with Mars's savage love of violence and bloodshed.

Athens was her chosen seat, her own city, awarded to her as the prize of a contest with Neptune, who also **aspired to it**. The tale ran that in the reign of Cecrops, the first king of Athens, the two deities **contended** for the possession of the city. The gods decreed that it should be awarded to that one who produced the gift most useful to mortals. Neptune gave the horse; Minerva produced the olive. The gods gave judgment that the olive was the more useful of the two, and awarded the city to the goddess; and it was named after her, Athens, her name in Greek being Athene.

Part Two

There was another contest, in which a mortal dared to come in competition with Minerva. That mortal was Arachne, a maiden who had attained such skill in the arts of weaving and embroidery that the nymphs themselves would leave their groves and fountains to come and gaze upon her work. It was not only beautiful when it was done, but beautiful also in the doing. To watch her, as she took the wool in its **rude** state and formed it into rolls, or separated it with her fingers and **carded** it till it looked as light and soft as a cloud, or twirled the **spindle** with skilful touch, or wove the **web**, or, after it was woven, **adorned it with her needle**, one would have said that Minerva herself had taught her. But this she denied, and could not bear to be thought a pupil even of a goddess. "Let Minerva try her skill with mine," said she; "if beaten I will pay the penalty."

Minerva heard this and was displeased. She assumed the form of an old woman and went and gave Arachne some friendly advice "I have had much experience," said she, "and I hope you will not despise my counsel. Challenge your fellow-mortals as you will, but do not compete with a goddess. On the contrary, I advise you to ask her forgiveness for what you have said, and as she is merciful perhaps she will pardon you." Arachne stopped her spinning and looked at the old dame with anger in her countenance. "Keep your counsel," said she, "for your daughters or handmaids; for my part I know what I say, and I stand to it. I am not afraid of the goddess; let her try her skill, if she dare venture." "She comes," said Minerva; and dropping her disguise stood confessed. The nymphs bent low in **homage**, and all the bystanders paid reverence. Arachne alone was unterrified. She blushed, indeed; a sudden color dyed her cheek, and then she grew pale. But she stood to her resolve, and with a foolish conceit of her own skill rushed on her fate.

[*omission*]

Part Three

They proceed to the contest. Each takes her station and **attaches the web to the beam**. Then the slender shuttle is passed in and out among the threads. The reed with its fine teeth strikes up the **woof** into its place and compacts the web. Both work with speed; their skilful hands move rapidly, and the excitement of the contest makes the labor light. Wool of Tyrian dye is contrasted with that of other colors, shaded off into one another so adroitly that the joining deceives the eye. **Like the [rain]bow, whose long arch tinges the heavens, formed by sunbeams reflected from the shower**, in which, where the colors meet they seem as one, but at a little distance from the point of contact are wholly different.

Minerva wrought on her web the scene of **her contest with Neptune**. Twelve of the heavenly powers are represented, Jupiter, with august gravity, sitting in the midst. Neptune, the ruler of the sea, holds his trident, and appears to have just smitten the earth, from which a horse has leaped forth. Minerva depicted herself with helmed head [and holding] her **Aegis**. Such was the central circle; and in the four corners were represented incidents illustrating the displeasure of the gods at such presumptuous mortals as had dared to contend with them. These were meant as warnings to her rival to give up the contest before it was too late.

Arachne filled her web with subjects designedly chosen to exhibit the **failings and errors of the gods**. One scene represented **Leda caressing the swan**, under which form Jupiter had disguised himself; and another, **Danae**, in the brazen tower in which her father had imprisoned her, but where [Jupiter] effected his entrance in the form of a golden shower. Still another depicted **Europa** deceived by Jupiter under the disguise of a bull. Encouraged by the tameness of the animal, Europa ventured to mount his back, whereupon Jupiter advanced into the sea and swam with her to Crete. You would have thought it was a real bull, so naturally was it wrought, and so natural the water in which it swam. She seemed to look with longing eyes back upon the shore she was leaving, and to call to her companions for help. She appeared to shudder with terror at the sight of the heaving waves, and to draw back her feet from the water. Arachne filled her canvas with similar subjects, wonderfully well done, but strongly marking her presumption and impiety.

Minerva **could not forbear to admire**, yet felt indignant at the insult. She struck the web with her shuttle and **rent** it in pieces, she then touched the forehead of Arachne and made her feel her guilt and shame. She [Arachne] could not endure it and went and **hanged herself**.

Minerva pitied her as she saw her suspended by a rope. "Live," she said, "guilty woman! and that you may preserve the memory of this Lesson , continue to hang, both you and your descendants, to all future times." She sprinkled her with the juices of aconite, and immediately her hair came off, and her nose and ears likewise. Her form shrank up, and her head grew smaller yet; her fingers cleaved to her side and served for legs. All the rest of her is body, out of which she spins her thread, often hanging suspended by it, in the same attitude as when Minerva touched her and transformed her into a spider.

[*omission for length*]

Year Five: The Age of Fable

Narration and Discussion

> "What's miraculous about a spider's web?" said Mrs. Arable. "I don't see why you say a web is a miracle—it's just a web."
>
> "Ever try to spin one?" asked Dr. Dorian.
>
> Mrs. Arable shifted uneasily in her chair. "No," she replied. "But I can crochet a doily and I can knit a sock."
>
> "Sure," said the doctor. "But somebody taught you, didn't they?...A young spider knows how to spin a webs without any instructions from anybody. Don't you regard that as a miracle?"
>
> (E. B. White, *Charlotte's Web*)

What are some other "miracles" you have observed in nature?

Creative narration #1: "Let Minerva try her skill with mine," said she; "if beaten I will pay the penalty." Although this may not have been intended to rhyme, it could easily form two lines of a poem about the contest. Could you add more?

Creative narration #2: Using any medium you like (painting, drawing, etc.), "weave a web" to show a myth that has interested you particularly. This may take more than one week, and could be considered an alternative term examination.

(Lesson 33) The Sad Story of Niobe

Introduction

Niobe, the queen of Thebes, wasn't prideful over weaving or spinning, but only about her children. Still, that was enough to cause trouble.

Vocabulary

noised abroad: spread around

matron: married woman

that elated her: that made her happy

frankincense: aromatic gum resin burned as an offering

of pretensions worthy of my alliance: worth joining to our family

richly caparisoned: with rich coverings

satiate: fill up, satisfy

biers: platforms for bodies

torpid: without movement

cleaved: stuck

pediment: the triangular front part of a building, such as a temple

Names

her husband's: Amphion (see **Year Six Lesson 8**)

Latona and her offspring, Apollo and Diana: (see **Year Five Lesson 12**)

Tantalus: a figure in Greek mythology, known for his punishment of being eternally close to fruit and water that stayed just outside of his grasp. (Can you think of an English word that sounds like his name?)

Places

Phrygia: a kingdom in what is now Turkey

Reading

Prologue

The fate of Arachne was **noised abroad** through all the country, and served as a warning to all presumptuous mortals not to compare themselves with the divinities. But one, and she a **matron** too, failed to learn the Lesson of humility. It was Niobe, the queen of Thebes. She had indeed much to be proud of; but it was not **her husband's** fame, nor her own beauty, nor their great descent, nor the power of their kingdom **that elated her**. It was her children; and truly the happiest of mothers would Niobe have been if only she had not claimed to be so.

Part One

It was on occasion of the annual celebration in honor of **Latona and her offspring, Apollo and Diana,**—when the people of Thebes were assembled, their brows crowned with laurel, bearing **frankincense** to the altars and paying their vows,—that Niobe appeared among the crowd. Her attire was splendid with gold and gems, and her aspect beautiful as the face of an angry woman can be. She stood and surveyed the people with haughty looks.

"What folly," said she, "is this!—to prefer beings whom you never saw to those who stand before your eyes! Why should Latona be honored with worship, and none be paid to me? My father was **Tantalus**, who was received as a guest at the table of the gods; my mother was a goddess. My husband built and rules this city, Thebes, and **Phrygia** is my paternal inheritance. Wherever I turn my eyes I survey the elements of my power; nor is my form and presence unworthy of a goddess. To all this (let me add) I have seven sons and seven daughters, and look for sons-in-law and daughters-in-law **of pretensions worthy of my alliance**. Have I not cause for pride? Will you prefer to me this Latona, the Titan's daughter, with her two children? I have seven times as many. Fortunate indeed am I, and fortunate I shall remain! Will any one deny this? My abundance is my security. I feel myself too strong for Fortune to subdue. She may take from me much; I shall still have much left. Were I to lose some of my children, I should hardly be left as poor as Latona with her two only. Away with you from these solemnities,—put off the laurel from your brows,—have done with this worship!"

The people obeyed, and left the sacred services uncompleted.

Part Two

The goddess was indignant. On the Cynthian mountain top where she dwelt she thus addressed her son and daughter: "My children, I who have been so proud of you both, and have been used to hold myself second to none of the goddesses except Juno alone, begin now to doubt whether I am indeed a goddess. I shall be deprived of my worship altogether unless you protect me." She was proceeding in this strain, but Apollo interrupted her. "Say no more," said he; "speech only delays punishment." So said Diana also.

Darting through the air, veiled in clouds, they alighted on the towers of the city. Spread out before the gates was a broad plain, where the youth of the city pursued their warlike sports. The sons of Niobe were there with the rest,—some mounted on spirited horses **richly caparisoned**, some driving [brightly coloured] chariots. Ismenos, the first-born, as he guided his foaming steeds, [was] struck with an arrow from above, cried out "Ah me!", dropped the reins, and fell lifeless. Another, hearing the sound of the bow,—like a boatman who sees the storm gathering and makes all sail for the port,—gave the reins to his horses and attempted to escape. The inevitable arrow overtook him as he fled. Two others, younger boys, just from their tasks, had gone to the playground to have a game of wrestling. As they stood breast to breast, one arrow pierced them both. They uttered a cry together, together cast a parting look around them, and together breathed their last. Alphenor, an elder brother, seeing them fall, hastened to the spot to render assistance, and fell stricken in the act of brotherly duty. One only was left, Ilioneus. He raised his arms to heaven to try whether prayer might not avail. "Spare me, ye gods!" he cried, addressing all, in his ignorance that all needed not his intercessions; and Apollo would have spared him, but the arrow had already left the string, and it was too late.

Part Three

The terror of the people and grief of the attendants soon made Niobe acquainted with what had taken place. She could hardly think it possible; she was indignant that the gods had dared, and amazed that they had been able to do it. Her husband **Amphion**, overwhelmed with the blow, destroyed himself.

Alas! how different was this Niobe from her who had so lately driven away the people from the sacred rites, and held her stately course through the city, the envy of her friends, now the pity even of her foes! She knelt over the lifeless bodies, and kissed now one, now another of her dead sons. Raising her pallid arms to heaven, "Cruel Latona," said she, "feed full your rage with my anguish! **Satiate** your hard heart, while I follow to the grave my seven sons. Yet where is your triumph? Bereaved as I am, I am still richer than you, my conqueror."

Scarce had she spoken, when the bow sounded and struck terror into all hearts except Niobe's alone. She was brave from excess of grief. The sisters stood in garments of mourning over the **biers** of their dead brothers. One fell, struck by an arrow, and died on the corpse she was bewailing. Another, attempting to console her mother, suddenly ceased to speak, and sank lifeless to the earth. A third tried to escape by flight, a fourth by concealment, another stood trembling, uncertain what course to take. Six were now dead, and only one remained, whom the mother held clasped in her arms, and covered as it were with her whole body. "Spare me one, and that the youngest! O spare me one of so many!" she cried; and while she spoke, that one fell dead.

Desolate she sat, among sons, daughters, husband, all dead, and seemed **torpid** with grief. The breeze moved not her hair, no color was on her cheek, her eyes glared fixed and immovable, there was no sign of life about her. Her very tongue **cleaved** to the roof of her mouth, and her veins ceased to convey the tide of life. Her neck bent not, her arms made no gesture, her foot no step. She was changed to stone, within and without. Yet tears continued to flow; and borne on a whirlwind to her native mountain, she still remains, a mass of rock, from which a trickling stream flows, the tribute of her never-ending grief.

[*omission for length*]

Part Four

An illustration of this story is…a celebrated statue in the [Niobe Room in the Uffizi Gallery] in Florence. It is the principal figure of a group supposed to have been originally arranged in the **pediment** of a temple. The figure of the mother clasped by the arm of her terrified child is one of the most admired of the ancient statues. It ranks with the Laocoön and the Apollo among the masterpieces of art. The following is a translation of a Greek epigram supposed to relate to this statue:

"To stone the gods have changed her, but in vain;

The sculptor's art has made her breathe again."

[*omission for length and content*]

Narration and Discussion

"What folly," said she, "is this!—to prefer beings whom you never saw to those who stand before your eyes! Why should Latona be honored with worship, and none be paid to me?" In what respects might you agree with Niobe? How would you disagree?

Creative narration: Imagine a conversation between Arachne (in spider form?) and Niobe, perhaps before she boasted about her family. What advice might Arachne give?

(Lesson 34) Special Lesson: Statues of the Gods

Introduction

The reading for this Lesson is taken from *The Age of Fable*, Chapter 35 (the second part).

Vocabulary

Four: Bulfinch says that he is going to describe four statues, but he actually lists five.

extant: existing

The Olympian Jupiter: or *Statue of Zeus at Olympia*, one of the "Seven Wonders" of the ancient world. For more information, and an illustration, see Richard Halliburton's *Complete Book of Marvels*, Chapter 31 "Ephesus, City of Ancient Temples."

Minerva of the Parthenon: or *Athena Parthenos*, the statue is said to have measured 13 m (over 42 feet) high. (For more about the Parthenon and Phidias, see *Complete Book of Marvels*, Chapter 27 "Parthenon, Temple of Athena."

Venus de' Medici: Marble copy of an earlier bronze statue; sculpted in the first century B.C.; now in the Uffizi Gallery, Florence.

Apollo Belvedere: Roman marble copy of an earlier bronze sculpture; now located in the Vatican Museums Complex.

Python: (See **Year Five Lesson 7**)

Diana of Versailles: also called *Diana with a Doe* (French: *Diane à la biche*), and *Diana of Ephesus*. It is now in the Musée du Louvre, Paris.

Reading

Prologue

To adequately represent to the eye the ideas intended to be conveyed to the mind under the [various] names of deities was a task which called into exercise the highest powers of genius and art. Of the many attempts, **four** have been most celebrated, the first two known to us only by the descriptions of the ancients, the others still **extant** and the acknowledged masterpieces of the sculptor's art.

Part One: The Olympian Jupiter

The statue of the Olympian Jupiter by Phidias was considered the highest achievement of this department of Grecian art. It was of colossal dimensions, and was what the ancients called "chryselephantine;" that is, composed of ivory and gold; the parts representing flesh being of ivory laid on a core of wood or stone, while the drapery and other ornaments were of gold. The height of the figure was forty feet, on a pedestal twelve feet high. The god was represented seated on his throne. His brows were crowned with a wreath of olive, and he held in his right hand a sceptre, and in his left a statue of Victory. The throne was of cedar, adorned with gold and precious stones.

The idea which the artist essayed to embody was that of the supreme deity of the Hellenic (Grecian) nation, enthroned as a conqueror, in perfect majesty and repose, and ruling with a nod the subject world. Phidias avowed that he took his idea from the representation which Homer gives in the first book of the "Iliad," in the passage thus translated by Pope:

> "He spoke and awful bends his sable brows,
>
> Shakes his ambrosial curls and gives the nod,
>
> The stamp of fate and sanction of the god.
>
> High heaven with reverence the dread signal took,
>
> And all Olympus to the centre shook."

Cowper's version is less elegant, but truer to the original:

> "He ceased, and under his dark brows the nod
>
> Vouchsafed of confirmation. All around
>
> The sovereign's everlasting head his curls
>
> Ambrosial shook, and the huge mountain reeled."

[*omission for length*]

Part Two: The Minerva of the Parthenon

This [statue] was also the work of Phidias. It stood in the Parthenon, or temple of Minerva, at Athens. The goddess was represented standing. In one hand she held a spear, in the other a statue of Victory. Her helmet, highly decorated, was surmounted by a Sphinx. The statue was forty feet in height, and, like the Jupiter, composed of ivory and gold. The eyes were of marble, and probably painted to represent the iris and pupil. The Parthenon, in which this statue stood, was also constructed under the direction and superintendence of Phidias. Its exterior was enriched with sculptures, many of them from the hand of Phidias. The Elgin marbles, now in the British Museum, are a part of them.

Both the Jupiter and Minerva of Phidias are lost, but there is good ground to believe that we have, in several extant statues and busts, the artist's conceptions of the countenances of both. They are characterized by grave and dignified beauty, and freedom from any transient expression, which in the language of art is called repose.

Part Three: The Venus de' Medici

The Venus of the Medici is so called from its having been in the possession of the princes of that name in Rome when it first attracted attention, about two hundred years ago. An inscription on the base records it to be the work of Cleomenes, an Athenian sculptor of 200 B.C., but the authenticity of the inscription is doubtful. There is a story that the artist was employed by public authority to make a statue exhibiting the perfection of female beauty, and to aid him in his task the most perfect forms the city could supply were furnished him for models. It is this which Thomson alludes to in his "Summer":

> "So stands the statue that enchants the world;
>
> So bending tries to veil the matchless boast,
>
> The mingled beauties of exulting Greece."

Byron also alludes to this statue. Speaking of the Florence Museum, he says:

> "There, too, the goddess loves in stone, and fills
>
> The air around with beauty;" etc.

[*omission for length and content*]

Part Four: The Apollo Belvedere

The most highly esteemed of all the remains of ancient sculpture is the statue of Apollo, called the Belvedere, from the name of the apartment of the Pope's palace at Rome in which it was placed.

The artist is unknown. It is supposed to be a work of Roman art, of about the first century of our era. It is a standing figure, in marble, more than seven feet high, naked except for the cloak which is fastened around the neck and hangs over the extended left arm. It is supposed to represent the god in the moment when he has shot the arrow to destroy the monster **Python**.

The victorious divinity is in the act of stepping forward. The left arm, which seems to have held the bow, is outstretched, and the head is turned in the same direction. In attitude and proportion the graceful majesty of the figure is unsurpassed. The effect is completed by the countenance, where on the perfection of youthful godlike beauty there dwells the consciousness of triumphant power.

Part Five: The Diana of Versailles

The [statue of Diana], in the palace of the Louvre, may be considered the counterpart to the Apollo Belvedere. The attitude much resembles that of the Apollo, the sizes correspond and also the style of execution. It is a work of the highest order, though by no means equal to the Apollo. The attitude is that of hurried and eager motion, the face that of a huntress in the excitement of the chase. The left hand is extended over the forehead of the Hind, which runs by her side, the right arm reaches backward over the shoulder to draw an arrow from the quiver.

Narration and Discussion

What statues have you seen (in person or in photographs) that made a great impression? What was it about them that made them more than just something carved out of stone? (Think of the lines from the reading on Niobe: "To stone the gods have changed her, but in vain; / The sculptor's art has made her breathe again."

Something else to think about: There are many places in Scripture where God commands his people not to worship idols. Does this conflict with our admiration of these past and present statues?

Creative narration: Imagine that you can travel anywhere (even to the past). Create a picture postcard to send home from a spot where you have seen a great statue.

Year Six: *The Age of Fable*, by Thomas Bulfinch

Introduction to the Year Six Readings

The *Age of Fable* readings for Year Five are from Chapters 1 through 14, and you might expect Year Six to continue from there.

However, we are going to jump ahead to Chapter 22. As we have only twelve weeks of readings in Term One, and as many students will already have read some of the next stories in the book (such as Perseus, Jason, and Theseus), it seemed like a better use of reading time to move on to some stories that might not be as familiar, and that would challenge Year Six students in new ways.

We have included as much of Bulfinch's choices of poetry as seemed appropriate; and (here and there) you will find quotes from Charlotte Mason.

The final story of the term is a bit of a lead-in to Homer's *Iliad*, which is scheduled as Literature for Term Two (a retelling such as *Black Ships Before Troy* is fine; see **For Further Reading** for other suggestions). Those who are unable to access other books, or who just really like Bulfinch, are, of course, welcome to continue with the summaries of Homer as told in the later chapters of *Age of Fable*.

Year Six: The Age of Fable

Chapter Twenty-Two

(Lesson 1) The Rural Deities and Erisichthon

Introduction

Erisichthon is not a story for the squeamish, and Ovid's version (from which Bulfinch translates), has the grisliest ending of any. There are at least two other versions of the story; one says simply that Erisichthon was reduced to beggary; another says that a snake was sent to plague him, and that in the end they were both placed in the heavens to continue the punishment forever.

Vocabulary

grottos: small caves

agency: doing

wantonly: deliberately

several: various

profane: outside of or against the accepted religion

venerable: ancient

votive: consecrated, holy

suppliants: those who prayed or asked for favors

fifteen cubits: about 26 feet (8 m)

ventured to remonstrate: protested

prostrated a great part of the grove: knocked down a lot of other trees

made her assume that of a fisherman busy at his occupation: Another version of the story says that Neptune turned Mestra into a donkey, which her father sold; but that finally she was turned into a butterfly and flew away free.

Names

Erisichthon, or Erysichthon: pronounced Ehr-ih-SICH-thun

Oreads: Nymphs of mountains and grottoes (one is coming up in the story)

Ceres: the goddess of harvest and plenty (Greek: Demeter)

Famine or Fames: the goddess of hunger and starvation (Greek: Limos)

Places

Mount Caucasus: Mount Elbrus or Mount Kazbek, in the Caucasus Mountains, located where Europe meets Asia.

Reading

Part One: The Rural Deities

Pan, the god of woods and fields, of flocks and shepherds, dwelt in **grottos**, wandered on the mountains and in valleys, and amused himself with the chase or in leading the dances of the nymphs. He was fond of music, and as we have seen, the inventor of the syrinx, or shepherd's pipe, which he himself played in a masterly manner. Pan, like other gods who dwelt in forests, was dreaded by those whose occupations caused them to pass through the woods by night, for the gloom and loneliness of such scenes dispose the mind to superstitious fears. Hence sudden fright without any visible cause was ascribed to Pan, and called a "Panic" terror. As the name of the god signifies "all," Pan came to be considered a symbol of the universe and personification of Nature; and later still to be regarded as a representative of all the gods and of heathenism itself.

Sylvanus and Faunus were Latin divinities, whose characteristics are so nearly the same as those of Pan that we may safely consider them as the same personage under different names.

The wood-nymphs, Pan's partners in the dance, were but one class of nymphs. There were beside them the Naiads, who presided over brooks and fountains, the **Oreads**, nymphs of mountains and grottos, and the Nereids, sea-nymphs. The three last named were immortal, but the wood-nymphs, called Dryads or Hamadryads, were believed to perish with the trees which had been their abode and with which they had come into existence. It was therefore an impious act **wantonly** to destroy a tree, and in some aggravated cases were severely punished, as in the instance of Erisichthon, which we are about to record.

Part Two

Milton in his glowing description of the early creation, thus alludes to Pan as the personification of Nature:

"... Universal Pan,

Knit with the Graces and the Hours in dance,

Led on the eternal spring."

And describing Eve's abode:

> "... In shadier bower,
> More sacred or sequestered, though but feigned,
> Pan or Sylvanus never slept, nor nymph
> Nor Faunus haunted."

(Paradise Lost, B. IV.)

It was a pleasing trait in the old Paganism that it loved to trace in every operation of nature the agency of deity. The imagination of the Greeks peopled all the regions of earth and sea with divinities, to whose **agency** it attributed those phenomena which our philosophy ascribes to the operation of the laws of nature. Sometimes in our poetical moods we feel disposed to regret the change, and to think that the heart has lost as much as the head has gained by the substitution. The poet Wordsworth thus strongly expresses this sentiment [in "The World Is Too Much With Us"]:

> "... Great God, I'd rather be
> A Pagan, suckled in a creed outworn,
> So might I, standing on this pleasant lea,
> Have glimpses that would make me less forlorn;
> Have sight of Proteus rising from the sea,
> And hear old Triton blow his wreathed horn."

[*omission for length*]

[There is] an early Christian tradition that when the heavenly host told the shepherds at Bethlehem of the birth of Christ, a deep groan, heard through all the isles of Greece, told that the great Pan was dead, and that all the royalty of Olympus was dethroned and the **several** deities were sent wandering in cold and darkness. So Milton [says] in his "Hymn on the Nativity":

> "The lonely mountains o'er,
> And the resounding shore,
>   A voice of weeping heard and loud lament;
> From haunted spring and dale,
> Edged with poplar pale,
>   The parting Genius is with sighing sent;
> With flower-enwoven tresses torn,
> The nymphs in twilight shade of tangled thickets mourn."

Part Two: Erisichthon

Erisichthon was a **profane** person and a despiser of the gods. On one occasion he presumed to violate with the axe a grove sacred to **Ceres**. There stood in this grove a **venerable** oak so large that it seemed a wood in itself, its ancient trunk towering aloft, whereon **votive** garlands were often hung and inscriptions carved expressing the gratitude of **suppliants** to the nymph of the tree. Often had the Dryads danced round it hand in hand. Its trunk measured **fifteen cubits** round, and it overtopped the other trees as they overtopped the shrubbery.

But for all that, Erisichthon saw no reason why he should spare it and he ordered his servants to cut it down.

When he saw them hesitate he snatched an axe from one, and thus impiously exclaimed: "I care not whether it be a tree beloved of the goddess or not; were it the goddess herself it should come down if it stood in my way." So saying, he lifted the axe and the oak seemed to shudder and utter a groan. When the first blow fell upon the trunk blood flowed from the wound. All the bystanders were horror-struck, and one of them **ventured to remonstrate** and hold back the fatal axe. Erisichthon, with a scornful look, said to him, "Receive the reward of your piety;" and turned against him the weapon which he had held aside from the tree, gashed his body with many wounds, and cut off his head.

Then from the midst of the oak came a voice, "I who dwell in this tree am a nymph beloved of Ceres, and dying by your hands forewarn you that punishment awaits you." He desisted not from his crime, and at last the tree, sundered by repeated blows and drawn by ropes, fell with a crash and **prostrated a great part of the grove** in its fall.

The Dryads in dismay at the loss of their companion and at seeing the pride of the forest laid low, went in a body to Ceres, all clad in garments of mourning, and invoked punishment upon Erisichthon. She nodded her assent, and as she bowed her head, the grain ripe for harvest in the laden fields bowed also. She planned a punishment so dire that one would pity him, if such a culprit as he could be pitied–to deliver him over to **Famine**.

As Ceres herself could not approach Famine, for the Fates have ordained that these two goddesses shall never come together, she called an Oread from her mountain and spoke to her in these words: "There is a place in the farthest part of ice-clad Scythia, a sad and sterile region without trees and without crops. Cold dwells there, and Fear and Shuddering, and Famine. Go and tell the last to take possession of [*omission*] of Erisichthon. Let not abundance subdue her, nor the power of my gifts drive her away. Be not alarmed at the distance" (for Famine dwells very far from Ceres), "but take my chariot. The dragons are fleet and obey the rein, and will take you through the air in a short time." So she gave her the reins, and she drove away and soon reached Scythia.

On arriving at **Mount Caucasus**, she stopped the dragons and found Famine in a stony field, pulling up with teeth and claws the scanty herbage. Her hair was rough, her eyes sunk, her face pale, her lips blanched, her jaws covered with dust, and her skin drawn tight, so as to show all her bones. As the Oread saw her afar off (for she did not dare to come near), she delivered the commands of Ceres; and, though she stopped as short a time as possible, and kept her distance as well as she could, yet she began to feel hungry, and turned the dragons' heads and drove back to Thessaly.

Famine obeyed the commands of Ceres and sped through the air to the dwelling of Erisichthon, entered the bedchamber of the guilty man, and found him asleep. She enfolded him with her wings and breathed herself into him, infusing her poison into his veins.

Having discharged her task, she hastened to leave the land of plenty and returned to her accustomed haunts. Erisichthon still slept, and in his dreams craved food, and moved his jaws as if eating. When he awoke, his hunger was raging. Without a moment's delay he would have food set before him, of whatever kind earth, sea, or air produces; and complained of hunger even while he ate. What would have sufficed for a city or a nation, was not enough for him. The more he ate the more he craved. His hunger was like the sea, which receives all the rivers, yet is never filled; or like fire, that burns all the fuel that is heaped upon it, yet is still voracious for more.

Part Three

His property rapidly diminished under the unceasing demands of his appetite, but his hunger continued unabated. At length he had spent all and had only his daughter [Mestra] left, a daughter worthy of a better parent. Her too he sold.

She scorned to be the slave of a purchaser and as she stood by the seaside raised her hands in prayer to Neptune. He heard her prayer, and though her new master was not far off and had his eye upon her a moment before, Neptune changed her form and **made her assume that of a fisherman busy at his occupation**. Her master, looking for her and seeing her in her altered form, addressed her and said, "Good fisherman, whither went the maiden whom I saw just now, with hair dishevelled and in humble garb, standing about where you stand? Tell me truly; so may your luck be good and not a fish nibble at your hook and get away." She perceived that her prayer was answered and rejoiced inwardly at hearing herself inquired of about herself. She replied, "Pardon me, stranger, but I have been so intent upon my line that I have seen nothing else; but I wish I may never catch another fish if I believe any woman or other person except myself to have been hereabouts for some time." He was deceived and went his way, thinking his slave had escaped. Then she resumed her own form.

Her father was well pleased to find her still with him, and the money too that he got by the sale of her; so he sold her again. But she was changed by the favor of Neptune as often as she was sold–now into a horse, now a bird, now an ox, and now a stag–got away from her purchasers and came home.

By this base method the starving father procured food; but not enough for his wants, and at last hunger compelled him to devour his limbs, and he strove to nourish his body by eating his body, till death relieved him from the vengeance of Ceres.

Narration and Discussion

Was Erisichthon's punishment for chopping the tree a fair one?

What can happen if a desire (for anything) becomes insatiable? You can probably think of stories where someone's appetite got out of control (though not to the same extent as Erisichthon's). Charlotte Mason wrote about what happens when childhood indulgences become adult ones:

> Gluttony leads his victim to the confectioner's windows and makes him think how nice this or that would taste: all his pocket-money goes in tarts, sweets, and toffee. He thinks at breakfast what pudding he should like for dinner, and asks for it as a favour. Indeed, he is always begging for bits of cake, and spoonfuls of jam, and extra chocolates...Gluttony begins with the little boy and goes with him all through life, only that, instead of caring for chocolate creams when he is a man, he cares for great dinners two hours long. (*Ourselves Book 1*, pp. 12-13)

Creative narration: Retell the story of Erisichthon from the point of view of a) his daughter, or b) his cook.

Something more to think about (for older students and adults): The descriptions of the rural deities, and the poetry by Milton and Wordsworth, may seem less compelling than the story of a man who was so hungry that he ate himself up; however, they represent the best of English literature, and deserve to be noticed. Choose one of the three verses, and write about what you think it is saying.

(Lesson 2) Gods of Water and Winds

Introduction

Many of the Greek/Roman deities seemed to live in families: for instance, those who lived in the ocean, and those who ruled the winds. This Lesson is a catalogue of both.

Vocabulary

when she would admit his society: when he could come and see her

playing at draughts: playing checkers

watery element: oceans

gambolled: frolicked

type: example

rudeness: roughness

Names

Carpathian wizard: Proteus, the shapeshifter (see **Year Six Lesson 7**)

Reading

Part One: Rhoecus of Cnidus

The Hamadryads could appreciate services as well as punish injuries. The story of Rhoecus proves this.

Rhoecus, happening to see an oak just ready to fall, ordered his servants to prop it up. The nymph, who had been on the point of perishing with the tree, came and expressed her gratitude to him for having saved her life and bade him ask what reward he would. Rhoecus boldly asked her love and the nymph yielded to his desire. She at the same time charged him to be constant and told him that a bee should be her messenger and let him know **when she would admit his society**.

One time the bee came to Rhoecus when he was **playing at draughts**, and he carelessly brushed it away.

This so incensed the nymph that she deprived him of sight.

[*omission for length*]

Part Two: The Water Deities

Oceanus and Tethys were the Titans who ruled over the **watery element**. When Jove and his brothers overthrew the Titans and assumed their power, Neptune and Amphitrite succeeded to the dominion of the waters in place of Oceanus and Tethys.

NEPTUNE: Neptune was the chief of the water deities. The symbol of his power was the trident, or spear with three points, with which he used to shatter rocks, to call forth or subdue storms, to shake the shores and the like. He created the horse and was the patron of horse races. His own horses had brazen hoofs and golden manes. They drew his chariot over the sea, which became smooth before him, while the monsters of the deep **gambolled** about his path.

AMPHITRITE: Amphitrite was the wife of Neptune. She was the daughter of Nereus and Doris, and the mother of Triton. Neptune, to pay his court to Amphitrite, came riding on a dolphin. Having won her he rewarded the dolphin by placing him among the stars.

NEREUS AND DORIS: Nereus and Doris were the parents of the Nereids, the most celebrated of whom were Amphitrite, Thetis (the mother of Achilles), and Galatea, who was loved by the Cyclops Polyphemus. Nereus was distinguished for his knowledge and his love of truth and justice, whence he was termed an elder; the gift of prophecy was also assigned to him.

TRITON AND PROTEUS: Triton was the son of Neptune and Amphitrite, and the poets make him his father's trumpeter. Proteus was also a son of Neptune. He, like Nereus, is styled a sea-elder for his wisdom and knowledge of future events. His peculiar power was that of changing his shape at will.

THETIS: Thetis, the daughter of Nereus and Doris, was so beautiful that Jupiter himself sought her in marriage; but having learned from Prometheus the Titan that Thetis should bear a son who should grow greater than his father, Jupiter desisted from his suit and decreed that Thetis should be the wife of a mortal. By the aid of Chiron the Centaur, Peleus succeeded in winning the goddess for his bride and their son was the renowned Achilles [*omission*].

LEUCOTHEA AND PALAEMON: Ino, the daughter of Cadmus and wife of Athamas, flying from her frantic husband with her little son Melicertes in her arms, sprang from a cliff into the sea. The gods, out of compassion, made her a goddess of the sea, under the name of Leucothea, and him a god, under that of Palaemon. Both were held powerful to save from shipwreck and were invoked by sailors.

Palaemon was usually represented riding on a dolphin. The Isthmian games were celebrated in his honor. He was called Portunus by the Romans, and believed to have jurisdiction of the ports and shores.

[The English poet John Milton] alludes to all these deities in the song at the conclusion of [his long poem] "Comus." "Sabrina" is a water nymph.

> "... Sabrina fair,
>
> Listen and appear to us,
>
> In name of great Oceanus;
>
> By the earth-shaking Neptune's mace,
>
> And Tethys' grave, majestic pace,
>
> By hoary Nereus' wrinkled look,
>
> And the **Carpathian wizard's** hook,
>
> By scaly Triton's winding shell,
>
> And old soothsaying Glaucus' spell,
>
> By Leucothea's lovely hands,

And her son who rules the strands.

By Thetis' tinsel-slippered feet,

And the songs of Sirens sweet;" etc.

[*omission for length*]

Part Three: The Winds

[The winds, personified], were Boreas or Aquilo, the north wind; Zephyrus or Favonius, the west; Notus or Auster, the south; and Eurus, the east. The first two have been chiefly celebrated by the poets, the former as the **type** of **rudeness**, the latter of gentleness.

Boreas loved the nymph Orithyia, and tried to play the lover's part, but met with poor success. It was hard for him to breathe gently, and sighing was out of the question. Weary at last of fruitless endeavors, he acted out his true character, seized the maiden and carried her off. Their children were Zetes and Calais, winged warriors, who accompanied the Argonautic expedition, and did good service in an encounter with those monstrous birds the Harpies.

Zephyrus was the lover of Flora. Milton alludes to them in "Paradise Lost," where he describes Adam waking and contemplating Eve still asleep.

"... He on his side

Leaning half raised, with looks of cordial love,

Hung over her enamored, and beheld

Beauty which, whether waking or asleep,

Shot forth peculiar graces; then with voice,

Mild as when Zephyrus on Flora breathes,

Her hand soft touching, whispered thus: 'Awake!

My fairest, my espoused, my latest found,

Heaven's last, best gift, my ever-new delight.'"

[*omission for length*]

Narration and Discussion

Are there any common patterns or ideas you notice in these stories? What do they seem to say about the ancient world, or the people who lived then?

Creative narration #1: The American poet James Russell Lowell wrote a poem titled "Rhœcus." Here is a bit from it (you will notice that he changes checkers for dice). Could you add a few lines of your own in Lowell's style? (Afterwards, you might like to look up the whole poem.)

> Young Rhœcus had a faithful heart enough,
> But one that in the present dwelt too much,
> And, taking with blithe welcome whatsoe'er
> Chance gave of joy, was wholly bound in that,
> Like the contented peasant of a vale,
> Deemed it the world, and never looked beyond.
> So, haply meeting in the afternoon
> Some comrades who were playing at the dice
> He joined them and forgot all else beside.

Creative narration #2: Imagine a double date (maybe a picnic) between Boreas (the god of big gusty winds), Zephyrus (the god of gentle breezes), and their sweethearts Orithyia and Flora. What might happen?

Creative narration #3: You are looking through the Water Gods family album with one of the deities mentioned. What questions do you ask about who's who? What responses might you get?

Chapter Twenty-Three
(Lesson 3) Achelous and Hercules

Introduction

The river god Achelous likes to tell stories, and he has a good one about himself (although it's a little embarrassing).

Vocabulary

board: table

vesture: clothing

It was the labor of my infancy to conquer snakes: It is said that Hercules strangled snakes while he was still in his cradle.

rent: tore

Cornucopia (from the Latin for "horn" and "abundance"): This harvest symbol has ancient roots. In Greek it was called the "Horn of Amalthea," after Zeus's nursemaid.

Names

Achelous: the god of the Achelous, the largest river in Greece

Erisichthon: See **Year Six Lesson 1**

Theseus: a hero of Greek mythology, famous for killing the Minotaur

Hercules (Heracles, Herakles): another great hero

Dejanira (Deianira): the wife of Hercules, and sister of Meleager (one of Jason's Argonauts)

Plenty: A Roman goddess also called **Ops** or **Opis**; the word "opes" means "wealth." (If Hercules and Dejanira's wedding feast was "opulent," what might it look like?)

the goat Amalthea: In some versions she is a nymph who fed Zeus on goats' milk; in others she is the goat itself.

Reading

Prologue

The river-god **Achelous** told the story of **Erisichthon** to **Theseus** and his companions, whom he was entertaining at his hospitable **board**, while they were delayed on their journey by the overflow of his waters. Having finished his story, he added, "But why should I tell of other persons' transformations when I myself am an instance of the possession of this power? Sometimes I become a serpent, and sometimes a bull, with horns on my head. Or I should say I once could do so; but now I have but one horn, having lost one." And here he groaned and was silent.

Theseus asked him the cause of his grief, and how he lost his horn. To which question the river-god replied as follows.

Part One: Achelous Tells His Story

"Who likes to tell of his defeats? Yet I will not hesitate to relate mine, comforting myself with the thought of the greatness of my conqueror, for it was **Hercules**.

"Perhaps you have heard of the fame of **Dejanira**, the fairest of maidens, whom a host of suitors strove to win. Hercules and myself were of the number, and the rest yielded to us two. He urged in his behalf his descent from Jove, and his labors by which he had exceeded the exactions of Juno, his stepmother. I, on the other hand, said to the father of the maiden, 'Behold me, the king of the waters that flow through your land. I am no stranger from a foreign shore, but belong to the country, a part of your realm. Let it not stand in my way that royal Juno owes me no enmity, nor punishes me with heavy tasks. As for this man, who boasts himself the son of Jove, it is either a false pretence, or disgraceful to him if true, for it cannot be true except by his mother's shame.' As I said this Hercules scowled upon me, and with difficulty restrained his rage. 'My hand will answer better than my tongue,' said he. 'I yield to you the victory in words, but trust my cause to the strife of deeds.' With that he advanced towards me, and I was ashamed, after what I had said, to yield. I threw off my green **vesture** and presented myself for the struggle. He tried to throw me, now attacking my head, now my body. My bulk was my protection, and he assailed me in vain.

"For a time we stopped, then returned to the conflict. We each kept our position, determined not to yield, foot to foot, I bending over him, clenching his hand in mine, with my forehead almost touching his. Thrice Hercules tried to throw me off, and the fourth time he succeeded, brought me to the ground, and himself upon my back. I tell you the truth, it was as if a mountain had fallen on me. I struggled to get my arms at liberty, panting and reeking with perspiration. He gave me no chance to recover, but seized my throat. My knees were on the earth and my mouth in the dust.

"Finding that I was no match for him in the warrior's art, I resorted to others and glided away in the form of a serpent. I curled my body in a coil and hissed at him with my forked tongue.

"He smiled scornfully at this, and said, '**It was the labor of my infancy to conquer snakes.**' So saying he clasped my neck with his hands. I was almost choked, and struggled to get my neck out of his grasp. Vanquished in this form, I tried what alone remained to me and assumed the form of a bull. He grasped my neck with his arm, and dragging my head down to the ground, overthrew me on the sand.

"Nor was this enough. His ruthless hand **rent** my horn from my head. The Naiads took it, consecrated it, and filled it with fragrant flowers. **Plenty** adopted my horn and made it her own, and called it 'Cornucopia.'"

Part Two: An Explanation

The ancients were fond of finding a hidden meaning in their mythological tales. They explain this fight of Achelous with Hercules by saying Achelous was a river that in seasons of rain overflowed its banks. When the fable says that Achelous loved Dejanira, and sought a union with her, the meaning is that the river in its windings flowed through part of Dejanira's kingdom.

It was said to take the form of a snake because of its winding, and of a bull because it made a brawling or roaring in its course.

When the river swelled, it made itself another channel. Thus its head was "horned." Hercules prevented the return of these periodical overflows by embankments and canals; and therefore he was said to have vanquished the river-god and cut off his horn. Finally, the lands formerly subject to overflow, but now redeemed, became very fertile, and this is [what is] meant by the "horn of plenty."

There is another account of the origin of the Cornucopia. Jupiter at his birth was committed by his mother Rhea to the care of the daughters of Melisseus, a Cretan king. They fed the infant deity with the milk of **the goat Amalthea**. Jupiter broke off one of the horns of the goat and gave it to his nurses, and endowed it with the wonderful power of becoming filled with whatever the possessor might wish.

[*omission for length*]

Narration and Discussion

If you were a river god, do you think you could have come up with a better way to beat Hercules?

Why did Achelous comfort himself with the thought of the greatness of his conqueror? Would you rather compete with someone of famous skill or strength, or someone you know you can easily beat?

Something more to think about: In the explanation, Hercules (the super-big and super-strong) is said to have built embankments and canals in Greece. Does this remind you of any stories from your own country?

Creative narration: You are a sportscaster covering the fight between Achelous and Hercules. How do you describe what is happening?

(Lesson 4) Admetus and Alcestis

Introduction

This unusual story starts with a resurrection, moves on to a life sacrificed through love, and ends with another unexpected resurrection.

Vocabulary

>**by his father:** see notes in the text
>
>**one year:** or nine years, depending on the version
>
>**impending loss:** In Bulfinch's version of the story, Hercules arrives before the death of Alcestis. Other versions have him come just after her death.

Names

>**Aesculapius (Asclepius):** Like Jason, Orpheus, and other heroes including his half-brother **Aristaeus** (see **Year Six Lesson 7**), he was schooled by the centaur Chiron.

Jove's great son: Hercules

Reading

Prologue: How It Started

Aesculapius, the son of Apollo, was endowed **by his father** with such skill in the healing art that he even restored the dead to life.

[*Bulfinch is perhaps too economical with details here. It is important to understand that Aesculapius was half human, the son of Apollo and Coronis. As noted under "Names," he was taught by Chiron, and became particularly skilled in all the healing arts. At one point he was offered a reward if he would restore the life of Theseus' son Hippolytus, and he did so. This, however, was viewed by the gods as presumptuous on the part of a mortal (even a half-mortal. And so we go on... but it is also worth pointing out that Aesculapius, even after his death, continued to be honoured for his healing gifts.*]

At this Pluto took alarm, and prevailed on Jupiter to launch a thunderbolt at Aesculapius.

Apollo was indignant at the destruction of his son, and wreaked his vengeance on the innocent workmen who had made the thunderbolt. (These were the Cyclopes, who have their workshop under Mount Aetna, from which the smoke and flames of their furnaces are constantly issuing.) Apollo shot his arrows at the Cyclopes, which so incensed Jupiter that he condemned him as a punishment to become the servant of a mortal for the space of **one year**.

Part One

Accordingly Apollo went into the service of Admetus, king of Thessaly, and pastured his flocks for him on the verdant banks of the river Amphrysos. Admetus was a suitor, with others, for the hand of Alcestis, the daughter of Pelias, who promised her to him who should come for her in a chariot drawn by lions and boars. This task Admetus performed by the assistance of his divine herdsman [*i.e. Apollo*], and was made happy in the possession of Alcestis.

But Admetus fell ill, and being near to death, Apollo prevailed on the Fates to spare him on condition that someone would consent to die in his stead.

Admetus, in his joy at this reprieve, thought little of the ransom, and perhaps remembering the declarations of attachment which he had often heard from his courtiers and dependents fancied that it would be easy to find a substitute. But it was not so. Brave warriors, who would willingly have periled their lives for their prince, shrunk from the thought of dying for him on the bed of sickness; and old servants who had experienced his bounty and that of his house from their childhood up, were not willing to lay down the scanty remnant of their days to show their gratitude. Men asked, "Why does not one of his parents do it? They cannot in the course of nature live much longer, and who can feel like them the call to rescue the life they gave from an untimely end?" But the parents, distressed though they were at the thought of losing him, shrunk from the call.

Then [his wife] Alcestis, with a generous self-devotion, proffered herself as the substitute. Admetus, fond as he was of life, would not have submitted to receive it at such a cost; but there was no remedy. The condition imposed by the Fates had been met, and the decree was irrevocable. Alcestis sickened as Admetus revived, and she was rapidly sinking to the grave.

[*We must reiterate that Admetus did not want his wife to die; it seems that the choice was already out of his hands.*]

Part Two

Just at this time Hercules arrived at the palace of Admetus, and found all the inmates in great distress for the **impending loss** of the devoted wife and beloved mistress.

[*We break in one more time to say that other tellers of this story, such as Edith Hamilton, take more time to explain that Admetus, being an excellent host, did not immediately say that he was in mourning (or, in Bulfinch's version, that his wife was close to death). When Hercules finally dragged that fact out of a servant, he was shocked and embarrassed that he (being Hercules) had arrived with his usual boisterousness, and had caused extra pain to his friend. He wanted to make it up somehow, and thought of an obvious solution: go and get Alcestis back.*]

Hercules, to whom no labor was too arduous, resolved to attempt her rescue. He went and lay in wait at the door of the chamber of the dying queen, and when Death came for his prey, he seized him, [wrestled him], and forced him to resign his victim.

[*And Alcestis was restored to her husband.*]

Milton alludes to the story of Alcestis in his Sonnet "On His Deceased Wife."

"Methought I saw my late espoused saint
  Brought to me like Alcestis from the grave,
  Whom **Jove's great son** to her glad husband gave,
  Rescued from death by force, though pale and faint."

[*omission for length*]

Narration and Discussion

Did Alcestis expect to be resurrected?

Who do you think was the true hero (or heroine) of this story?

Creative narration #1: The story of Admetus and Alcestis may get most of our interest, but the events leading up to it (the murder of Aesculapius, the revenge and then the punishment of Apollo) are also worth considering. Choose a creative format to retell an earlier part of the story; for example, write some diary entries for Apollo when he is sent to earth.

Creative narration #2: The American poet John Charles McNeill (1874-1907) wrote a poem where Alcestis speaks a farewell to her husband. A few lines are given below; can you write a response from Admetus?

> Not long the living weep above their dead,
> And you will grieve, Admetus, but not long.
> The winter's silence in these desolate halls
> Will break with April's laughter on your lips;
> The bees among the flowers, the birds that mate,
> The widowed year, grown gaunt with memory
> And yearning toward the summer's fruits, will come
> With lotus comfort, feeding all your veins.

Something to think about: For those who have read *The Lion, the Witch and the Wardrobe*, do you think this is perhaps another illustration of the Deep Magic?

(Lesson 5) Antigone

Introduction

This is the sad and shocking story of Antigone and her family, made famous by the plays of Sophocles. As great tragedies should do, it brings up deep questions of love, hate, family loyalty, and hard decisions.

Please note the long list of characters, each of whom will be on stage here only briefly. It might be helpful to make or to print out a family tree; a search for *family tree Antigone* or *Royal House of Thebes* will show examples.

Year Six: The Age of Fable

Vocabulary

filial and sisterly fidelity: family loyalty

connubial devotion: married love

an unrelenting fate…: To this family belong some of the most tragic stories in Greek mythology (often told through plays and poetry).

reign alternately year by year: Other versions say that **Eteocles** took the throne and expelled his brother, who then went to **Argos**.

collar of Harmonia: the wedding necklace of Harmonia (see **Year Five Lesson 28**)

issue: outcome

depriving it of those rites…: In Greek belief, the souls of the unburied would be forced to wander forever; so to bury the dead was considered a most sacred duty.

dissuading counsel: advice not to do something

set at naught the solemn edict: ignored the ruling

Names

Antigone: usually pronounced Ann-TIG-a-nee

Alcestis: see **Year Six Lesson 4**

Oedipus, Jocasta: the parents of **Antigone** and the others

Eteocles: the younger brother, who tried to protect the city of **Thebes**

Polynices (Polyneices): the older brother, who tried to recapture **Thebes**

Adrastus: the king of Argos

Amphiaraus: the brother-in-law of **Adrastus**, married to **Eriphyle**; he was a prophet who knew that most of the attackers would not come home alive

Eriphyle: the wife who convinced her husband to go to the war (which he knew would be his death)

Tiresias (Teiresias): a prophet who had served the royal family for seven generations, beginning with Cadmus

Menoeceus, the son of Creon: Creon refused to allow **Menoeceus** to die, even if it meant saving the city. **Menoeceus** was braver than his father gave him credit for, but he was indeed quickly killed when he joined the fight.

Creon: Antigone's uncle (her mother's brother), who had acted as regent (caretaker king) after Oedipus abdicated his throne.

an affectionate but timid sister: Ismenes

Places

Argos: a city in **Argolis**, in the **Peloponnese** (the southern part of **Greece**)

Reading

Part One

A large proportion both of the interesting persons and of the exalted acts of legendary Greece belongs to the female sex. **Antigone** was as bright an example of **filial and sisterly fidelity** as was **Alcestis** of **connubial devotion**. She was the daughter of **Oedipus** and **Jocasta**, who with all their descendants were the victims of **an unrelenting fate, dooming them to destruction**.

Oedipus in his madness had torn out his eyes, and was driven forth from his kingdom [of] Thebes, dreaded and abandoned by all men, as an object of divine vengeance. Antigone, his daughter, alone shared his wanderings and remained with him till he died [near Athens]. She then returned to Thebes.

Her brothers, **Eteocles** and **Polynices**, had agreed to share the kingdom between them, and **reign alternately year by year**. The first year fell to the lot of Eteocles, who, when his time expired, refused to surrender the kingdom to his brother. Polynices fled to **Adrastus**, king of **Argos**, who gave him his daughter [Argia] in marriage, and aided him with an army to enforce his claim to the kingdom.

[*omission for length*]

Part Two

Amphiaraus, the brother-in-law of Adrastus, opposed the enterprise, for he was a soothsayer, and knew by his art that no one of the leaders except Adrastus would live to return. But Amphiaraus, on his marriage to **Eriphyle**, the king's sister, had agreed that whenever he and Adrastus should differ in opinion, the decision should be left to Eriphyle. Polynices, knowing this, gave Eriphyle the **collar of Harmonia**, and thereby gained her to his interest. This collar or necklace was a present which Vulcan had given to Harmonia on her marriage with Cadmus, and Polynices had taken it with him on his flight from Thebes.

Eriphyle could not resist so tempting a bribe, and by her decision the war was resolved on, and Amphiaraus went to his certain fate. He bore his part bravely in the contest, but could not avert his destiny. Pursued by the enemy, he fled along the river, when a thunderbolt launched by Jupiter opened the ground, and he, his chariot, and his charioteer were swallowed up.

[*omission for length and content*]

Part Three

Early in the contest Eteocles consulted the soothsayer **Tiresias** as to the **issue**. (Tiresias in his youth had by chance seen Minerva bathing. The goddess in her wrath deprived him of his sight, but afterwards relenting gave him in compensation the knowledge of future events.) When consulted by Eteocles, he declared that victory should fall to Thebes if [*and only if*] **Menoeceus, the son of Creon**, gave himself a voluntary victim. The heroic youth, learning the response, threw away his life in the first encounter.

The siege continued long, with various success. At length both hosts agreed that the brothers should decide their quarrel by single combat. They fought and fell by each other's hands. The armies then renewed the fight, and at last the invaders were forced to yield, and fled, leaving their dead unburied.

Part Four

Creon, the uncle of the fallen princes, now became king. He caused Eteocles to be buried with distinguished honor, but suffered the body of Polynices to lie where it fell, forbidding every one on pain of death to give it burial.

Antigone, the sister of Polynices, heard with indignation the revolting edict which consigned her brother's body to the dogs and vultures, **depriving it of those rites which were considered essential to the repose of the dead**. Unmoved by the **dissuading counsel** of **an affectionate but timid sister**, and unable to procure assistance, she determined to brave the hazard, and to bury the body with her own hands.

She was detected in the act, and Creon gave orders that she should be buried alive [in a tomb], as having deliberately **set at naught the solemn edict** of the city.

[Antigone said to Creon, "The unwritten laws of heaven are not of today nor yesterday, but from all time." As she was led away to her death, she said, "…Behold me, what I suffer / Because I have upheld that which is high." (Hamilton's *Mythology*)]

[*Omission for length and content. Bulfinch continues the chapter with the story of Penelope (the wife of Odysseus); but as that will be covered in other books, it is unnecessary to include it here.*]

Narration and Discussion

Were there any clear winners in this story? Why or why not?

Are there any times in the story where it seemed like things could have gone a different way? Or was it all doomed to happen, as prophets like Amphiarus and Tiresias said?

Something to think about: Charlotte Mason wrote about people who live by Will, meaning that they have a purpose outside of their own interests. Habits help our lives go more smoothly; but sometimes (often!) we need to make choices, between good things and bad things, or even between good things and other good things. Building up our "choice muscles" helps us stay strong and focused when others try to persuade us to take a wrong path.

> ...and yet most men go through life without a single definite act of willing. Habit, convention, the customs of the world have done so much for us that we get up, dress, breakfast, follow our morning's occupations, our later relaxations, without an act of choice. For this much at any rate we know about the will. Its function is to *choose*, to decide... (*Philosophy of Education*, p. 128)

Who in this story might be said to have acted with Will?

Something else to think about: The Greeks said that a **tragedy** was a story that allows the audience to experience "a pain that awakens pleasure." The philosopher Aristotle explained that we feel pity or fear along with the characters, which then helps us to feel better ourselves. Do you agree? Are there stories that are just too frightening or sad to read?

Chapter Twenty-Four

(Lesson 6) Orpheus and Eurydice

Introduction

Orpheus, the famous maker of music (and one of Jason's Argonauts), was happily married to Eurydice. Like Admetus and Alcestis, however, their happiness was interrupted by her sudden death. The grieving husband Orpheus came up with a wild idea: if his music could tame wild beasts, might it also coax the underworld spirits to send Eurydice home? The lovers were reunited in the end, but not quite in the way that they hoped.

Vocabulary

lyre: harp with a U-shaped frame

lay: song

sensible: sensitive

prognostics: predictions

among the stars: the constellation Lyra

shade: spirit, ghost

Names

son of Apollo and the Muse Calliope: Some sources say the father of Orpheus was not Apollo but a mortal man, and the exact identity of his mother is also unsure (though she was probably one of the Muses).

Aristaeus: the god of "rustic and rural arts," such as dairying, leather-making, and bee-keeping. He is believed to be the father of **Actaeon** (**Year Five Lesson 11**), as well as others; his story will be told in **Lesson 7**.

Tantalus: See **Year Five Lesson 33**. (Do you recognize any of the other spirits listed?)

Maenads: female followers of Dionysus (Bacchus). Apparently their anger at Orpheus was caused by his worship of Apollo, the sun and music god (and quite possibly his father), rather than Bacchus.

Pentheus: a king of Thebes, grandson of **Cadmus**. Mentioned in **Year Five Lesson 28**.

St. Cecilia: the patron saint of musicians

the fatal sisters: The three Fates, those believed to hold the threads of someone's life

the Bacchanals: The **Maenads**, noted above

Places

at the Stygian realm: in the underworld

Rhodope: the Rhodope Mountains of southeastern Europe

Haemus: the Balkan Mountains

Reading

Part One

Orpheus was the **son of Apollo and the Muse Calliope**. He was presented by his father with a **lyre**, and taught to play upon it, which he did to such perfection that nothing could withstand the charm of his music. Not only his fellow-mortals but wild beasts were softened by his strains, and, gathering round him, laid by their fierceness, and stood entranced with his **lay**. Nay, the very trees and rocks were **sensible** to the charm. The former crowded round him, and the latter relaxed somewhat of their hardness, softened by his notes.

[The god of wedding ceremonies] had been called to bless with his presence the nuptials of Orpheus with Eurydice; but though he attended, he brought no happy omens with him. His very torch smoked and brought tears into their eyes. In coincidence with such **prognostics**, Eurydice, shortly after her marriage, while wandering with the nymphs, her companions, was seen by the shepherd **Aristaeus**, who was struck with her beauty and made advances to her. She fled, and in flying trod upon a snake in the grass, was bitten in the foot, and died.

Part Two

Orpheus sang his grief to all who breathed the upper air, both gods and men; and, finding it all unavailing, resolved to seek his wife in the regions of the dead.

He descended by a cave situated on the side of the promontory of Taenarus, and arrived **at the Stygian realm**. He passed through crowds of ghosts and presented himself before the throne of Pluto and Proserpine. Accompanying the words with the lyre, he sang,

> O deities of the underworld, to whom all we who live must come,
> hear my words, for they are true.
>
> I come not to spy out the secrets of Tartarus, nor to try my strength
> against the three-headed dog with snaky hair who guards the
> entrance.
>
> I come to seek my wife, whose opening years the poisonous viper's
> fang has brought to an untimely end.
>
> Love has led me here, Love, a god all powerful with us who dwell on
> the earth, and, if old traditions say true, not less so here.
>
> I implore you by these abodes full of terror, these realms of silence
> and uncreated things, unite again the thread of Eurydice's life.
>
> We all are destined to you and sooner or later must pass to your
> domain.
>
> She too, when she shall have filled her term of life, will rightly be
> yours.
>
> But till then grant her to me, I beseech you.
>
> If you deny me I cannot return alone; you shall triumph in the death
> of us both.

As he sang these tender strains, the very ghosts shed tears. **Tantalus**, in spite of his thirst, stopped for a moment his efforts for water, Ixion's wheel stood still, the vulture ceased to tear the giant's liver, the daughters of Danaus rested from their task of drawing water in a sieve, and Sisyphus sat on his rock to listen. Then for the first time, it is said, the cheeks of the Furies were wet with tears. Proserpine could not resist, and Pluto himself gave way.

Eurydice was called. She came from among the new-arrived ghosts, limping with her wounded foot. Orpheus was permitted to take her away with him on one condition, that he should not turn around to look at her till they should have reached the upper air. Under this condition they proceeded on their way, he leading, she following, through passages dark and steep, in total silence, till they had nearly reached the outlet into the cheerful upper world, when Orpheus, in a moment of forgetfulness, to assure himself that she was still following, cast a glance behind him, when instantly she was borne away.

Stretching out their arms to embrace each other, they grasped only the air! Dying now a second time, she yet cannot reproach her husband, for how can she blame his impatience to behold her? "Farewell," she said, "a last farewell,"—and was hurried away, so fast that the sound hardly reached his ears.

Part Three

Orpheus endeavored to follow her, and besought permission to return and try once more for her release; but the stern ferryman repulsed him and refused passage.

Seven days he lingered about the brink [of the river], without food or sleep; then bitterly accusing of cruelty the powers of Erebus, he sang his complaints to the rocks and mountains, melting the hearts of tigers, and moving the oaks from their stations.

[*Bulfinch gets a little hard to follow at this point. Hamilton is easier to understand:* "But at last a band of **Maenads** came upon him. They were as frenzied as those who killed Pentheus so horribly." *See the note under* **Names** *for further explanation.*]

[The Maenads] tore him limb from limb, and threw his head and his lyre into the river Hebrus, down which they floated, murmuring sad music, to which the shores responded a plaintive symphony.

The Muses gathered up the fragments of his body and buried them at [the foot of Mount Olympus], where the nightingale is said to sing over his grave more sweetly than in any other part of Greece.

His lyre was placed by Jupiter **among the stars**. His **shade** passed a second time to Tartarus, where he sought out his Eurydice and embraced her with eager arms. They roam the happy fields together now, sometimes he leading, sometimes she; and Orpheus gazes as much as he will upon her, no longer incurring a penalty for a thoughtless glance.

Part Four

The story of Orpheus has furnished [the English poet Alexander] Pope (1688-1744) with an illustration of the power of music, for his "Ode On **St. Cecilia's** Day." [Here is one part of it.]

"But soon, too soon the lover turns his eyes;

>   Again she falls, again she dies, she dies!
>   How wilt thou now **the fatal sisters** move?
>   No crime was thine, if't is no crime to love.
>   Now under hanging mountains,
>   Beside the falls of fountains,
>   Or where Hebrus wanders,
>   Rolling in meanders,
>   All alone,
>   He makes his moan,
>   And calls her ghost,
>   Forever, ever, ever lost!
>   Now with furies surrounded,
>   Despairing, confounded,
>   He trembles, he glows,
>   Amidst **Rhodope's** snows
>   See, wild as the winds o'er the desert he flies;
>   Hark! **Haemus** resounds with **the Bacchanals'** cries;
>   Ah, see, he dies!
>   Yet even in death Eurydice he sung,
>   Eurydice still trembled on his tongue:
>   Eurydice the woods
>   Eurydice the floods
>   Eurydice the rocks and hollow mountains rung"

[*omission for length*]

Narration and Discussion

Have you ever heard music so beautiful that it might have made wild beasts stand entranced or ghosts shed tears? What was it?

Why do you think that Orpheus wasn't allowed a second try at rescuing Eurydice?

Something to think about: "Orpheus sang his grief…" Can you sing grief as well as joy? In C. S. Lewis's novel *Out of the Silent Planet*, the main character Ransom attends the funeral of a creature from a very different world:

> "Lifting their heads, and with no signal given as far as Ransom could see, they began to sing…he began, ever so little, to hear it with their

ears. A sense...of giants dancing, of eternal sorrows eternally consoled, of he knew not what and yet what he had always known, awoke in him with the very first bars of the deep-mouthed dirge, and bowed down his spirit as if the gate of heaven had opened before him."

Creative narration #1: Dramatize the scene of Orpheus trying to gain the sympathies of the underworld beings, and his attempt to get home with Eurydice.

Creative narration #2: Note the last few lines given from Pope's poem, and especially how they are structured with each line beginning with "Eurydice." Could you write something in a similar pattern, but perhaps on a different topic? The possibilities are many: "Winter"; "Rain"; some other nature theme; or a character from a story.

(Lesson 7) Aristaeus the Bee-Keeper

Introduction

In this sequel to the story of Orpheus and Eurydice, we find out what happened to Aristaeus, who caused all of their trouble in the first place.

Vocabulary

the carcass of a dead animal would be occupied by the bees: Judges 14:8-9

engendered: created, caused

libations: drink-offerings

mortality: deaths

repose: nap, rest

fetters: chains

elude me: get away from me

Names

Virgil: Roman poet; author of the *Aeneid*

Proteus: see also **Year Six Lesson 2**

Reading

Prologue

Man avails himself of the instincts of the inferior animals for his own advantage. Hence sprang the art of keeping bees. Honey must first have been known as a wild product, the bees building their structures in hollow trees or holes in the rocks, or any similar cavity that chance offered. Thus occasionally **the carcass of a dead animal would be occupied by the bees f**or that purpose. It was no doubt from some such incident that the superstition arose that the bees were **engendered** by the decaying flesh of the animal; and **Virgil**, in the following story, shows how this supposed fact may be turned to account for renewing the swarm when it has been lost by disease or accident.

Part One

Aristaeus, who first taught the management of bees, was the son of the water-nymph Cyrene. His bees had perished, and he resorted for aid to his mother. He stood at the riverside and thus addressed her: "O mother, the pride of my life is taken from me! I have lost my precious bees. My care and skill have availed me nothing, and you, my mother, have not warded off from me the blow of misfortune."

His mother heard these complaints as she sat in her palace at the bottom of the river, with her attendant nymphs around her. They were engaged in female occupations, spinning and weaving, while one told stories to amuse the rest. The sad voice of Aristaeus interrupting their occupation, one of them put her head above the water and seeing him, returned and gave information to his mother, who ordered that he should be brought into her presence.

The river at her command opened itself and let him pass in, while it stood curled like a mountain on either side. He descended to the region where the fountains of the great rivers lie; he saw the enormous receptacles of waters, and was almost deafened with the roar, while he surveyed them hurrying off in various directions to water the face of the earth.

Arriving at his mother's apartment, he was hospitably received by Cyrene and her nymphs, who spread their table with the richest dainties. They first poured out **libations** to Neptune, then regaled themselves with the feast; and after that, Cyrene thus addressed him:

"There is an old prophet named **Proteus**, who dwells in the sea and is a favorite of Neptune, whose herd of sea-calves he pastures. We nymphs hold him in great respect, for he is a learned sage and knows all things, past, present, and to come. He can tell you, my son, the cause of the **mortality** among your bees, and how you may remedy it. But he will not do it voluntarily, however you may entreat him. You must compel him by force. If you seize him and chain him, he will answer your questions in order to get released, for he cannot by all his arts get away if you hold fast the chains. I will carry you to his cave, where he comes at noon to take his midday **repose**. Then you may easily secure him.

"But when he finds himself captured, his resort is to a power he possesses of changing himself into various forms. He will become a wild boar or a fierce tiger, a scaly dragon or lion with yellow mane. Or he will make a noise like the crackling of flames or the rush of water, so as to tempt you to let go the chain, when he will make his escape. But you have only to keep him fast bound, and at last when he finds all his arts unavailing, he will return to his own figure and obey your commands."

So saying, she sprinkled her son with fragrant nectar, the beverage of the gods; and immediately an unusual vigor filled his frame, and courage his heart, while perfume breathed all around him.

Part Two

The nymph led her son to the prophet's cave and concealed him among the recesses of the rocks, while she herself took her place behind the clouds. When noon came and the hour when men and herds retreat from the glaring sun to indulge in quiet slumber, Proteus issued from the water, followed by his herd of sea-calves which spread themselves along the shore. He sat on the rock and counted his herd; then stretched himself on the floor of the cave and went to sleep.

Aristaeus hardly allowed him to get fairly asleep before he fixed the **fetters** on him and shouted aloud. Proteus, waking and finding himself captured, immediately resorted to his arts, becoming first a fire, then a flood, then a horrible wild beast, in rapid succession. But finding all would not do, he at last resumed his own form and addressed the youth in angry accents: "Who are you, bold youth, who thus invade my abode, and what do you want of me?"

Aristaeus replied, "Proteus, you know already, for it is needless for anyone to attempt to deceive you. And do you also cease your efforts to **elude me**. I am led hither by divine assistance, to know from you the cause of my misfortune and how to remedy it."

At these words the prophet, fixing on him his gray eyes with a piercing look, thus spoke: "You receive the merited reward of your deeds, by which Eurydice met her death, for in flying from you she trod upon a serpent, of whose bite she died. To avenge her death, the nymphs, her companions, have sent this destruction to your bees. You have to appease their anger, and thus it must be done: Select four bulls, of perfect form and size, and four cows of equal beauty, build four altars to the nymphs, and sacrifice the animals, leaving their carcasses in the leafy grove. To Orpheus and Eurydice you shall pay such funeral honors as may allay their resentment. Returning after nine days, you will examine the bodies of the cattle slain and see what will befall."

Aristaeus faithfully obeyed these directions. He sacrificed the cattle, he left their bodies in the grove, he offered funeral honors to the shades of Orpheus and Eurydice; then returning on the ninth day he examined the bodies of the animals, and, wonderful to relate! a swarm of bees had taken possession of one of the carcasses and were pursuing their labors there as in a hive.

Narration and Discussion

Was it fair to kill off Aristaeus' bees without explaining the reason? Does that mean that every bad thing that happens to people is some kind of punishment?

Something else to think about: Did all this sacrificing help Orpheus and Eurydice? (Did Aristaeus actually repent of or change his behavior?)

Creative narration: Find some creative way to dramatize the scene with Proteus.

Going further: Hanging on while something shifts its shapes is an old theme in folk tales. (A variation is a battle between not one but two shapeshifters.) One example is Rosemary Sutcliff's retelling of the Scottish tale "Tam Lin" in her book *The Armourer's House*.

(Lesson 8) Who Can Tell the Strangest Story?

Introduction

This reading is a bit different in structure, as we hear about not one but three different characters, each with a strange story to tell.

[*Note: The original text contains other stories as well.*]

Vocabulary

exposed: left to die

usurping king: one who had stolen someone else's throne

when he played on his lyre…: Hamilton's *Mythology* points out that Zetheus, as someone who was used to physical tasks, might have been scornful of Amphion's ability to help build the wall. However, Amphion had his own methods.

auditors: listeners

flaying: beating, whipping

woodworms: the larvae of beetles that bore into wood

Names

the queen of Thebes: Edith Hamilton's *Mythology* says that Antiope was only a princess, and that she left the babies on the mountain out of fear of the king's anger.

Reading

Part One: Amphion

Amphion was the son of Jupiter and Antiope, **the queen of Thebes**. With his twin brother Zethus he was **exposed** at birth on Mount Cithaeron, where they grew up among the shepherds, not knowing their parentage. Mercury gave Amphion a lyre and taught him to play upon it; and his brother occupied himself in hunting and tending the flocks.

Meanwhile Antiope, their mother, who had been treated with great cruelty by Lycus, the **usurping king** of Thebes, and by Dirce, his wife, found means to inform her children of their rights and to summon them to her assistance. With a band of their fellow-herdsmen they attacked and slew Lycus, and tying Dirce by the hair of her head to a bull, let him drag her till she was dead.

[Later on], Amphion, having become king of Thebes, fortified the city with a wall. It is said that **when he played on his lyre the stones moved of their own accord** and took their places in the wall.

[A postscript that Bulfinch doesn't mention here: Amphion married Niobe, and it appears that they ruled without trouble in Thebes until the tragic incident told of in **Year Five Lesson 33**.]

Part Two: Marsyas

[The goddess] Minerva invented the flute, and played upon it to the delight of all the celestial **auditors**. But the mischievous urchin Cupid having dared to laugh at the [strange faces] which the goddess made while playing, Minerva threw the instrument indignantly away.

It fell down to earth, and was found by [a satyr named] Marsyas. He blew upon it, and drew from it such ravishing sounds that he was tempted to challenge Apollo himself to a musical contest.

The god of course triumphed, and punished Marsyas by **flaying** him [*omission*].

Part Three: Melampus

Melampus was the first mortal endowed with prophetic powers. Before his house there stood an oak tree containing a serpent's nest. The old serpents were killed by the servants, but Melampus took care of the young ones and fed them carefully. One day, when he was asleep under the oak, the serpents licked his ears with their tongues. On awaking he was astonished to find that he now understood the language of birds and creeping things. This knowledge enabled him to foretell future events, and he became a renowned soothsayer.

At one time his enemies took him captive and kept him strictly imprisoned. Melampus, in the silence of the night, heard the **woodworms** in the timbers talking together, and found out by what they said that the timbers were nearly eaten through and the roof would soon fall in. He told his captors and demanded to be let out, warning them also.

They took his warning, and thus escaped destruction, and rewarded Melampus and held him in high honor.

Narration and Discussion

If you could have just one of the skills described here, which would you choose, and what would you do with it?

Creative narration: The three characters meet at a restaurant or a party, and play a game of "My day was harder than yours." (This could be acted out, or done in writing.)

Chapter Twenty-Five
(Lesson 9) Arion and the Pirates

Introduction

This entertaining story shows that good musicians must have sharp wits along with skill on the lyre.

Vocabulary

festal board: celebration feast

propitious: favorable

firmament: sky

as becomes a bard: in a way that is fitting for a poet/musician

held on their way: kept sailing

wend: travel

avarice: greed

Names

Arion: pronounced AIR-ree-on

Periander: king of Corinth, died in 585 B.C. He is called one of the "Seven Sages of Greece," but he is also said to have been cruel to family members. Some think there might have been two Perianders, since there are such conflicting stories about him.

Thou, who didst find thy Eurydice: Who is Arion addressing here?

Galatea (#2): a Nereid; not the same Galatea as in the story of Pygmalion

Places

Corinth: a major city (or city-state) located on the **Isthmus of Corinth**, which connects the northern and southern parts of **Greece**

Sicily: the large island across from the "toe" of **Italy's** "boot"; there were Greek cities there such as **Syracuse**, which was founded by **Corinth**.

Tarentum: a coastal city in Apulia, southern Italy

Reading

Part One

Arion was a famous musician, and dwelt in the court of **Periander**, king of **Corinth**, with whom he was a great favorite. There was to be a musical contest in **Sicily**, and Arion longed to compete for the prize. He told his wish to Periander, who besought him like a brother to give up the thought. "Pray stay with me," he said, "and be contented. He who strives to win may lose."

Arion answered, "A wandering life best suits the free heart of a poet. The talent which a god bestowed on me, I would fain make a source of pleasure to others. And if I win the prize, how will the enjoyment of it be increased by the consciousness of my widespread fame!" He went, won the prize, and embarked with his wealth in a Corinthian ship for home.

On the second morning after setting sail, the wind breathed mild and fair. "O Periander," he exclaimed, "dismiss your fears! Soon shall you forget them in my embrace. With what lavish offerings will we display our gratitude to the gods, and how merry will we be at the **festal board**!"

The wind and sea continued **propitious**. Not a cloud dimmed the **firmament**. He had not trusted too much to the ocean—but he had to man. He overheard the seamen exchanging hints with one another, and found they were plotting to possess themselves of his treasure. Presently they surrounded him, loud and mutinous, and said, "Arion, you must die! If you would have a grave on shore, yield yourself to die on this spot; but if otherwise, cast yourself into the sea."

"Will nothing satisfy you but my life?" said he. "Take my gold, and welcome. I willingly buy my life at that price."

"No, no; we cannot spare you. Your life would be too dangerous to us. Where could we go to escape from Periander, if he should know that you had been robbed by us? Your gold would be of little use to us, if on returning home, we could never more be free from fear."

"Grant me, then," said he, "a last request, since nought will avail to save my life: that I may die, as I have lived, **as becomes a bard**. When I shall have sung my death song, and my harp-strings shall have ceased to vibrate, then I will bid farewell to life, and yield uncomplaining to my fate."

This prayer, like the others, would have been unheeded–they thought only of their booty–but to hear so famous a musician, that moved their rude hearts.

"Suffer me," he added, "to arrange my dress. Apollo will not favor me unless I be clad in my minstrel garb."

Part Two

He clothed his well-proportioned limbs in gold and purple, fair to see; his tunic fell around him in graceful folds; jewels adorned his arms; his brow was crowned with a golden wreath; and over his neck and shoulders flowed his hair perfumed with odors. His left hand held the lyre, his right the ivory wand with which he struck its chords. Like one inspired, he seemed to drink the morning air and glitter in the morning ray. The seamen gazed with admiration.

He strode forward to the vessel's side and looked down into the deep blue sea. Addressing his lyre, he sang,

> Companion of my voice, come with me to the realm of shades.
>
> Though Cerberus may growl, we know the power of song can tame his rage.
>
> Ye heroes of Elysium, who have passed the darkling flood,—ye happy souls, soon shall I join your band. Yet can ye relieve my grief? Alas, I leave my friend behind me.
>
> **Thou, who didst find thy Eurydice**, and lose her again as soon as found; when she had vanished like a dream, how didst thou hate the cheerful light!
>
> I must away, but I will not fear. The gods look down upon us.
>
> Ye who slay me unoffending, when I am no more, your time of trembling shall come.
>
> Ye Nereids, receive your guest, who throws himself upon your mercy!

So saying, he sprang into the deep sea.

Part Three

The waves covered him, and the seamen **held on their way**, fancying themselves safe from all danger of detection.

But the strains of his music had drawn round him the inhabitants of the deep to listen, and dolphins followed the ship as if chained by a spell. While he struggled in the waves, a dolphin offered him his back, and carried him mounted thereon safe to shore. At the spot where he landed, a monument of brass was afterwards erected upon the rocky shore, to preserve the memory of the event.

When Arion and the dolphin parted, each to his own element, Arion thus poured forth his thanks: "Farewell, thou faithful, friendly fish! Would that I could reward thee; but thou canst not **wend** with me, nor I with thee. Companionship we may not have. May **Galatea**, queen of the deep, accord thee her favor, and thou, proud of the burden, draw her chariot over the smooth mirror of the deep."

[Some versions of the story say that the dolphin did not make it back to the sea, and that Periander put up a monument to it; also, that the dolphin became the constellation Delphinus. There is an extrasolar planet in that constellation, now called 18 Delphini b, or Arion.]

Part Three

Arion hastened from the shore, and soon saw before him the towers of Corinth. He journeyed on, harp in hand, singing as he went, full of love and happiness, forgetting his losses, and mindful only of what remained, his friend and his lyre.

He entered the hospitable halls, and was soon clasped in the embrace of Periander. "I come back to thee, my friend," he said. "The talent which a god bestowed has been the delight of thousands, but false knaves have stripped me of my well-earned treasure; yet I retain the consciousness of wide spread fame." Then he told Periander all the wonderful events that had befallen him, who heard him with amazement.

"Shall such wickedness triumph?" said he. "Then in vain is power lodged in my hands. That we may discover the criminals, you must remain here in concealment, and so they will approach without suspicion."

When the ship arrived in the harbor, he summoned the mariners before him. "Have you heard anything of Arion?" he inquired. "I anxiously look for his return."

They replied, "We left him well and prosperous in **Tarentum**."

As they said these words, Arion stepped forth and faced them. His well-proportioned limbs were arrayed in gold and purple fair to see, his tunic fell around him in graceful folds, jewels adorned his arms, his brow was crowned with a golden wreath, and over his neck and shoulders flowed his hair perfumed with odors; his left hand held the lyre, his right the ivory wand with which he struck its chords.

They fell prostrate at his feet, as if a lightning bolt had struck them. "We meant to murder him, and he has become a god. O Earth, open and receive us!"

Then Periander spoke. "He lives, the master of the lay! Kind Heaven protects the poet's life. As for you, I invoke not the spirit of vengeance; Arion wishes not your blood. Ye slaves of **avarice**, begone! Seek some barbarous land, and never may aught beautiful delight your souls!"

Part Four

[Sir Edmund Spenser, in *The Fairie Queene*, Book the Fourth], represents Arion, mounted on his dolphin, accompanying the train of Neptune and Amphitrite:

> "Then was there heard a most celestial sound
> Of dainty music which did next ensue,
> And, on the floating waters as enthroned,
> Arion with his harp unto him drew
> The ears and hearts of all that goodly crew;
> Even when as yet the dolphin which him bore
> Through the Aegean Seas from pirates' view,
> Stood still, by him astonished at his lore,
> And all the raging seas for joy forgot to roar."

[*omission for length*]

Narration and Discussion

What do you think of Periander's choice not to "invoke the spirit of vengeance?"

Something to think about: Arion said, "The talent which a god bestowed on me, I would fain make a source of pleasure to others." Does that remind you of any Scriptures? (Maybe this one: Matthew 5:15)

Creative narration: Lucian of Samosata lived in the second century A.D., and was a "Hellenized" Syrian (meaning that he wrote in Greek and lived according to Greek customs). He was a witty writer, probably a travelling lecturer, possibly a government official, but we don't know a lot about him outside of his own writings. One of his works is translated as "Dialogues of the Sea-Gods," and in it he includes a conversation between Poseidon and the dolphins. Here are a few lines:

> **Pos.** Well done, Dolphins!... Those sailors had almost had their wicked will of him; but you were not going to stand that.
>
> **Dol.** You need not be surprised to find us doing a good turn to a man, Poseidon; we were men before we were fishes.
>
> **Pos.** Yes; I think it was too bad of Dionysus to celebrate his victory

by such a transformation scene; he might have been content with adding you to the roll of his subjects.— Well, Dolphin, tell me all about Arion.

Can you continue the scene? (This could be dramatized or written.)

(Lesson 10) Ibycus: A Greek Whodunit

Introduction

Unlike many characters in *The Age of Fable*, Ibycus was a real poet who lived in Samos during the second half of the sixth century B.C. It is in the fragments of writings by Ibycus, strangely enough, that we have the first mention of Orpheus. Ibycus is perhaps best remembered, though, for the strange events of his death.

Vocabulary

despoiled: plundered, robbed

entwine your temples: cover your head

strife of song: music contest

expiation: amends, reparation

amphitheatre: an open performance area with tiers of seats

awful: inspiring reverence or fear; "awe"-ful

rending: tearing, breaking

Names

Eumenides: also called the **Erinyes** or the **Furies**; the goddesses of vengeance

Reading

Prologue

In order to understand the story of Ibycus which follows it is necessary to remember, first, that the theatres of the ancients were immense fabrics capable of containing from ten to thirty thousand spectators, and as they were used only on festival occasions, and admission was free to all, they were usually filled. They were without roofs and open to the sky, and the performances were in the daytime. Secondly, the appalling representation of the Furies is not exaggerated in the story. It is recorded that Aeschylus, the tragic poet, having on one occasion represented the Furies in a chorus of fifty performers, the terror of the spectators was such that many fainted and were thrown into convulsions, and the magistrates forbade a like representation for the future.

Part One

Ibycus, the pious poet, was on his way to the chariot races and musical competitions held at the Isthmus of Corinth, which attracted all of Grecian lineage. Apollo had bestowed on him the gift of song, the honeyed lips of the poet, and he pursued his way with lightsome step, full of the god. Already the towers of Corinth crowning the height appeared in view, and he had entered with pious awe the sacred grove of Neptune. No living object was in sight, only a flock of cranes flew overhead taking the same course as himself in their migration to a southern clime. "Good luck to you, ye friendly squadrons," he exclaimed, "my companions from across the sea. I take your company for a good omen. We come from far and fly in search of hospitality. May both of us meet that kind reception which shields the stranger guest from harm!"

He paced briskly on, and soon was in the middle of the wood. There suddenly, at a narrow pass, two robbers stepped forth and barred his way. He must yield or fight. But his hand, accustomed to the lyre, and not to the strife of arms, sank powerless. He called for help on men and gods, but his cry reached no defender's ear. "Then here must I die," said he, "in a strange land, unlamented, cut off by the hand of outlaws, and see none to avenge my cause."

Sore wounded, he sank to the earth, when hoarse screamed the cranes overhead. "Take up my cause, ye cranes," he said, "since no voice but yours answers to my cry." So saying he closed his eyes in death.

Part Two

The body, **despoiled** and mangled, was found, and though disfigured with wounds, was recognized by the friend in Corinth who had expected him as a guest. "Is it thus I find you restored to me?" he exclaimed. "I who hoped to **entwine your temples** with the wreath of triumph in the **strife of song**!"

The guests assembled at the festival heard the tidings with dismay. All Greece felt the wound, every heart owned its loss. They crowded round the tribunal of the magistrates, and demanded vengeance on the murderers and **expiation** with their blood.

But what trace or mark shall point out the perpetrator from amidst the vast multitude attracted by the splendor of the feast? Did he fall by the hands of robbers or did some private enemy slay him? The all-discerning sun alone can tell, for no other eye beheld it. Yet not improbably the murderer even now walks in the midst of the throng, and enjoys the fruits of his crime, while vengeance seeks for him in vain. Perhaps in their own temple's enclosure he defies the gods mingling freely in this throng of men that now presses into the **amphitheatre**.

For now crowded together, row on row, the multitude fill the seats till it seems as if the very fabric would give way. The murmur of voices sounds like the roar of the sea, while the circles widening in their ascent rise tier on tier, as if they would reach the sky.

Part Three

And now the vast assemblage listens to the **awful** voice of the chorus personating the Furies, which in solemn guise advances with measured step, and moves around the circuit of the theatre. Can they be mortal women who compose that awful group, and can that vast concourse of silent forms be living beings?

The choristers, clad in black, bore in their fleshless hands torches blazing with a pitchy flame. Their cheeks were bloodless, and, in place of hair, writhing and swelling serpents curled around their brows. Forming a circle, these awful beings sang their hymns, **rending** the hearts of the guilty, and enchaining all their faculties. It rose and swelled, overpowering the sound of the instruments, stealing the judgment, palsying the heart, curdling the blood.

> "Happy the man who keeps his heart pure from guilt and crime!
>
> Him we avengers touch not; he treads the path of life secure from us.
>
> But woe! woe! to him who has done the deed of secret murder.
>
> We the fearful family of Night fasten ourselves upon his whole being.
>
> Thinks he by flight to escape us? We fly still faster in pursuit, twine our snakes around his feet, and bring him to the ground.
>
> Unwearied we pursue; no pity checks our course; still on and on, to the end of life, we give him no peace nor rest."

Thus the **Eumenides** sang, and moved in solemn cadence, while stillness like the stillness of death sat over the whole assembly as if in the presence of superhuman beings; and then in solemn march completing the circuit of the theatre, they [filed] out at the back of the stage.

Every heart fluttered between illusion and reality, and every breast panted with undefined terror, quailing before the awful power that watches secret crimes, and winds unseen the skein of destiny.

Part Four

At that moment a cry burst forth from one of the uppermost benches— "Look! look! comrade, yonder are the cranes of Ibycus!"

And suddenly there appeared sailing across the sky a dark object which a moment's inspection showed to be a flock of cranes flying directly over the theatre. "Of Ibycus! did he say?" The beloved name revived the sorrow in every breast.

As wave follows wave over the face of the sea, so ran from mouth to mouth the words, "Of Ibycus! him whom we all lament, whom some murderer's hand laid low! What have the cranes to do with him?"

And louder grew the swell of voices, while like a lightning's flash the thought sped through every heart, "Observe the power of the Eumenides! The pious poet shall be avenged! the murderer has informed against himself. Seize the man who uttered that cry and the other to whom he spoke!"

The culprit would gladly have recalled his words, but it was too late. The faces of the murderers, pale with terror, betrayed their guilt. The people took them before the judge, they confessed their crime, and suffered the punishment they deserved.

Part Five: An Addition to Bulfinch

The German poet Friedrich Schiller wrote a ballad on this topic called "The Cranes of Ibycus" (or "Ibykus"). Here is the beginning of it (translated by William F. Wertz).

> Unto the songs and chariot fighting
> Which all the strains of Greece are joining,
> On Corinth's isthmus festive gay,
> Made Ibycus, gods' friend, his way.
> The gift of song Apollo offer'd,
> To him the sweeten'd voice of song;
> Thus on a light staff forth he wander'd,
> From Rhegium, with god along.
>
> Now beckons high on mountain ridges
> High Corinth to the wand'rer's glances,
> And then doth he, with pious dread,
> To Poseidon's spruce grove tread.
> Naught stirs about him, just a swarming
> Of cranes which join him on his way,
> Which towards the distant southern warming
> Are flying forth in squadrons grey.
>
> "Receive my greetings, squads befriended,
> Which o'er the sea have me escorted!
> I take you as a goodly sign,
> Your lot, it doth resemble mine
> From distant lands we are arriving
> And pray for a warm dwelling place.
> Be the hospitable good willing,
> Who wards the stranger from disgrace!"

Narration and Discussion

The chorus playing the Furies sang, "We give him no peace or rest." Do you think the guilty consciences of the murderers might have caught up with them, even without the cranes that gave them away?

Creative narration: Could there have been any other suspects in the murder of Ibycus? A jealous competitor? Someone he had insulted in a poem? Imagine you are a Corinthian detective trying to solve the case. This might be a drama activity, or you could write out your investigative notes.

For those who like to write: Examine the verses by Schiller, and compare it with Bulfinch's version. Do you see some close similarities? This is not a coincidence: there is a note in *The Age of Fable* saying that he based his retelling on Schiller's ballad; he felt this was, in a way, acknowledging the inspiration that is passed down from one poet to another. Could you take something written in verse, and retell it in story form?

Chapter Twenty-Six
(Lesson 11) Two Stories About Diana

Introduction

Diana (or Artemis) was a twin to Apollo, as we read in the story of Latona (**Year Five Lesson 12**); we have already read about her in "Diana and Actaeon" (**Year Five Lesson 11**). She was the goddess of many things: hunting and wild animals, childbirth, the moon, and other aspects of nature. Diana/Artemis was a very popular deity for both the Greeks and the Romans, as we see in Acts 19:28.

The story of Orion is also a "why story" about some of the constellations.

Vocabulary

perpetual: everlasting

chid: scolded

their number was seven: It is now known that there are more stars in the cluster, but at that time only seven were able to be seen.

Places

Mount Latmos (Latmus): part of the Beşparmak Mountains in Turkey

Reading

Part One: Diana and Endymion

Endymion was a beautiful youth who fed his flock on **Mount Latmos**.

One calm, clear night Diana, the moon, looked down and saw him sleeping. The cold heart of the virgin goddess was warmed by his surpassing beauty, and she came down to him, kissed him, and watched over him while he slept. Another story was that Jupiter bestowed on him the gift of **perpetual** youth, united with perpetual sleep.

Of one so gifted we can have but few adventures to record. Diana, it was said, took care that his fortunes should not suffer by his inactive life, for she made his flock increase, and guarded his sheep and lambs from the wild beasts.

[*omission for length and content*]

[John Fletcher, who also collaborated with Shakespeare, was the author of a play called "The Faithful Shepherdess." It contains these lines that reflect the simple story of Diana's love for Endymion.]

> "How the pale Phoebe, hunting in a grove,
>
> First saw the boy Endymion, from whose eyes
>
> She took eternal fire that never dies;
>
> How she conveyed him softly in a sleep,
>
> His temples bound with poppy, to the steep
>
> Head of old Latmos, where she stoops each night,
>
> Gilding the mountain with her brother's light,
>
> To kiss her sweetest."

[Edith Hamilton (in *Mythology*) retells the story as it was told by the third-century poet Theocritus. That version ends with these words: "But it is said, too, that her passion brings her only a burden of pain, fraught with many sighs."]

Part Two: Orion

Orion was the son of Neptune. He was a handsome giant and a mighty hunter. His father gave him the power of wading through the depths of the sea, or, as others say, of walking on its surface.

[*Omission for content: Orion's attempt to win the love of Merope*]

After this he dwelt as a hunter with Diana, with whom he was a favorite, and it is even said she was about to marry him. Her brother [Apollo] was highly displeased and often **chid** her, but to no purpose. One day, observing Orion wading through the sea with his head just above the water, Apollo pointed it out to his sister and maintained that she could not hit that black thing on the sea. The archer-goddess discharged a shaft with fatal aim.

The waves rolled the dead body of Orion to the land, and bewailing her fatal error with many tears, Diana placed him among the stars, where he appears as a giant, with a girdle, sword, lion's skin, and club. Sirius, his dog, follows him, and the **Pleiades** fly before him.

[How did the Pleiades get into the sky?] The Pleiades were daughters of Atlas, and nymphs of Diana's train. One day Orion saw them and became enamoured and pursued them. In their distress they prayed to the gods to change their form, and Jupiter in pity turned them into pigeons, and then made them a constellation in the sky. Though **their number was seven**, only six stars are visible, for Electra, one of them, it is said left her place that she might not behold the ruin of Troy, for that city was founded by her son Dardanus. The sight had such an effect on her sisters that they have looked pale ever since.

[*omission for length and content*]

[An astronomical guide written by Hyginus, early in the first century A.D., mentions a different story about the missing sister, saying that the faint or invisible star might be Merope, not Electra. Merope was believed to have married a mortal, and that is why we don't see her star. But Hyginus includes the other version as well, saying that the missing Pleiad is Electra mourning the destruction of Troy; and Ovid's writings also mention both. So you can choose the version you prefer.]

Part Three: A Lost Sister

Felicia Dorothea Hemans (1793-1835), the author of "Casabianca," or "The boy stood on the burning deck", also wrote a poem called "The Lost Pleiad," about the invisible star, whichever sister it might be. Bulfinch mentions the poem but does not include it; but we think it deserves a place in the book.

    And is there glory from the heavens departed?

    O void unmarked!—thy sisters of the sky

    Still hold their place on high,

    Though from its rank thine orb so long hath started,—

    Thou that no more art seen of mortal eye.

    Hath the night lost a gem, the regal night?

    She wears her crown of old magnificence,

    Though thou art exiled thence;

    No desert seems to part those urns of light,

Midst the far depth of purple gloom intense.
They rise in joy, the starry myriads burning:
The shepherd greets them on his mountains free;
And from the silvery sea
To them the sailor's wakeful eye is turning—
Unchanged they rise, they have not mourned for thee.
Couldst thou be shaken from thy radiant place,
E'en as a dewdrop from the myrtle spray,
Swept by the wind away?
Wert thou not peopled by some glorious race,
And was there power to smite them with decay?
Why, who shall talk of thrones, of sceptres riven?
Bowed be our hearts to think of what *we* are,
When from its height afar
A world sinks thus—and yon majestic heaven
Shines not the less for that one vanished star!

Narration and Discussion

Why might Diana's love for Endymion be "fraught with many sighs?"

Does Apollo's trick remind you of any other myths or stories?

Creative narration #1: Imagine a conversation between the Pleiades in the sky.

Creative narration #2 (for those who like to write): A contemporary writer, Danith McPherson, has written a short poem called "Pleiades," which you should be able to find on her website. In comparison with Felicia Hemans' style, McPherson uses very short lines in her poem, often only one word, or three at the most. Which do you prefer? Your challenge: choose another subject (something from nature?), and write some lines in McPherson's style. Is it easy or hard to write extremely short lines?

(Lesson 12) Aurora, Tithonus, and Memnon

Introduction

In our final Lesson for this term, we continue the theme of love: between gods and mortals, but also between mothers and sons. The story of Memnon is also a bit of a lead-in to the *Iliad*.

Vocabulary

mortification: embarrassment, shame

raiment: clothing

kindred: relatives

Names

Aethiopians: If you remember the beginning chapter of this book, "Aethiopia" was more of a mystical, far-off land than an actual geographical place.

Memnon: In the *Iliad*, he is a king of Aethiopia who helps defend Troy.

King Priam: the king of Troy

Reading

Part One: Aurora and Tithonus

[Aurora/Eos], the goddess of the Dawn, like her sister the Moon, was at times inspired with the love of mortals. Her greatest favorite was Tithonus, son of Laomedon, king of Troy. She stole him away, and prevailed on Jupiter to grant him immortality; but, forgetting to have youth [included] in the gift, after some time she began to discern, to her great **mortification**, that he was growing old.

When his hair was quite white she left his society; but he still had the range of her palace, lived on ambrosial food, and was clad in celestial **raiment**.

At length he lost the power of using his limbs, and then she shut him up in his chamber, whence his feeble voice might at times be heard.

Finally she turned him into a grasshopper.

Part Two: Memnon at Troy

Memnon was the son of Aurora and Tithonus. He was king of the **Aethiopians**, and dwelt in the extreme east, on the shore of Ocean.

He came with his warriors to assist the **kindred** of his father in the war of Troy. **King Priam** received him with great honors, and listened with admiration to his narrative of the wonders of the ocean shore.

The very day after his arrival, Memnon, impatient of repose, led his troops to the field. Antilochus, the brave son of Nestor, fell by his hand, and the Greeks were put to flight, when Achilles appeared and restored the battle. A long and doubtful contest ensued between him and the son of Aurora; at length victory declared for Achilles, Memnon fell, and the Trojans fled in dismay.

Aurora, who from her station in the sky had viewed with apprehension the danger of her son, when she saw him fall, directed his brothers, the Winds, to convey his body to the banks of the river Esepus in Paphlagonia. In the evening Aurora came, accompanied by the Hours and the Pleiads, and wept and lamented over her son. Night, in sympathy with her grief, spread the heaven with clouds; all nature mourned for the offspring of the Dawn. The Aethiopians raised his tomb on the banks of the stream in the grove of the Nymphs, and Jupiter caused the sparks and cinders of his funeral pile to be turned into birds, which, dividing into two flocks, fought over the pile till they fell into the flame. Every year at the anniversary of his death they return and celebrate his obsequies in like manner.

Aurora remains inconsolable for the loss of her son. Her tears still flow, and may be seen at early morning in the form of dew-drops on the grass.

Part Three: The Statues in Egypt

Unlike most of the marvels of ancient mythology, there still exist some memorials of this. On the banks of the river Nile, in Egypt, are two colossal statues, one of which is said to be the statue of Memnon. Ancient writers record that when the first rays of the rising sun fall upon this statue a sound is heard to issue from it, which they compare to the snapping of a harp-string. There is some doubt about the identification of the existing statue with the one described by the ancients, and the mysterious sounds are still more doubtful. Yet there are not wanting some modern testimonies to their being still audible. It has been suggested that sounds produced by confined air making its escape from crevices or caverns in the rocks may have given some ground for the story. Sir Gardner Wilkinson, a late traveller, of the highest authority, examined the statue itself, and discovered that it was hollow, and that "in the lap of the statue is a stone, which on being struck emits a metallic sound, that might still be made use of to deceive a visitor who was predisposed to believe its powers."

[**Want to know more?** The ancient geographer Pausanias saw the Colossi of Memnon, a pair of giant (59 foot high) stone statues on the west bank of the Nile. They are now known to represent Pharaoh Amenhotep III, but because of certain inscriptions, at least one was thought to represent Memnon. Following an earthquake in 27 B.C., the "Memnon" statue collapsed, and, at sunrise, it began to produce an eerie musical sound that people interpreted as Memnon calling out to his mother. Apparently this sound continued and made the statue a great attraction for visitors (including the Roman emperor Hadrian). The Romans restored the statue and set it up on sandstone blocks; however, the story has one more twist: Emperor Septimius Severus had some more repair work done on it around the turn of the second century, and the musical sounds haven't been heard since. But, as Bulfinch says, someone clever enough might still be able to produce them.]

[*omission for content*]

Narration and Discussion

How did Aurora and the other gods show their continuing love for Memnon, and their grief at his death? Can you think of any myths or other stories where nature mourned the loss of someone beloved?

> I heard a voice, that cried,
> "Balder the Beautiful
> Is dead, is dead!"
> And through the misty air
> Passed like the mournful cry
> Of sunward sailing cranes.

("Tegnér's Drapa," by Henry Wadsworth Longfellow)

Something more to think about: Was Aurora's enchantment of Tithonus simply out of impatience at his aging, or out of pity because he could not die? Does this say anything about our attitude towards old age and the loss of beauty or strength?

Creative narration: You have now read through many of the stories of Greek and Roman mythology. Choose any creative format you like to tell what you have learned.

Postscript: In Which Bulfinch Tells of Ovid, a Poet of Mythology

Ovid, often alluded to in poetry by his other name of Naso, was born in the year 43 B.C. He was educated for public life and held some offices of considerable dignity, but poetry was his delight, and he early resolved to devote himself to it. He accordingly sought the society of the contemporary poets, and was acquainted with Horace and saw Virgil, though the latter died when Ovid was yet too young and undistinguished to have formed his acquaintance.

Ovid spent an easy life at Rome in the enjoyment of a competent income. He was intimate with the family of Augustus, the emperor [see *Augustus Caesar's World*, p. 225]; and it is supposed that some serious offence given to some member of that family was the cause of an event which reversed the poet's happy circumstances and clouded all the latter portion of his life. [He himself explained it only as "a poem and a mistake."] At the age of fifty he was banished from Rome, and ordered to betake himself to Tomis [now Constanța in Romania], on the borders of the Black Sea.

Here, among the barbarous people and in a severe climate, the poet, who had been accustomed to all the pleasures of a luxurious capital and the society of his most distinguished contemporaries, spent the last ten years of his life, worn out with grief and anxiety. His only consolation in exile was to address his wife and absent friends, and his letters were all poetical. Though these poems (the "Trista" and "Letters from Pontus") have no other topic than the poet's sorrows, his exquisite taste and fruitful invention have redeemed them from the charge of being tedious, and they are read with pleasure and even with sympathy.

The two great works of Ovid are his "Metamorphoses" and his "Fasti." They are both mythological poems, and from the former we have taken most of our stories of Grecian and Roman mythology. [The nineteenth-century publisher and writer Charles Knight, in his "Cyclopedia,"] thus characterizes these poems:

> "The rich mythology of Greece furnished Ovid, as it may still furnish the poet, the painter, and the sculptor, with materials for his art. With exquisite taste, simplicity, and pathos he has narrated the fabulous traditions of early ages, and given to them that appearance of reality which only a master hand could impart. His pictures of nature are striking and true; he selects with care that which is appropriate; he rejects the superfluous; and when he has completed his work, it is neither defective nor redundant. The 'Metamorphoses' are read with pleasure by youth, and are re-read in more advanced age with still greater delight. The poet ventured to predict that his poem would survive him, and be read wherever the Roman name was known."

The prediction above alluded to is contained in the closing lines of the "Metamorphoses," of which we give a literal translation below:

"And now I close my work, which not the ire

Year Six: The Age of Fable

Of Jove, nor tooth of time, nor sword, nor fire
Shall bring to nought. Come when it will that day
Which o'er the body, not the mind, has sway,
And snatch the remnant of my life away,
My better part above the stars shall soar,
And my renown endure forevermore.
Where'er the Roman arms and arts shall spread
There by the people shall my book be read;
And, if aught true in poet's visions be,
My name and fame have immortality."

For Further Reading

You will notice that we have stopped partway through *The Age of Fable*. The main reason for this is that AmblesideOnline students will be working through retellings, or even adult translations, of the *Iliad* and the *Odyssey*, so they do not need to read those stories again here. Another reason is that, if they have read *Heroes of Asgard* in Year Four, they will have covered that section of Bulfinch (although *Asgard* does not cover the "Teutonic" Mythology). Finally, some of the other myths will be covered in assigned reading; for instance, Egyptian mythology and a short retelling of the Aeneid are included in *Augustus Caesar's World* by Genevieve Foster.

We have listed some suggestions, from both assigned reading and "extras," that cover the same or similar material as the remaining chapters of *The Age of Fable*.

Chapters 15-21: More Greek Myths

D'Aulaires' Book of Greek Myths. A favourite with many young students; contains short readings and vivid illustrations.

Mythology, by Edith Hamilton. Written for adults, but accessible and enjoyable for students.

Chapters 27 & 28: The *Iliad* (The Trojan War)

The Story of the Greeks, by Helene A. Guerber, chapters 13-18

Mythology, by Edith Hamilton, pp. 247-281

Black Ships Before Troy, by Rosemary Sutcliff

The Iliad for Boys and Girls, by Alfred Church

The Iliad of Homer, by Barbara Leonie Picard

Chapters 29 & 30: The *Odyssey*

Mythology, by Edith Hamilton, pp. 282-307

The Odyssey for Boys and Girls, by Alfred Church

The Wanderings of Odysseus, by Rosemary Sutcliff

The Odyssey of Homer, by Barbara Leonie Picard

Year Six: The Age of Fable

The Children's Homer, by Padraic Colum (a useful option if time is limited, as it combines stories from both the *Iliad* and the *Odyssey*)

Chapters 31-33: The Aeneid

Augustus Caesar's World, pp. 152-158, 164-165

The Story of the Romans, by Helene A. Guerber, chapters 2-5

Mythology, by Edith Hamilton, pp. 308-330

The Aeneid of Virgil, by N. B. Taylor

Chapter 34: Egyptian Mythology; Oracles

Augustus Caesar's World, pp. 199-209, 216-217

Complete Book of Marvels, by Richard Halliburton; chapters on Egypt.

Chapter 35-36: The Origins and Authors of Mythology; "Modern Monsters"

Augustus Caesar's World, pp. 159-165

Chapter 37: "Eastern Mythology" (Hinduism, Buddhism)

Augustus Caesar's World, pp. 171-174, 258-264, 267-272

Kim, by Rudyard Kipling

Chapters 38-40: Norse and Teutonic Mythology

Augustus Caesar's World, pp. 174-176 (very brief)

Mythology, by Edith Hamilton, pp. 427-449

D'Aulaires' Norse Gods and Giants. Similar to their *Book of Greek Myths*; the illustrations can get quite wild at times.

Gods and Heroes from Viking Mythology, by Brian Branston. This 1970's book would appeal to older children who like a bit of gore (zombies! blood!), but aren't up for the "edginess" of more recent books.

The Children of Odin, by Padraic Colum. Literary, thorough, never in bad taste. The order of the stories is a bit confusing.

Myths of the Norsemen, by Roger Lancelyn Green. Literary, challenging, and mostly free of mature content; a top recommendation among these books. One caution: it contains numerous references to spells and wizardry.

Norse Mythology, by Neil Gaiman. Current, readable, but does contain mature content; previewing is strongly recommended.

Chapter 41: Druids and Iona (a bit of British mythology)

Augustus Caesar's World, pp. 137-140 (Warning: includes descriptions of violent deaths.)

Made in the USA
Columbia, SC
15 August 2025